T0326455

Globalisms and Power

GLOBAL
STUDIES IN
EDUCATION

A.C. (Tina) Besley, Michael A. Peters,
Cameron McCarthy, Fazal Rizvi
General Editors

Vol. 14

The Global Studies in Education series is part of the Peter Lang Education list.
Every volume is peer reviewed and meets
the highest quality standards for content and production.

PETER LANG
New York • Washington, D.C./Baltimore • Bern
Frankfurt • Berlin • Brussels • Vienna • Oxford

Globalisms and Power

Iberian Education and
Curriculum Policies

João M. Paraskeva & Jurjo Torres Santomé, Editors

PETER LANG
New York • Washington, D.C./Baltimore • Bern
Frankfurt • Berlin • Brussels • Vienna • Oxford

Library of Congress Cataloging-in-Publication Data

Globalisms and power: Iberian education and curriculum
policies / edited by João M. Paraskeva, Jurjo Torres Santomé.
p. cm. — (Global studies in education; v. 14)
Includes bibliographical references and index.
1. Education and globalization—Portugal.
2. Education and globalization—Spain.
3. Education—Curricula—Portugal. 4. Education—Curricula—Spain.
5. Neoliberalism. I. Paraskeva, João M. II. Torres, Jorge (Torres Santomé)
LC93.P8G56   379.46—dc23   2012012212
ISBN 978-1-4331-1554-7 (hardcover)
ISBN 978-1-4331-1553-0 (paperback)
ISBN 978-1-4539-0814-3 (e-book)
ISSN 2153-330X

Bibliographic information published by **Die Deutsche Nationalbibliothek**.
Die Deutsche Nationalbibliothek lists this publication in the "Deutsche
Nationalbibliografie"; detailed bibliographic data is available
on the Internet at http://dnb.d-nb.de/.

Contents

INTRODUCTION

Pouring Old Philosophical Wine into New Ideological Bottles

Globalisms and the Rebooting of Mankind's Revolution

João M. Paraskeva & Jurjo Torres Santomé

The last three decades of the twentieth century might be considered crucial for the transformations that were about to take place around the world (Apple, 2009; Conversi, 2010; Dasgupta & Kiely, 2006; Giroux, 2008; Harvey, 2005; Paraskeva, 2009, 2010a, 2010b; Sousa Santos, 2006; Steger, 2005; Torres Santomé, 2005). The staggering economic upheaval in post-Allende Chile, the great contemporary revolution in the People's Republic of China (which adopted the *Xiaopingian* formula: one nation, two states), and the elections of Margaret Thatcher in the United Kingdom and Ronald Reagan in the United States signified the emergence of a "new world economic configuration—often subsumed under the term [neoliberal] globalization" (Harvey, 2005, p. 2).

Given the inefficiency and inoperability of the political and economic architecture determined by the post–World War II Bretton Woods agreement, which established a kind of *embedded liberalism* that imposed unreasonable restrictions and regulations on a greedy market, the succession of events listed above must be seen as the harbinger of a new world order that advocates the liberation of the market and its mechanisms from the shackles of state dynamics. As Harvey (2005) accurately claims, neoliberalism has led to the destruction "not only of prior institutional frameworks and powers, but also of divisions of labour, social relations, welfare provisions, technological mixes, ways of life and thought, reproductive activities, attachments to the land and habits of the heart" (p. 3). The survival of capitalism depended on a new model of internationalization; in this context, the consequent unregulated and senseless globalization, which Foster (2008) would have called the newer financialization of capital, was called into being. Žižek's (1989) comment is quite insightful:

> Far from constricting [capitalism limits] is the very impetus of its development. Herein lies the paradox proper to capitalism, its last resort: capitalism is capable of transforming its limit, its very impotence, in the source of its power—the more it "putrefies" the more its immanent contradiction is aggravated, the more it must revolutionize itself to survive. It is paradox that defines surplus enjoyment: it is not a surplus which attaches itself to some "normal" fundamental enjoyment because *enjoyment as such emerges only in the surplus*, because it is constitutively an "excess." If we subtract the surplus we lose enjoyment itself, just as capitalism, which can survive only by incessantly revolutionizing its own material conditions, ceases to exist if it "stays the same," if it achieves an internal balance. (p. 52)

Within this context, and arguably, like never before, the social apparatus began to be overwhelmingly subsumed in the overbearing capitalist financial powers, without any control by the state per se. This paved the way for gargantuan scams, such as the infamous "Madoff-gate"—the biggest social fraud in history. The fact that large financial corporations would have gone bankrupt without a government bailout demonstrates the inhuman excesses of capitalism and its need to exist within a permanent state of imbalance. It goes without saying that not only the middle and working classes, but also social spheres such as health care, public education, and public institutions, are actually funding the rescue and recovery from the havoc created by capitalism, suffering cuts to social programs and the elimination of certain civil rights—changes that would have been unimaginable a few years ago.

However, neoliberal globalization is much more than economics; it also is a form of cultural politics that produces greater cultural and economic rewards (cf. Mennell, 2009; Strange, 1996) for the globalized few (Bauman, 1998). It would be unreasonable to suggest that these economic, cultural, and social transformations would not interfere with educational policies and politics. Indeed, education has been used to support one of the key arguments of neoliberal global policies, especially since the fall of the Berlin Wall—the fading of the "iron curtain of ideology and the vigorous emergence of the velvet curtain of culture" (cf. Žižek, 2008, p. 661).

The creed promulgated and fervently advocated by Bell (1960), Huntington (1987), Fukuyama (1992), and others about the emergence of a de-ideologized world brought together followers who claimed that Marxism-Leninism and classical liberalism were exhausted political ideologies. The end of ideology was precipitately defended not only as an irrevocable process, but also as the pipeline for free-market globalization (cf. Steger, 2002). This neoliberal shift prompted a new definition of the state rather than its disappearance, as neoliberalists desired.

States take charge of creating or adapting their infrastructures to attract significant financial and industrial capital. In other words, states are now responsible for "modernizing" their constitutions, and subsequently their penal codes, in order to ensure the circulation of capital, by decriminalizing fraudulent transactions, by cutting taxes, reducing salaries, and abolishing certain civil rights, as well as by reforming the labor market—that is, by facilitating the dismissal of workers and employees, the cutting of wages, increases in working hours, and so on, based on a magic word: flexibility.

Supporters of the so-called third way subsequently amplified this faith in the end of ideology. Third-way mentor-strategist Anthony Giddens (2000) argued that the weakening of state policies, the multiplication of inequalities, and severe changes in the daily life of the people must be perceived as natural side effects and moral procedures of transitions triggered by economic globalization. What matters, Giddens insisted, is that globalization attempts to promote a dominant global cosmopolitan society, and thus to overcome traditions and parochialisms that are harmful to individuals, and to offer lifestyle choices.

However, we agree with Steger (2002) that "ideology is not only very much with us today, but represents just as powerful a force as it did a century ago" (p. 4). In fact, "It took the al-Qaeda attacks of 11 September 2001 to expose the naïveté of [the] premature hopes for a de-ideologized world" (Steger, 2009, p. 3). As Kellner (2005) straightforwardly notes:

> The terrorist acts on the United States on September 11 and the subsequent Terror War throughout the world dramatically disclose the downside of globalization and the ways that global flows of technology, goods, information, ideologies and people can have destructive as well as productive effects. The experience of September 11 points to the objective ambiguity of globalization, that the positive and negative sides are interconnected, that the institutions of the open society unlock the possibilities of destruction and violence, as well as destruction of and violence against democracy, free trade, and cultural and social change. (p. 32)

The attacks on New York City and Washington, D.C., on 9/11/2001, the bombings in Madrid in 2004 and in London in 2005, together with the 1991

Gulf War (the first Gulf War), distracted society from political issues, thus constructing a new social reality that buried—once and for all—the dynamics of class struggle. Naturally, any new social clashes were attributed to religious and cultural causes. The structural dimensions of society, such as the economy and politics, play a less visible role in the lives of the vast majority of the population and are left primarily in the hands of professional economists.

After 9/11, Islamism replaced Communism as the next great enemy of the West that had to be defeated by whatever means necessary. Forces in the West decided that Islamic-majority countries needed to be liberated from Islamist extremism. Needless to say, that implied that Western powers had carte blanche to embark on the Crusades of the twenty-first century and to expropriate the natural resources of the enemy Islamic countries, especially their oil.

Thus, "far from condemning people to ideological boredom in a world without history, the opening decade of the twenty-first century has become a teeming battlefield of clashing ideologies" (Steger, 2005, p. 4). As Žižek (2008) adamantly claims, "[Huntington's] clash of civilizations is politics at [Fukuyama's] . . . end of history" (p. 2). Neoliberal globalization, as the practice of corporate populism, carries in itself an ideological scaffold—neoliberal globalism (cf. Conversi, 2010; Kaplinsky, 2005; Rapley, 2004). No one has more effectively unmasked the ideological backbone of neoliberal globalization than Harvey (2005):

> [Neoliberal globalization] is particularly assiduous in seeking privatization of assets. The absence of clear property rights . . . is seen as one of the greatest of all institutional barriers to economic development and the improvement of human welfare. Enclosure and the assignment of private property rights is considered the best way to protect against the so-called tragedy of the commons. Sectors formerly run or regulated by the state must be turned over to the private sphere and be deregulated. Competition—between individuals, between firms, between territorial entities—is held to be a primary virtue....Privatization and deregulation, combined with competition, it is claimed, eliminate bureaucratic red tape, increase efficiency and productivity, improve quality, and reduce costs both directly to the consumer through cheaper commodities and services and indirectly through reduction of the tax burden. (p. 65)

Conversi (2010) claims that to the globalist ideologue, "Globalization is largely an integrative process, leading to convergence, efficiency, development, and generally more harmony" (p. 40). Neoliberal ideologues were quite able to present "a benevolent mask full of wonderful-sounding words like freedom, liberty, choice, and rights, to hide the grim realities of the restoration or reconstruction of naked class power, locally as well as transnationally, but most particularly in the main financial centers of global capitalism" (Harvey, 2005, p. 159). One should not forget that neoliberal globalization is really about "restoring or in some instances (as in Russia and China) creating the power of an economic elite" (p. 19), and "legalizing" corruption as a new model within which political institutions operate.

Following Steger's (2002) arguments, we can clearly identify five ideological claims within the globalist discourse: (1) globalization is about the liberalization and global integration of markets; (2) globalization is inevitable and irreversible; (3) nobody is in charge of globalization; (4) globalization benefits everyone; and (5) globalization furthers the spread of democracy in the world (p. 73). Global neoliberal devotion to a self-regulating market merges "nineteenth-century ideals to fashionable globalization talk"; that is, "Neoliberal globalization is a gigantic repacking enterprise—the pouring of old philosophical wine into new ideological bottles" (Steger, 2002, p. 65). However, as Paraskeva (2011a; 2011b) has claimed, any attempt to de-ideologize is always a segregated practice of de-historicizing and domesticating the historical processes. Such de-ideologization masks spurious attempts to sterilize history from history itself—as if it were adialectical and existed in a social vacuum, rather than determining and determined by an integrative totality of a given social formation:

> We are experiencing processes of de-rooting of key concepts such as democracy, equality, freedom, and justice, from its own ideological dimension and trying to line them up in a neutral dimension. However odd it might be, any ideologicide is an ideological act. That is, you can only kill ideology ideologically. Indubitably the ideologies underpinning any form of de-ideologization strictly define who is exhausting the public from the public good, as well as who and how has been decided the social function of public institutions. The end of ideologies is a graphic metaphor that allows us to unveil the contradictory excesses of capitalism. (Paraskeva, 2011b, p. 14)

What we are facing is indeed the reboot of mankind's ideological revolution. The idea of globalization, Sousa Santos (2006) claims, "far from being innocent, must be considered an ideological and political move" (p. 395; see also ch. 1 of this volume). Sousa Santos recognizes two main modes of production of globalization:

> The first one consists of a twin process of globalized localisms/localized globalisms. Globalized localism is the process by which a particular phenomenon is successfully globalized, whether it is the worldwide activities of the multinational, the transformation of the English language into a lingua franca, the globalization of American fast food or popular music or the worldwide adoption of the same laws of intellectual own-

ership, patents or telecommunications aggressively promoted by the USA. The second process of globalization is the localized globalism. It consists of the specific impact on local conditions produced by transnational practices and imperatives that arise from globalized localisms. To respond to these transnational imperatives, local conditions are disintegrated, oppressed, excluded, destructured, and, eventually, restructured as subordinate inclusion. (2006, pp. 396–397)

Yet, as many of us have argued (Giroux, 2010; Harvey, 2005; Paraskeva, 2010a, 2010b; Sousa Santos, 2005, 2006; Steger 2002; Torres Santomé, 2001, 2011), neoliberal globalization has encountered serious resistance from ideological challengers around the world. Sousa Santos (2006) felicitously situates such counter-dominant global perspectives as a second mode of production of globalization—insurgent cosmopolitanism:

It consists of the transnationally organized resistance against the unequal exchanges produced or intensified by globalized localisms and localized globalisms. This resistance is organized through local/global linkages between social organizations and movements representing those classes and social groups victimized by hegemonic globalization and united in concrete struggles against exclusion, subordinate inclusion, destruction of livelihoods and ecological destruction, political oppression, or cultural suppression, etc. They take advantage of the possibilities of transnational interaction created by the world system in transition, including those resulting from the revolution in information technology and communications and from the reduction of travel costs. (p. 397; cf. ch. 1 of this volume)

Education in general and curriculum in particular are not immune to such ideological quarrels between dominant and counter-dominant forms of globalization. The language of globalization, Spring (2008) argues, "has quickly entered discourses about globalization" (p. 331). Spring goes on to note that today,

Most of the world's governments discuss similar educational agendas that include investing in education to develop human capital or better workers and to promote economic growth. As a consequence, educational discourses around the world often refer to human capital, lifelong learning for improving job skills, and economic development. Also, the global economy is sparking a mass migration of workers, resulting in global discussions about multicultural education. Intergovernmental organizations (IGOs), such as the United Nations, the OECD, and the World Bank, are promoting global educational agendas that reflect educational discourses about human capital, economic development, and multiculturalism. Information and communication technology is speeding the global flow of information and creating a library of world knowledges. Global nongovernmental organizations (NGOs), in particular those concerned with human rights and environmentalism, are trying to influence school curricula throughout the world. Multinational corporations, in particular those involved

in publishing, information, testing, for-profit schooling, and computers, are marketing their products to governments, schools, and parents around the world. (p. 332)

In this context, it is crucial to highlight the role of the Organisation for
Economic Co-operation and Development (OECD) and its famous comparative Programme for International Student Assessment reports, which became
one of the most effective ways to put pressure on states to rethink and change
their educational policies—that is, an efficient resource to challenge the hidden control of the educational agendas (Torres Santomé, 2011). Educational
policy in the social sciences, humanities, and the arts were relegated to a secondary priority; areas such as math and the so-called hard sciences became a
non-negotiable priority, which helped to establish a world exclusively paced by
economic interests. It's a way to encourage and consolidate *homo economicus* and
homo consumens.

Neoliberal globalization, or as Giroux (2008) put it, negative globalization-
al forms, became hegemonic because it has systematically won the battle over
common sense, which is deeply implicated in what is going on inside classrooms. Debates about what to teach and how to teach, what should and should
not be part of education, the relevance of school curriculum content, and various testing/grading philosophies are in fact part of the heated ideological tangle of objectives imposed by a selfish and ambitious market in which education,
curriculum, knowledge, and even students are seen as commodities. Global educational discourse, Spring (2008) claims, "play[s] an important role in creating
common educational practices and policies [driven by the faith in] a global
knowledge-based economy" (p. 338). This is one source of the ferment in the
debates surrounding "technology, human capital, lifelong learning, and the global migration of workers" (p. 338; cf. Borg & Mayo, 2005; Dale, 2005; Robertson
& Keeling, 2010; Stoer & Magalhães, 2004; Stromquist, 2002). The global discourse about "the knowledge economy has set the agenda for many national
educational policies" (Spring, 1998, 2006). Education, therefore, is profoundly implicated in this "new moral economy" (Ball, 2006, p. 11).

Arguably, schools in general and the curriculum in particular are immersed
like never before in the dynamics of ideological production, in which the
dynamics of class, race, gender, and sexual orientation are crossed unequally
with economic, cultural, and political categories (Carlson & Apple,1998;
Apple & Weis, 1983; McCarthy & Apple, 1988; Paraskeva, 2011a; Torres
Santomé, 2001). What is at stake with the current neoliberal global momentum is not just reform that drives the public educational system into a for-profit private arena, but an attempt to accomplish global uniformity through a

global curriculum, instruction, testing, and the coloniality of the English language (Spring, 2008). The attempts to achieve such global uniformity at all costs mask a eugenic claim of the need to westernize the West (Paraskeva, 2010a). As Gopal Balakrishnan (2009) argues, globalization is indeed an attempt to foster and perpetuate a "West-run global empire [in which the smell] of a long term systemic chaos" is overtly noticed (p. 25). Our task, as critical educators genuinely concerned with a society and schools that foster cognitive justice, is to challenge this dangerous trend. Peters (2005) is of great help here:

> More radically, education must actively reach beyond the confines of the modern state and the project of nation-building to establish an orientation to the Other in cultural and political terms as a basis of a new internationalism and world civic culture....Certainly the promise of Western education in long term is more to do with renouncing its ethnocentrism in order to debate with other cultural and educational traditions philosophical and theological questions concerning religious faith and its role in the political order and in the process of modernization. (p. 3)

Globalisms and Power: Iberian Educational and Curriculum Policies examines the current effects neoliberal globalization is having on Spanish and Portuguese educational and curriculum policies. In so doing, the volume dissects the nexus between globalization or globalisms and power under a global policy momentum and analyzes how neoliberal globalization strategies eagerly led by nongovernmental institutions determine and drive the educational agenda in each nation.

Portugal and Spain were the last countries in Western Europe to recover democracy—Portugal with the Carnation Revolution on April 25, 1974, and Spain with the death of the dictator General Francisco Franco on November 20, 1975. The two countries were subjugated by menacing and murderous military dictatorships; therefore, their education systems were laced with an authoritarian, militaristic, racist, and xenophobic ideology. For example, foreigners were seen as supporters of or related to socialist and communist ideologies, or simply as democrats.

In Spain, the fascist uprising of General Franco in 1936 essentially wiped out the governments of the autonomous communities and installed a highly centralized state. Franco's regime aimed to exterminate the various cultures and languages that existed within the Spanish state, such as Galicia, Cataluña, and the País Vasco (Basque Country). In Portugal, Salazar's strategy was not that different: During his dictatorship, the borders of Portugal were the borders of the world. Any historical analysis of the contemporary Portuguese and Spanish epoch cannot ignore the sanguinary events in these nations, which help explain the routines of many teachers, especially older teachers, and their "common sense" arguments. Portugal and Spain's secular authoritarian traditions and the strong influence of a conservative church are now dangerously entangled with the demands of neoliberal ideologies.

By digging into contentious themes such as globalization, democracy, and educational reform; teacher education and technology; official discourses in educational systems; and curriculum policies and politics, the contributors to this volume have engaged in a deeply critical exegesis that addresses the arenas of elementary, middle, and high school, as well as higher education. They bring to the fore how education and curriculum policies are determined and how they in turn determine the dynamics of ideological production in society. The analyses in this volume demonstrate that "globalization masks more than it reveals of what is happening in the world" (Sousa Santos, 2006, p. 395; cf. ch. 1 of this volume); in so doing, this volume not only unmasks the "paraphernalia borrowed from the private sector" (Ball, 2006, p. 11) to fix public education, it also lays bare the fact that nothing is natural, normal, or inevitable in this corporate global momentum (cf. Faraclas, 2001; Norberg-Hodge, 2001; Sousa Santos, 2006; see also ch. 1 of this volume). As this volume shows, understanding the relationship between globalism, power, and education implies completing "the study of intertwined worldwide discourses, processes, and institutions affecting local educational practices and policies" (Spring, 2008, p. 330).

In chapter 1, "Globalizations," Boaventura de Sousa Santos examines globalization as the vast arena in which hegemonic or dominant social groups, states, interests, and ideologies collide with counter-hegemonic or subordinate social groups, states, interests, and ideologies on a world scale. According to Sousa Santos, despite its inner contradictions and conflicts, the hegemonic camp has been able to produce and secure a basic consensus among its most influential members (in political terms, the G7), and it is precisely this consensus that confers on neoliberal globalization its dominant characteristics. Despite its dominance, hegemonic globalization clashes openly with a counter-hegemonic or subordinate form of globalization—what Sousa Santos calls "insurgent cosmopolitanism." Insurgent cosmopolitanism consists of the transnational resistance that has been organized against the unequal exchanges produced or intensified by globalized localisms and localized globalisms.

In chapter 2, "Secondary Education in Spain," Rafael Feito Alonso examines the effects of trends in neoliberal globalization on secondary education in Spain. The Spanish sociologist unveils how market-driven education and curriculum policies have been reinforcing behavioristic psychological approaches of the worst kind in the way we teach, thereby sharpening the irrelevance of curriculum content, putting the emphasis on grading and not on evaluation, and legitimizing the inefficacy of a fragmented educational and curriculum framework. As Feito Alonso demonstrates, schools cannot anticipate what kind of knowledge workers will need in their future working lives.

João Formosinho and Joaquim Machado argue in chapter 3, "Democratic Governance of Public Mass Schools in Portugal," that the universal character of the postprimary school induces not only quantitative but also important qualitative transformations in the education system. As Formosinho and Machado demonstrate, the first act to promote diversity was based on the assumption that extending a grammar school education to all was the natural democratic answer. However, as the authors explain, application of the traditional homogeneous recipe to more culturally diverse contexts led to massive failure among the new school populations. According to Portuguese educationalists, this massive failure prompted the government to promote reforms in the areas of teacher education and school curriculum and to launch specific national programs to combat school failure. This social and cultural diversity and discussions about the social mandate for the new elementary school also led to successive reforms in the democratic governance of the massive accessibility of public of schools in Portugal.

In chapter 4, "Crisis and Trends in Spanish Universities: The Bologna Process, Year Zero," Gloria Braga Blanco and José Luis San Fabián Maroto look at some problems and trends in Spanish universities at a time when a general crisis in the university model provides a background for the construction of the common European university space. Braga Blanco and Fabián Maroto expose the transformations in Spanish higher education that were sparked by the Bologna Declaration (1999). As they demonstrate, in a system that was already struggling to address democratic needs, the Bologna Declaration emphasized the agony of a system struggling to address social justice.

In chapter 5, "Bologna Process(ors): Knowing Very Well What They Are Doing, but Still Doing It," João Paraskeva analyzes the interplay between the Bologna Declaration (1999) and what Slaughter and Rhoades (2004) called "academic capitalism" as it was developed in Portugal. Paraskeva situates the Bologna Declaration in the context of what he calls "neoradical centrist" policies, which are forcing a new and dangerous role for higher education within the European Union (EU). Paraskeva claims that the current silent revolution in the EU higher education system must be seen not only as an attempt to market higher education, but also as an ideological and cultural strategy that attempts to westernize the West.

In chapter 6, "The Professional Career for Teachers," José Gimeno Sacristán claims that the teaching profession has become merely a forum for the recognition of teachers' merit in their professional development. This means dealing with teachers' improved cognitive abilities as well as their reflective-practical competence, the aims of which are to motivate them for their practices, to reinforce their commitment to education in general, and to recognize the merits of the best professionals with fairness. From a strictly educational point of view, Gimeno Sacristán argues that the teaching career must serve to improve teaching practices, which in turn should improve learning. This requires us to clarify the criteria that determine what we understand as good practices and specify the criteria used to assess them. Moreover, as Gimeno Sacristán claims, the complexity of teaching requires having the appropriate methodologies to deal with processes of a qualitative nature. Regulation of the teaching career has to overcome the easy quantification of methods and the bureaucratic regulation of the level of quality, and consider incentives other than salary.

Maria Alfredo Moreira and Flávia Vieira argue in chapter 7, "Preservice Teacher Education in Portugal and the Transformative Power of Local Reform," that even though theoretical and official discourses value the teacher's role as an agent of change in moving toward democratic education, beginning teacher education practices may run counter to this purpose. Moreira and Vieira discuss their own experiences as teacher educators and take a critical stance toward current reforms in beginning teacher education in Portugal. They argue for the need to implement local reforms through a scholarship of teacher education that has two main goals: to develop a critical vision for pedagogy and teacher education and to disclose the forces that impinge on teaching and teacher education and envision new possibilities.

In chapter 8, "ICT as Discourse of Salvation," José Félix Angulo Rasco and César Bernal examine the impact of information and communication technologies (ICT) in schools. The authors discuss the dangers of blindly applying technological devices in schools and curriculum and highlight the way ICT has been extolled as the solution for all the malaise within the education system. Angulo Rasco and Bernal situate their analyses within the global focus on ICT and its impact on work, on the economy of knowledge, and on student learning.

In chapter 9, "National Technology Plan for Education and Public Schooling: Myths, Limits, and False Promises," Lia Raquel Oliveira examines the Technological Plan for Education (TPE) imposed by the neoliberal

Portuguese government. Oliveira analyzes the main objectives of the TPE, exposing not only its market trends and impulses but also its limits, myths, and false promises. According to Oliveira, understanding public school as a leader in social transformation requires a reconceptualization of the interface between TPE and public education that, among other things, will set aside the technological determinism that arises as a discourse of salvation for all the problems public schools face nowadays.

In chapter 10, "Official Discourses in the Educational Systems: Competencies—The New Curriculum Password?" José Bravo Nico and Lurdes Prata Nico examine some of the main elements of the official discourse in Portuguese education. Bravo Nico and Pratas Nico delve critically into the tension over knowledge versus competence, thereby unveiling how the discourse of the competencies—the great buzzword of the Portuguese education system today—needs to be understood within the very core of the complex polyhedron that defines learning: contents (what), time (when), utility (what for). As the authors demonstrate, the discourse of the competencies is rediscovering the old reproduction of differences.

Juan Bautista Martínez Rodríguez claims in chapter 11, "Competencies: The Key to the New Curriculum," that within the Spanish context, there has been a widescale process of dissemination in terms of key competencies throughout the autonomous communities and at universities. According to Martínez Rodríguez, although this concept is not new in the field of education, it has been applied in diverse ways with inevitably varying effects. Martínez Rodríguez examines the role played by different national and international bodies in the introduction of competence training in Spain. He also identifies the conditions under which the language of competence take root and considers the impact it has on the selection of knowledge matter and the structure of curricular areas, in addition to the implications it has for practice.

In chapter 12, "Disability and Education: Transforming Difficulties into Possibilities," Miguel Lopez Melero asserts that the discourse over disability and education implies that there are educational answers to diversity and the way they have been implemented in schools. As Lopez Melero argues, the basis of the school curriculum is *what* the disabled student has to learn and *how* this will happen. He shows how educational responses to disability went from disabled students being totally excluded (they did not count at all, and were hidden in their homes) to their present recognition and request to participate in school life (inclusion). The path moved through the most common responses, from educating them in specific schools (segregation) to educational reforms that recommend educating these individuals with the rest of the students (integration), but failed to produce significant institutional transformation or change teachers' minds.

In chapter 13, "Curricular Tensions and Struggle for Justice in Neoliberal Times," Jurjo Torres Santomé claims that the current worldwide economic crisis, beyond its disastrous consequences, actually provides an excellent opportunity to rethink our position regarding the types of societies we wish to aim for, given the enormous authoritarian power now exercised by large economic corporations whose operations are supported by insufficient regulation from the political establishment. According to Torres Santomé, this situation arises as a result of policies that have progressively weakened citizenship, thus allowing for the creation of more impediments and obstacles to keep citizens from analyzing and evaluating events. In the last few decades, progressive social and community organizations have suffered attacks that have left them completely debilitated; at the same time, individuals concerned with the public sphere have become suspect. As Torres Santomé shows, community ties have been severed, and it is now becoming clear that only by recovering these community institutions and reinforcing the values of a democratic and responsible citizenship, including solidarity—or, in other words, by regaining the true value and significance of politics—will we be able to find our way out of the crisis. According to Torres Santomé, we should be guided by a key objective: to transform the world, its institutions, and the obscurantism that underlies their functions in order to build societies that are more open-minded and just, and that include strong democratic frameworks that enable citizens to regain their true role—to exercise control and make decisions about what the present and future of humanity should be like.

In chapter 14, "Deconstructing Discourses on Racism in Educational Contexts in Spain: Along a Continuum of Racialization, New and Old," Cathryn Teasley argues that the mainstream discourse on racism in Spain has centered on its supposed novelty, as if the racism that typifies reactions to the recent sharp increase in Spain's immigrant population was previously nonexistent. By means of critical historical analysis, Teasley argues that such reactions represent just one more eruption along a continuum of racism that extends far back into the multicultural contours of Iberian history. Teasley further asserts that public schooling, as one of the "final frontiers" of cosmopolitan encounters in the public sphere, must be prioritized as a privileged site for the collective deconstruction of racism in *all* of its forms and for the creative construction of cross-cultural justice.

In chapter 15, "Social Class and Education in Spain," Jaime Rivière and Mariano Fernández Enguita examine how the burden of social class in school achievement is still alive despite four decades of educational and curriculum reforms—some of them quite profound. According to Rivière and Fernández Enguita, regardless of the areas in which the reform has taken place—at the level of the cycles, pedagogy, or policies—social class continues to be the determining element. Yet, Rivière and Fernández Enguita argue, although social class maintains its predominance in multiplying segregation, increasingly detailed data show that the most advantaged students are not necessarily the children of those who are richer, but those who are more cultured; not those who have economic capital, but those who have *cultural capital*—an issue that cannot be minimized in the midst of an information and knowledge society.

In chapter 16, "Gendered Agenda in Education," Ana Sánchez Bello argues that in Spanish education, concerns about gender run parallel to women's movements. From feminist theoretical perspectives, such concerns begin to develop curriculum frameworks and organizational practices, and thereby to promote gender equality. Sánchez Bello examines crucial works published since the dictatorship that situate Spain among the countries with more educational initiatives directed at minimizing this inequality. In the proposals for gender equality, she analyzes gender violence, "the glass ceiling," revision of the curriculum, and new ways of relating in educational institutions.

Acknowledgements

In writing books scholars incur many debts along the way. Special thanks go to the contributors of this volume for the constant support and solidarity, and to Dody Riggs, who reviewed the entire manuscript in depth and clarified each chapter. We would like to express our gratitude to Provost Tony Garro (UMass Dartmouth) for the publication subvention grant that helped this project to become a reality. We also are grateful to Chris Myers and Peter Lang for their support and solidarity in this project. Intellectual debts, although no less real, are often more difficult to pinpoint. Both editors would like to thank Michael Peters, Donaldo Macedo, Henry Giroux, Richard Quantz, Shirley Steinberg, Antonia Darder, Peter McLaren, Clyde Barrow, Cameron McCarthy, David Hursh, João Rosa, Gustavo Fishman, Dennis Carlson, Alvaro Hypolito, Jarbas Vieira, Elizabeth Macedo, Alice Lopes, Jacqueline Zapata, Tristan McCowan, and Boaventura de Sousa Santos. Last but not least, thank you to our grad students at the University of Massachusetts, Dartmouth and Universidade de A Coruña, Espana.

References

Apple, M. (2009). *Global crises, social justice and education.* New York: Routledge.

Apple, M. and Weis, L. (1983). (Eds.) *Ideology and the practice of schooling.* Philadelphia: Temple University Press.

Balakrishnan, G. (2009, September–October). Speculations on the stationary state. *New Left Review, 59,* 5–26.

Ball, S. (2006). *Educational policy and social class: The selected works of Stephen Ball.* London: Routledge.

Bauman, Z. (1998). *Globalization: The human consequences.* New York: Columbia University Press.

Bell, D. (1960). *The end of ideology: On the exhaustion of political ideas in the fifties.* New York: Free Press.

Borg, C., & Mayo, P. (2005). The EU memorandum on lifelong learning: Old wine in new bottles? *Globalization, Societies and Education, 3,* 203–225.

Carlson, D., and Apple, M. (1998). *Power, knowledge, pedagogy.* Boulder: Westview Press.

Conversi, D. (2010). Limits of cultural globalization. *Journal of Critical Globalization Studies, 3,* 36–59.

Dale, R. (2005). Globalization, knowledge economy and comparative education. *Comparative Education, 41,*117–149.

Dasgupta, S., & Kiely, R. (Eds.). (2006). *Globalization and after.* Thousand Oaks, CA: Sage.

Faraclas, N. (2001). Melanesia, the banks and the BINGOS: Real alternatives are everywhere (except in the consultants' briefcases). In V. Bennholdt-Thomsen, N. Faraclas, & C. Von Werlhof (Eds.), *There is an alternative: Subsistence and worldwide resistance to corporate globalization* (pp. 67–76). London: Zed Books.

Foster, J. B. (2008, April). The financialization of capital and the crisis. *Monthly Review,* 1–15.

Fukuyama, F. (1992). *The end of history and the last man.* New York: Avon Books.

Giddens, A. (2000). *Runaway world: How globalization is reshaping our lives.* New York: Routledge.

Giroux, H. (2008). *Against the terror of neoliberalism.* Boulder, CO: Paradigm.

Giroux, H. (2010). *Contra o terror do neoliberalismo.* Lisbon: Edicoes Pedago.

Harvey, D. (2005). *A brief history of neoliberalism.* Cambridge, UK: Oxford University Press.

Huntington, S. (1987). *The clash of civilizations and the remaking of world order.* New York: Touchstone.

Kaplinsky, R. (2005) *Globalization, poverty and inequality: Between a rock and a hard place.* Cambridge: Polity

Kellner, D. (2005). The conflicts of globalization and restructuring of education. In M. Peters (Ed.), *Education, globalization and the state in the age of terrorism* (pp. 31–70). Boulder, CO: Paradigm.

McCarthy, C., & Apple, M. (1988). "Race, class, and gender in American education. Towards a nonsynchronous parallelist position," in L. Weis (Ed) *Class, race, and gender in American education.* Albany: State University of New York Press, pp., 3–39.

Mennell, B. (2009). Globalization and Americanization. In B. Turner (Ed.), *The Routledge international handbook of globalization studies.* New York: Routledge.

Norberg-Hodge, H. (2001). Local lifeline: Rejecting globalization—embracing localization. In V. Bennholdt-Thomsen, N. Faraclas, & C. Von Werlhof (Eds.), *There is an alternative: Subsistence and worldwide resistance to corporate globalization* (pp. 178–188). London: Zed Books.

Paraskeva, João (2009). Mozambique: Remasculimization of democracy. In Dave Hill and Ellen Rosskam (Eds.) (Vol. 3) *The Developing World and State Education: Neo-liberal Depredation and Egalitarian Alternatives* (pp. 197–215). New York: Routledge.

Paraskeva, J. (2010a). Highjacking public education. In S. Macrine, P. McLaren, & D. Hill (Eds.), *Revolutionizing pedagogies: Education for social justice within and beyond global neoliberalism* (pp. 167–185). New York: Palgrave Macmillan.

Paraskeva, J. (2010b). Academic capitalism in Portugal: Westernizing the west. In J. Paraskeva (Ed.), *Unaccomplished utopia: Neoconservative dismantling of public higher education in the European Union* (pp. 15–40). New York: Sense.

Paraskeva, J. (2011a). *Conflicts in curriculum theory: Challenging hegemonic epistemologies.* New York: Palgrave Macmillan.

Paraskeva, J. (2011b). Existem [mesmo] pecados para lá do Equador.' Por uma nova teoria crítica. *Revista Angolana de Sociologia*, 7 (2), 9—17.

Peters, M. (2005). Introduction: Education in the age of terrorism. In M. Peters (Ed.), *Education, globalization and the state in the age of terrorism* (pp. 1–30). Boulder, CO: Paradigm.

Rapley, J. (2004). *Globalization and inequality. Neoliberalism's downward spiral.* Boulder: Lynne Rienner Publishers.

Robertson, S., & Keeling, R. (2010). The role of the Bologna Process in the global struggle for "minds" and "markets." In J. Paraskeva (Ed.), *Unaccomplished utopia: Neoconservative dismantling of public higher education in the European Union* (pp. 41–63). New York: Sense.

Slaughter, S,. & Rhoades, G. (2004). *Academic capitalism and the new economy.* Baltimore: John Hopkins University.

Sousa Santos, B. (2005). *Democratizing democracy. Beyond the liberal democratic canon.* London: Verso.

Sousa Santos, B. (2006). *A gramatica do tempo.* Porto: Afrontamento.

Spring, J. (1998). *Education and the rise of the global economy.* Mahwah, NJ: Lawrence Erlbaum.

Spring, J. (2006). *Pedagogies of globalization: The rise of the educational security state.* Mahwah, NJ: Lawrence Erlbaum.

Spring, J. (2008). Research on globalization and education. *Review of Educational Research*, 78, 330–363.

Steger, M. (2002). *Globalism: The new market ideology.* Lanham, MD: Rowman & Littlefield.

Steger, M. (2005). *Globalism: Market ideology meets terrorism.* Lanham, MD: Rowman & Littlefield.

Steger, M. (2009). Political ideologies and social imaginaries in a global age. *Global Justice: Theory and Practice Rhetoric*, 29(2), 1–17.

Stoer, S., & Magalhães, A. (2004). Education, knowledge and the network society. *Globalisation, Societies and Education*, 2, 319–335.

Strange, S. (1996). *The retreat of the state: The definition of power in the world economy.* Cambridge, UK: Cambridge University Press.

Stromquist, N. (2002). *Education in a globalized world: The connectivity of economic power, technology, and knowledge.* Lanham, MD: Rowman & Littlefield.

Torres Santomé, J. (2001). *Educación en tiempos de neoliberalismo.* Madrid: Morata.

Torres Santomé, J. (2011). *La justicia curricular: El caballo de Troya de la cultura escolar.* Madrid: Morata.

Žižek, S. (1989). *The sublime object of ideology.* London: Verso.

Žižek, S. (2008). Tolerance as an ideological category. *Critical Inquiry*, 34, 660–682.

· 1 ·

Globalizations[1]

Boaventura de Sousa Santos

O ver the past three decades, transnational interactions have intensified dramatically, from production systems and financial transfers to the worldwide dissemination of information and images through the media, and through the mass movements of people, whether tourists or migrant workers or refugees. The extraordinary range and depth of these transnational interactions have led social scientists and politicians to view them as a rupture with previous forms of cross-border interactions—a new phenomena they have termed *globalization*. The term *global* is used to refer to both the processes and the results of globalization.

Whether new or old, the processes of globalization are a multifaceted phenomenon with economic, social, political, cultural, religious, and legal dimensions that are interlinked in a complex fashion. Strangely enough, globalization seems to combine universality and the elimination of national borders, on the one hand, with rising particularity, local diversity, ethnic identity, and a return to communitarian values on the other. In other words, globalization appears to be the other side of localization, and vice versa. Moreover, it seems to be related to a vast array of transformations across the globe, such as the dramatic rise in inequality between rich and poor countries and between rich and poor within each country, environmental disasters, ethnic conflicts, mass international migration, the emergence of new states and the collapse or decline of others, the proliferation of civil wars, ethnic cleansing, globally organized crime, and formal democracy as a political condition for international aid, terrorism, and militarism, etc.

The globalization debate has centered around the following questions: (1) Is globalization a new or old phenomenon? (2) Is globalization monolithic, or does it have different political meanings and both positive and negative aspects? (3) Is it as important in the social, political, and cultural domains as it is in the economic domain? and (4) Assuming that globalization is intensifying, where is it leading, what is the future of national societies, economies, polities, and cultures? These questions demonstrate that what is generally called globalization is a vast social field in which hegemonic or dominant social groups, states, interests, and ideologies collide with counter-hegemonic or subordinate social groups, states, interests, and ideologies on a world scale (Fisher & Ponniah, 2003; Sen et al., 2004). Although the hegemonic camp is fraught with conflicts, there is nevertheless a basic consensus among its most influential members (in political terms, the G7) that confers on globalization its dominant characteristics. As with the concepts that preceded it, such as modernization and development, the concept of globalization contains both descriptive and prescriptive components.

The prescription is, in fact, a vast set of prescriptions anchored in the hegemonic consensus. This consensus is known as the neoliberal consensus or the Washington consensus, because it was in Washington, D.C., in the mid-1980s that the core capitalist states in the world system subscribed to it. It covers a vast set of domains: world economy, social policies, relations in state and civil society, and international relations. Although it has weakened in recent years due to rising conflicts within the hegemonic camp and resistance from social movements and progressive NGOs around the world (Fisher & Ponniah, 2003), this consensus has brought us to where we are today and therefore warrants this analysis.

The Washington consensus encompasses four major issues: the consensus of the liberal (or, rather, neoliberal) economy, the consensus of the weak state, the consensus of liberal democracy, and the consensus of the primacy of the rule of law and the judicial system. The consensus of the neoliberal economy addresses several basic elements:

1. national economies must open themselves up to the world market, and domestic prices must accommodate international prices;
2. priority must be given to the export sector;

3. monetary and fiscal policies must be guided toward a reduction in inflation;
4. the rights of private property must be protected effectively and internationally;
5. the entrepreneurial sector of the state must be privatized;
6. there must be free mobility of resources (except labor), invest-ments, and profits;
7. state regulation of the economy must be minimal; and
8. social policies must be a low priority in the state budget, no longer universally applied but implemented as compensatory measures for means-tested, vulnerable social strata.

The consensus of the weak state is based on the idea that the state, rather than being the mirror of civil society, is its opposite, and potentially its enemy. The state inherently oppresses and limits civil society, and only by reducing the size of the state is it possible to reduce its harmful effects and thus strengthen civil society. Hence, the weak state tends also to be a minimal state. According to the consensus of liberal democracy, civic and political rights have absolute pri-ority over social and economic rights. Free elections and free markets are two sides of the same coin—the common good achieved through the actions of util-itarian individuals involved in competitive exchanges with the minimum of state interference.

Finally, the consensus of the primacy of the rule of law and the judicial sys-tem establishes the need for a new legal framework that is suited to the regu-latory needs of the new economic and social model, which is based on privatization, liberalization, and market relations. Property rights and con-tractual obligations must be guaranteed by the law and the judicial system, which are conceived of as independent and universal mechanisms that create standard expectations for businesses and consumers and resolve litigation through legal frameworks that are presumed to be accepted by everyone.

These four types of consensus share a core idea that constitutes a kind of meta-consensus—that is, that we are entering a period in which deep politi-cal rifts are disappearing. The imperialist rivalries between the hegemonic countries, which in the twentieth century provoked two world wars, have dis-appeared, giving rise to interdependence between the great powers, coopera-tion, and regional integration. Nowadays, only small wars exist, many of which are of low intensity and almost always on the periphery of the world system. In any case, through various mechanisms—selective military intervention, manip-ulation of international aid, and control of multilateral agencies such as the

World Bank and the International Monetary Fund—the core countries have the means to keep these focuses for instability under control (Patomäki & Teivainen, 2005). Moreover, conflicts between capital and labor have become relatively deinstitutionalized without causing serious instability. This is due to the fact that labor has become a global resource and because no institutionalized global labor market exists or ever will exist.

The idea that rifts between the different models of social transformation are disappearing also forms part of this meta-consensus. The first three-quarters of the twentieth century were dominated by rivalries between two antagonistic models: revolution and reformism. If the collapse of the Soviet Union and the fall of the Berlin Wall meant the end of the revolutionary paradigm, then the crises of the welfare state in the developed countries and of the developmentalist state in the developing countries means that the reformist paradigm is equally condemned. In the face of this, social transformation from now on will no longer be a political question but a technical question. The idea of the end of history is the extreme manifestation of this meta-consensus.

Moving from the descriptive/prescriptive level to the analytical level, it becomes evident that the dominant characteristics of globalization are the characteristics of dominant or hegemonic globalization. Therefore, a crucial distinction must be made between hegemonic and counter-hegemonic globalization.

The Nature of Globalization

The idea of globalization as a linear, homogenizing, and irreversible phenomenon, although false, is prevalent nowadays, and it is all the more so as we move from scientific discourse into political discourse and everyday talk. Apparently transparent and without complexity, the idea of globalization masks more than it reveals of what is happening in the world. When viewed from a different perspective, what it masks or hides is so important that the transparency and simplicity of the idea of globalization, far from being innocent, must be considered an ideological and political move.

Two motives for such a move should be stressed. The first is what we could call the determinist fallacy. It consists of inculcating the idea that globalization is a spontaneous, automatic, unavoidable, and irreversible process that intensifies and advances according to inner logic and dynamism strong enough to impose themselves on any external interference. The fallacy exists in transforming the causes of globalization into its effects, which obscures the fact that globalization results from a set of political decisions that are identifiable in time and space, as mentioned above. The second political motive is the fallacy of the disappearance of the South. Whether at a financial level or at the level of production or even of consumption, the world has become integrated into a global economy in which, faced with multiple interdependencies, it no longer makes sense to distinguish between North and South or between the core, periphery, and semi-periphery of the world system. In the terms of this fallacy, even the idea of the Third World is becoming obsolete. Contrary to this discourse, the inequalities between North and South have dramatically increased in the past three decades; therefore, this fallacy seems to have no other objective than to trivialize the negative, exclusionary consequences of neoliberal globalization by denying them analytical centrality. Thus, declaring the "end of the South" and the "disappearance of the Third World" is, above all, a product of ideological changes that must themselves become an object of scrutiny (Sousa Santos, 2005; Sen et al., 2004).

Both the determinist fallacy and the fallacy of the disappearance of the South have lost credibility in recent years. On the one hand, although some still consider globalization a great triumph of rationality, innovation, and liberty capable of producing infinite progress and unlimited abundance, for others it is anathema, as it brings misery, loss of food sovereignty, and social exclusion for increasingly vast populations of the world, ecological destruction, and so on On the other hand, a contradiction has been growing between those who see in globalization the indisputable and unconquerable energy of capitalism and those who discover in some of its features, such as the revolution in information and communication technologies, new opportunities to broaden the scale and the nature of transnational solidarity and anticapitalist struggle (Buey, 2005).

In light of these disjunctions and confrontations, it becomes clear that what we term *globalization* is, in fact, a set of different processes of globalization and, in the last instance, of different and sometimes contradictory globalizations. What we generally call globalization is different sets of social relationships that give rise to different phenomena of globalization. In these terms, there is not, strictly speaking, one sole entity called globalization, but many globalizations; to be precise, this term should only be used in the plural. As they are sets of social relationships, globalizations involve conflicts, and therefore, winners and losers.

The dominant discourse on globalization is the history of the winners, told by the winners. At an abstract level, only a process-based definition of globalization is possible. Here is my definition: globalization is a set of unequal exchanges in which a certain artifact, condition, entity, or local identity extends its influence beyond its local or national borders and, in so doing, develops an ability to designate as local another rival artifact, condition, entity, or identity.

The most important implications of this concept are as follows: First, there is no originally global condition; what we call globalization is always the successful globalization of a particular localism. In other words, there are no global conditions for which we cannot find local roots. The second implication is that globalization presupposes localization. The process that creates the global as the dominant position in unequal exchanges is the same one that produces the local as the dominated—and, therefore, hierarchically inferior—position. In fact, we live as much in a world of globalizations as we live in a world of localizations. Therefore, in analytical terms, it would be equally correct if our current situation and our research topics were defined in terms of localization instead of globalization. The reason why the latter term is preferred is basically because hegemonic scientific discourse tends to favor the history of the world as told by the winners.

There are many examples of how globalization produces localization. English as a lingua franca is one. Its spread as a global language implies the localization of other languages, even those that not long ago saw themselves as global, such as French. An analogy can be seen in the French or Italian actors of the 1960s—Brigitte Bardot and Alain Delon, or Marcello Mastroianni and Sophia Loren—who at the time symbolized the universal style of acting but nowadays seem provincially European, if not curiously ethnic. The difference lies in the way the Hollywood style of acting has managed to globalize itself in the ensuing decades. That is to say, once a certain process of globalization has been identified, its integral meaning and explanation cannot be understood without taking into account the adjacent processes of relocalization occurring simultaneously or in sequence with it.

One transformation most frequently associated with the processes of globalization is the compression of time and space, or, rather, the social process by which phenomena accelerate and are spread throughout the world. Although apparently monolithic, this process combines highly differentiated situations and conditions. Because of this, it cannot be analyzed independently of the power relations that respond to the different forms of temporal and spatial mobility. On the one hand, there is the global capitalist class that in reality controls the space-time compression and is capable of transforming it in its favor. On the other hand, there are the lower classes and subordinate groups, such as migrant workers and refugees, who in recent decades have represented much cross-border traffic but who do not in any way control the space-time compression. Between the executives of the multinational companies and the emigrants and refugees are the tourists, who represent a third mode of production of the compression of space and time.

There are also those who contribute greatly to globalization but nevertheless remain prisoners in their own local time and space. For example, by cultivating coca, the peasants of Bolivia, Peru, and Colombia contribute decisively to the world drug culture, but they remain localized in their villages, as they always have been. The same is true of the Rio slum-dwellers, who are prisoners of their marginal urban lifestyle while their songs and dances, particularly the samba, are now part of a globalized music culture. The production of globalization therefore entails the production of localization.

I identify two main modes of the production of globalization. The first consists of a twin process of globalized localisms/localized globalisms. Globalized localism is the process by which a particular phenomenon is successfully globalized, such as the worldwide activities of the multinational, the transformation of the English language into a lingua franca, the globalization of American fast food and popular music, and the worldwide adoption of the laws of intellectual ownership, patents, and telecommunications aggressively promoted by the United States. In this mode of the production of globalization, what is globalized is the winner of a struggle for the appropriation or valorization of resources, or for the hegemonic recognition of a given cultural, racial, sexual, ethnic, religious, or regional difference. This victory translates into the capacity to dictate the terms of integration, competition, and inclusion.

The second process of globalization is localized globalism, which consists of the specific impact on local conditions produced by transnational practices and imperatives that arise from globalized localisms. To respond to these transnational imperatives, local conditions are disintegrated, oppressed, excluded, destructured, and eventually restructured as subordinate inclusion. Such localized globalisms include the elimination of traditional commerce and subsistence agriculture; the creation of free-trade enclaves or zones; the deforestation and massive destruction of natural resources in order to pay off external debt; the use of historic treasures, religious ceremonies or places, craftsmanship, and wildlife for the benefit of the global tourism industry; ecological dumping— that is, the "purchase" by Third World countries of toxic waste produced in the core capitalist countries in order to pay off foreign debt; the conversion of subsistence agriculture into agriculture for export as part of "structural adjustment"; and the ethnicization of the workplace—in other words, devaluing salaries because the workers belong to an ethnic group considered "inferior."

These two processes operate in conjunction with each other and constitute the hegemonic type of globalization also called *top-down neoliberal globalization,* or *globalization from above.* The processes should be dealt with separately, because the factors, agents, and conflicts that intervene in one or the other are partially distinct. The sustained production of globalized localisms and localized globalisms is increasingly determining or conditioning the various hierarchies that constitute the global capitalist world. The international division of the production of globalization tends to assume the following pattern: Core countries specialize in globalized localisms, while peripheral countries only have the choice of localized globalisms.

Insurgent Cosmopolitanism

There is, however, a second mode of the production of globalization, which I call *insurgent cosmopolitanism.* It consists of the transnationally organized resistance against the unequal exchanges produced or intensified by globalized localisms and localized globalisms. This resistance is organized through local/global linkages between social organizations and movements that represent those classes and social groups victimized by hegemonic globalization and united in concrete struggles against exclusion, subordinate inclusion, destruction of livelihoods and local environments, political oppression, cultural suppression, and so on. They take advantage of the possibilities of transnational interaction created by a world system in transition, including those resulting from the revolution in information technology and communications, and from lower travel costs. Insurgent cosmopolitan activities include, among many others, egalitarian transnational North–South and South–South networks of solidarity among social movements and progressive NGOs; the new working-class internationalism (dialogues between workers organizations in regional blocs); transnational coalitions among workers of the same multinational corporation operating in different countries; coalitions of workers and citizens groups in the struggle against sweatshops, discriminatory labor practices, and slave labor; international networks of alternative legal aid; transnational human rights organizations; worldwide networks of feminist, indigenous, ecological, or alternative development movements and associations; and literary, artistic, and scientific movements on the periphery of the world system in search of alternative non-imperialist, counter-hegemonic cultural values that are involved in studies using postcolonial or minority perspectives. The confrontations outside the World Trade Organization meeting in Seattle on November 30, 1999, were the first eloquent demonstration of insurgent cosmopolitanism (Fisher & Ponniah, 2003; Sen et al., 2004). The World Social Forum is today its most accomplished manifestation.

Use of the term *cosmopolitanism* to describe global resistance against the unequal exchanges produced by hegemonic globalization may seem inadequate in the face of its modernist or Western ascendancy. The idea of cosmopolitanism, like universalism, world citizenship, and the rejection of political and territorial borders, has a long tradition in Western culture, from the cosmic law of Pythagoras and the philallelia of Democritus to the *Homo sum, humani nihil a me alienum puto* of Terence; from the medieval *res publica christiana* to the Renaissance humanists; and from Voltaire, for whom "to be a good patriot, it is necessary to become an enemy of the rest of the world," to working-class internationalism. This ideological tradition has often been put to the service of European expansionism, colonialism, and imperialism—the same historical processes that today generate globalized localisms and localized globalisms. Insurgent cosmopolitanism, in contrast, refers to the aspiration of oppressed groups to organize their resistance on the same scale and through the same type of coalitions used by the oppressors to victimize them; that is, the global scale and local/global coalitions. Insurgent cosmopolitanism is also different from that invoked by Marx, which referred to the universality of those who, under capitalism, have nothing to lose but their chains—the working class. The oppressed classes in the world today cannot be encompassed by the class-that-has-only-its-chains-to-lose category. Insurgent cosmopolitanism includes vast populations in the world that are not sufficiently useful or skilled enough to "have chains"—in other words, to be directly exploited by capitalism.

Insurgent cosmopolitanism aims to unite social groups on a non-class basis—the victims of exploitation as well as the victims of social exclusion, and of sexual, ethnic, racist, and religious discrimination. For this reason, contrary to the Marxist concept, insurgent cosmopolitanism does not imply uniformity, a general theory of social emancipation and the collapse of differences, autonomies, and local identities. Giving equal weight to the principle of equality and to the principle of recognzing difference, insurgent cosmopolitanism is no more than a global emergence resulting from the fusion of local progressive struggles with the aim of maximizing their emancipatory potential in loco (however defined) through translocal/local linkages.

This is both the strength and the weakness of insurgent cosmopolitanism. The progressive or counter-hegemonic character of cosmopolitan coalitions cannot be taken for granted. On the contrary, it is intrinsically unstable and problematic and demands constant self-reflection by those who share its objectives. Cosmopolitan initiatives conceived and created by a counter-hegemonic character can later come to assume hegemonic characteristics, and even run the risk of becoming converted into globalized localisms. It is enough to think of the local initiatives in participatory democracy, which had to fight for years against authoritarian populism, the absolutism of representative democracy, and the mistrust of the conservative political elites, and which nowadays are beginning to be recognized and even adopted by the World Bank, seduced by the efficiency and lack of corruption they have applied to managing funds and development loans. Self-reflexive vigilance is essential in order to distinguish between the technocratic concept of participatory democracy sanctioned by the World Bank and the democratic and progressive concept of participatory democracy as an embryo of counter-hegemonic globalization (Bell, 2002).

The instability of the progressive or counter-hegemonic character is also derived from another factor: the different concepts of emancipatory resistance held by cosmopolitan initiatives in different regions of the world system. For example, the struggle for minimum standards in working conditions (so-called labor standards)—a struggle led by trade unions and human rights organizations in the more developed countries, to prevent from circulating freely in the world market products produced by labor that does not reach these required minimum standards—is certainly seen by the organizations that promote it as counter-hegemonic and emancipatory, since it aims to improve the conditions of the workers' lives. However, it can be seen by similar organizations in peripheral countries as one more hegemonic strategy of the North to create one more form of protectionism that favors the rich countries and harms the poor ones. But despite all these difficulties, insurgent cosmopolitanism has succeeded in credibly demonstrating that there is an alternative to hegemonic, neoliberal, top-down globalization, and that is counter-hegemonic solidarity, bottom-up globalization.

From now on, what we call global and globalization cannot but be conceived of as the provisory, partial, and reversible result of a permanent struggle between two modes of the production of globalization—indeed, between two globalizations.

Note

1. A version of this chapter appears in *Theory, Culture & Society*, 23(2–3), 393–399. Published with authors' permission.

References

Bell, W. (2002). *Deglobalization: Ideas for a new economy*. London: Zed Books.

Bue, F. (2005). *Guía para una globalización alternativa*. Barcelona: Ediciones.

Fisher, W., & Ponniah, T. (Eds.). (2003). *Another world is possible: Popular alternatives to globalization at the world social forum*. London: Zed Books.

Houtart, F., & Polet, F. (Eds.). (2001). *The other Davos: The globalization of resistance to the world economic system*. London: Zed Books.

Patomäki, H., & Teivainen, T. (2005). *A possible world: Democratic transformation of global institutions*. London: Zed Books.

Sen, J., Anand, A., Escobar, A., & Waterman, P. (Eds.). (2004). *World Social Forum: Challenging empires*. New Delhi: Viveka Foundation.

Sousa Santos, B. de. (2005). *O forum social mundial: Manual de uso*. São Paulo: Cortez Editora.

· 2 ·

Secondary Education in Spain

Rafael Feito Alonso

The *educación secundaria obligatoria* (compulsory secondary education)—the four years that serve pupils aged 12 to 16 in Spain—has become quite controversial in recent years; most accusations of poor performance in international academic rankings point directly to failings in secondary education. Comprehensive reform, which started in Spain in the 1990s with the passing of the Ley de Ordenación General del Sistema Educativo (LOGSE) that addressed the general organization of education, is considered by some to be the main reason for most of the recent troubles in education. Conservatives consider it a mistake to educate struggling and academically successful pupils together in the same classrooms and advocate for a more selective secondary education with vocational and academic branches, as was the case in Spain before 1990.

Yet, educational reforms in Europe and elsewhere are leaning a different direction. The European Union (EU) has committed itself to school success including upper secondary school—which in Spain means either a baccalaureate or intermediate-level vocational education degree—for most youngsters. In an agreement signed in Lisbon in 2000 (i.e. the Lisbon Treaty) leaders of EU nations proposed that a minimum of 85% of people aged 20 to 24 will get at least an upper secondary degree. This proposal was passed in the context of the need for a knowledgeable and participative citizenry able to face twenty-first-century variegated challenges. As citizens, we are asked about more and more complex topics such as climate change or stem cell research. In almost every workplace, in our neighbourhoods, and in our schools we meet people coming from different cultures which with we must live in cooperatively. Furthermore, our homes and our daily lives are overflowing with gadgets that make life more convenient, but in order to use them we must keep up with innovation. Our life expectancy is increasing, which means that older people will likely develop new roles as they enter more lengthy retirement periods. And finally, scientific production more than doubles every few years, and the greatest number of scientists in the history of mankind are alive and active in research today.

Beyond elementary literacy and the three Rs—reading, writing, and arithmetic—there is great uncertainty about what knowledge schools must deliver and how knowledge will develop in the near and distant future. Today's schools, therefore, should provide students with the analytic tools they will need to continue to learn long after they leave compulsory education. Schools must aim to produce inquiring readers, lively citizens, devoted parents, and innovative and reliable workers—in short, people who are able to learn continually and perhaps even reinvent themselves throughout their lives.

The most efficient economies are those that, besides producing more knowledge and information, are able to make both items universally accessible. Schools should get rid of their function of creating or perpetuating social hierarchy. If we want most of the people to get at least an upper secondary education many things have to change, and to start with, we need to acknowledge that secondary education is no longer for just a single minority of the population.

> According to Barth (2004), in the United States in 1973, 51% of manufacturing work was performed by high school dropouts; in 2000 that figure had dropped to 19%. It is crucial to note that in constant dollars, annual earnings for dropouts fell 19% during that period. Manufacturing work performed by people with a secondary school education rose from 37% in 1973 to 45% in 2000 (Barth, 2004). The ten most in-demand jobs in the United States in 2010 did not exist in 2004, and it is likely this trend will continue.

The message for schools seems absolutely crystal: In order to ensure that 85% of youngsters earn an upper secondary degree, schools will have to provide a high-quality education that gives students the skills and knowledge they will need to be successful in the twenty-first century. It is not enough to teach by rote memorization material that has no applicability or relevance outside the school setting.

School failure is becoming less and less socially acceptable. A report on education from the Bill and Melinda Gates Foundation expressed that concern:

> Imagine that an overnight mail service failed to deliver a third of its packages on time, or that three-quarters of the stereos produced by an electronics company failed to meet industry standards. Imagine that a retail clothing company provided high-quality customer service, but only to certain types of customers. Would these companies stay in business? Now, consider that American high schools:
> - Allow one-quarter of students to read below basic levels.
> - Fail to graduate 30% of their students.
> - Prepare far fewer low-income than high-income students for college.
> (Gates & Gates, 2010, p. 2)

Yet, the problem is not exclusively school failure. Many people who succeed at school fail in real life. Gardner (2004) pointed out that many astrophysics students are unable to give a correct explanation to the question of why summer is hotter than winter: Most of them answer that the earth is closer to the sun in summer, which left unexplained why it is winter in one hemisphere and summer in the other.

Allowing everyone to gain access to secondary education means educating people from very different backgrounds. Obviously this can be a source of social problems, but also it can be a source of richness, as demonstrated by Stockholm's Rinkeby School, which is famous for being visited by every Nobel literature winner. It is quite different to work with a minority of pupils who leaves education for work at age 14 than to work with a mixed, unsegregated cohort. This does not necessarily entail a decline in educational level. On the contrary, despite the claims of some teachers and journalists that school results are declining, data from the ministry of education and a large body of educational research never have supported that claim, even when conservatives were in office.

Struggling students bring up a challenge for school in terms of their curricula, internal workings, and rules. These students' attitudes toward school suggest that academic knowledge is not enough for a successful adult life and that there are many ways of understanding the world. Typical academic language sometimes does not go beyond empty jargon. Perhaps it is possible to learn more, and more deeply, when students of different ages work together.

After an enthusiastic experimental period, secondary schools in Spain seem to have become isolated from the people they serve. They gradually returned to a transmissive, passive pedagogy that upholds the supremacy of conceptual knowledge, which has resulted in increased educational inequality and greater school failure among the less socially and economically privileged groups.

Secondary schools favour compensatory or remedial education for struggling students. Pupils who do not achieve acceptable educational standards are considered to be victims of an intellectual deficit; in short, they suffer from a culture of deprivation. It is common for secondary schools to put into different tracks struggling and successful pupils. Remedial math and language classes are filled with struggling pupils, while successful students are placed into classes in which French or other foreign languages are taught. This kind of tracking often follows ethnic lines. Typically, Spaniards fill the foreign language group, whereas immigrants are overrepresented in the remedial classes. This becomes a self-fulfilling prophesy, because students in the remedial classes often are stigmatized. Furthermore, more often than not most experienced teachers will not choose to teach these pupils.

Retention Grade Rates

Whereas promotion at primary level occurs at the end of each of three two-year periods in which this level is organized (first and second course make a period, third and fourth the second one, and finally fifth and sixth make the third one), promotion at secondary level is decided after every course, after every academic year. So, primary education allows longer periods to evaluate students while secondary education seems to rush evaluations.

Grade retention is far from controversial in Spain, and what is worse, the international controversy surrounding grade retention it is not well known in Spain, though the experience of other European countries is quite conspicuous. Belgium is a case in point (see Gates & Gates, 2010). Three educational systems coexist in this country: Dutch, German, and French. The retention level is quite high in the French system: One in four pupils has repeated at least one course. Automatic promotion is the norm in the Belgian Dutch and German systems, which show better results for every evaluation, national and international, than the French one. Several other countries with better international results than Spain—including Finland, Norway, Sweden, Denmark, the United Kingdom, Ireland, and Japan—also enjoy automatic promotion. Moreover, data indicate that the rate of admission to upper level secondary education is greater in countries that make use of automatic promotion than in those that do not (see Gates & Gates, 2010).

At first sight, grade retention seems quite a logical thing to do: The pupil who fails is slow, and it is better to give him enough time to acquire the required knowledge and skills. Nevertheless, retention is not recommended due to its negative or, at best, neutral effects.

Slight improvements can be detected for retained pupils which leads to the belief that retention is a useful measure. But what is not immediately apparent is that pupils are much less productive in a repeated year than they would be if they were promoted. Research made in France in 1984 (cited in Seibel, 1996) found that pupils who remain with their cohort instead of being retained are less likely to fail (4% versus 6%). Second, the data showed retention to be barely efficacious. Five groups of pupils were under research: three groups of students who had never been retained (high-, medium-, and low-level pupils), one group was made up of pupils retained for the first time, and the last group were pupils who previously had been retained. As the table below shows (Seibel, 1996), the benefits of retention generally are quite low. For example, low-level pupils made better progress when not retained. Moreover, students are emotionally at their best when they remain with their classmates of the same age, and being retained often means being stigmatized.

Table 1. Comparative Results for Retained and Promoted Pupils in French and Maths

Subpopulation	%	French results			Maths results		
		June	Dif. June-Dec	Dec	June	Dif. June-Dec	Dec
Not retained							
** High performance	12.0	86.6	-2.6	84.0	98.2	+0.9	99.1
** Intermediate performance	61.3	70.0	+5.5	75.5	77.9	+8.0	85.0
** Low performance	6.2	36.3	+17.2	53.5	51.1	+11.7	62.8
Previously retained	11.0	60.0	+1.8	61.8	71.8	+3.8	75.6
Newly retained	9.5	33.4	+4.1	37.5	47.8	+3.3	51.1
Sample	100.0	66.1	+4.7	70.8	76.2	+6.5	84.7

Note. Adapted from "Genèses et consequences de l'échec scolaire: Vers une politique de prévention," by Claude Seibel, 1996, Revue Française de Pédagogie, 67, 7-28. Adapted with permission.

The coordinator of the Programme for International Student Assessment (PISA), Andreas Schleicher, considers grade retention, especially in Spain, to be expensive and not efficacious and just a way to pass the problem from one teacher to another rather than solving pupils' problems within their age groups, as it is the case in Finland (interview with Andreas Schleicher, *Escuela*, 3689, December 22, 2006).

Regrettably, Spain's 2006 Ley de Ordenación Educativa (LOE) supports anti-egalitarian teachers, allowing soft tracking—curricular diversification—for pupils who have been retained for one year at the third course of compulsory secondary education. In addition, it allows 15-year-old pupils to take vocational courses, always under their parents' consent. Traditional daily secondary education seems to be out of question.

Curriculum Content

Quite often what is taught at school is irrelevant from an educational point of view because it does not increase students' level of understanding or help them develop their intellectual abilities. Moreover, irrelevant content is often forgotten after it has been taught a few days . Here is an example of what twelfth-year pupils are supposed to know:

- What was achieved with the Peace of Augsburg?
- Define and give an example of an indirect reciprocal clause.
- Write the number of faces, edges, and vertex of a hexahedron.
- What is the climate of the savannah?
- What are the main terrestrial biomes?
- Who organized the Congress of Berlin in 1855? What were the results?
- What is the name of the cells that produce *gametangia?*
- Name the mechanical and chemical processes that take place in the small intestine.
- What are the characteristics of the eukaryotic cells? (Examples taken from Vera & Esteve, 2001, p. 43)

It is doubtful that this kind of knowledge is essential for compulsory education, which prompts an obvious question: Who selects this knowledge? Socially valued knowledge usually is arbitrarily imposed by the upper and middle classes. For example, in fourteenth-century China and Europe the archetypical cultivated man of privilege was able to versify, to ride a horse, and to do fencing or archery. It becomes an issue when this kind of cultural formation is imposed upon every pupil, and particularly when it is done at the expense of more practical and useful knowledge

The Way We Teach

Most of the learning process at the secondary level consists of pupils taking notes from their teachers' lectures and reading textbooks. Our culture considers learning to be a process in which the teacher talks and pupils listen and occasionally pose a question. Evidence shows that pupils' concentration declines as a lecture moves forward, according to a distinct pattern: five minutes for adaptation, five minutes to assimilate information, followed by confusion and boredom and a sharp decline in attention, a low level of concentration during the rest of the lecture, and a small resurgence of interest at the end (Johnson & Johnson, 1999).

Our educational model seems to be based on behaviourist psychology in that it considers learning to be more effective when we simply gather small pieces of information that together will build knowledge. But as recent research on brain function shows, most people learn more easily when they are given a global or holistic view of the topics to be learned.[1] In an unconscious way, our schools thus favour the minority of the population with an analytic understanding.

Our schools tend to teach discrete subjects in separate classes, especially at the secondary level. In some innovative schools, however, rather than learning about literature in English class and history in History class, students tackle a subject such as the Great Depression and they explore how literature, art, and news reports depicted the period. Instead of lecturing, teachers serve as guides, pointing students to various source documents and giving examples of the quality of work expected for the final project.

Pupils learn deeper and better when they focus on a few topics, scrutinize them deeply, and examine how they relate to each other. But it is not only a question of learning about certain topics as analytic thinking can be applied to many different subjects, learned in or out of school.

A Fragmented Organization

Generally, secondary schools do not work with a global curriculum. Each teacher considers his or her subject to be the most important knowledge in the world and barely relates it to other subjects. Pupils in primary education study a few subjects and spend most of their time with just one teacher, and when they enter secondary school suddenly they are faced with thirteen subjects and, quite likely, thirteen teachers.

Secondary education teachers are specialists in one particular subject and they often know little to nothing about what their colleagues are teaching— and often they do not seem to be interested in knowing it. Many teachers consider their job to be transmitting knowledge, and they know little about their pupils except perhaps who the troublemakers are and which students are outstanding learners. Fanfani (2010) cited a text Freud wrote in 1910 to explain the moral bankruptcy students suffer in secondary education:

> Secondary school must be able to achieve much more than avoiding adolescent suicide. It must be able to arouse the desire for living…I consider it out of the question that it does not do that and that in many respects it does not live up to its mission which is to offer a substitute for family and raise interest in outside life. (p. 2)

A Diminished Vision of Compulsory Secondary Education

Quite likely due to the school enrolment of historically excluded people, the LOE presents an approach to secondary education akin to a kind of desert crossing. Contrasts between lower level secondary education and the baccalaureate level are outrageous. At the compulsory level, student learning is largely passive, and pupils are expected to know, value, respect, and assume basic knowledge, and to develop a very modest number of skills. At the baccalaureate level, in contrast, students are expected to develop an autonomous moral identity; the LOE describes their learning with expressions such as *exercise, consolidate, master, access,* and *develop.* What is more, despite the fact that the idea of entrepreneurial spirit is addressed at both secondary levels, at the baccalaureate level creative development is added.

Once again, we return to the obsessive focus on pupil effort. It goes without saying that pupils need to expend a great deal of effort to achieve their educational goals. This effort should be guided by the pleasure of learning and a natural curiosity that, regrettably, schools often stifle in young adolescents, who often are viewed with suspicion and mistrust. This brings to mind what Zweig wrote about education in Central Europe at the beginning of the twentieth century:

> They never get tired of saying to the young man that he was still not mature, that he did not understand anything at all, that he should listen and obey, and that he could not take the floor in conversations and, much less, contradict. (2001, p. 59)

It seems that school is viewed by many as a preparation for life, rather than an integral part of life in itself. In other words, they focus on what the child will become in the future rather than on who he or she is at the present time. The weight of a *propaedeutic* mentality—when each educational level has a meaning related to the next one—is a burden of the past that government proposals cannot avoid.

Where Is the Place for Reading, Researching, and Using ITCs?

Government regulations mandate a certain amount of time to reading in every academic subject, but there are no organizational settings in which to situate the reading. In fact, our schools fail to connect the library with daily teaching.

Michel Rocard reported that teaching based on research methods is much more effective than traditional teaching approaches. Moreover, empirical evidence shows a close connection between attitudes toward science and the way it is taught.[2] This suggests that teaching should focus more on concepts and scientific methods and less on rote memorization. As it is the case for gathering scientific data, there are two pedagogical approaches for teaching science. The first one is deductive, or transmissive—from the top down; it is the approach most often used in schools. In this model, teachers explain concepts and their logical implications and then provide examples. The second approach is inductive—from the bottom up. This method provides more space for the pupil to observe, experiment, and build, with teacher assistance. Clearly, this is the most appropriate approach to teaching. By definition, research is an intentional process in which participants diagnose problems, develop theories, look up information, build up patterns, and debate with their peers in coherent arguments.

In this approach, using the library and reading a variety of sources is critical for the learning process. There is a striking contrast in library use between pupils in primary and secondary education that reflects the dependence of academic culture on the textbook. In a paper published in *Cuadernos de Pedagogía*, Inés Miret wrote, based in her own research, that primary education pupils use libraries more often than secondary pupils.[3] In fact, seventy-five percent of secondary teachers say they do not visit the school library with their students; only 20% of teachers provide library access during lecture time; and a mere 9% work or lecture in the library. More than 60% of teachers say that they never recommend reading books to their students—so they do not learn to use different sources of information. When reading is recommended, it is usually literature rather than books on history, chemistry, or math. Obviously, we need a radical change in teaching methods to give the school library the crucial role it should have.

The same thing seems to happen with information and communication technologies (ICT). Traditionally, schools have been reluctant to utilize technological innovations. In its day, using a pen rather than a pencil was quite an upheaval; more recent generations have witnessed the absurd controversy around using calculators at school. Even today, many schools ban pupils from writing their essays using computers for fear of copying from Internet. The fact is, both books and new technologies—especially the Internet—open wide avenues for intellectual adventures into new, unexplored territories.

Lack of Deliverance Settings

In order to live in harmony and make democracy a daily practice, we need people to be able to express themselves, to listen to others carefully and politely, and to be able to participate in civilized debate.

Early childhood education offers daily opportunities for students to verbalize their experiences and feelings; similar opportunities should be offered in secondary education. Every subject should be organized to allow students to exchange their points of view about curricular matters. When pupils are allowed to speak, they discover new universes and are able to incorporate knowledge into their interpretation of the world. Regrettably, most school time consists of pupils listening rather than speaking and being listened to.

> Learning to speak, to handle a language that allows a minimum of precision, that allows going beyond a close circle of acquaintances is anything but spontaneous. Almost half of Argentinian students that finish secondary school experience dire difficulties in understanding a text. Daily experience proves that many younger—and not so young—people are unable to communicate accurately what they think. This happens not only in Argentina. It is the same, for instance, in France where one out of ten youngsters aged 17 to 25 years does not read or write correctly. French linguist Alain Bentolila believes this situation gives birth to what he calls linguistic insecurity. Being unable to accurately express oneself and to understand what others say locks young people into a social ghetto. This dooms them to exclusion, drives them to rebellion and, quite likely, also to violence. Linguistic insecurity results in dramatic social inequality. (Etcheverry, 2006, p. 1)

In an experiment at Monserrat School in Barcelona, third- and fourth-degree secondary education pupils researched the twentieth century using several documents.[4] All pupils said they considered the experience a very valuable way of learning history. They remembered the facts and were able to put them into context and make sense of them. Some of the pupils researched far beyond what was required and read a lot about recent history, read newspapers, watched the news, and asked their grandparents about the past.

In contrast, the fact of silencing pupils in the classroom allows empty intellectual spaces in which they can develop wrong ideas and prejudices. When asked about the importance of debates in the classroom, London University Kings College professor Jonathan Osborne said, "It is crucial. Teachers could promote debates in the classroom if they were less worried about teaching the right idea and thought more about explaining why a wrong idea is misguided."[5]

Government proposals do little to address the enormous social and ethnic inequalities in education; indeed, very few of the ideas discussed in this paper are addressed in the 2006 LOE. As Gimeno Sacristán (2006) wrote, legislators have avoided bothering corporate secondary education teachers—teachers who would like to return to an imagined paradise of compliant academic students. Notwithstanding the proposal of learning by competencies, the ministerial curricular regulations establish an academic knowledge strongly divided into discrete subjects. In any case, competencies are considered to be additional to the task of transmitting knowledge.

Fortunately, some primary and secondary schools work in a different way. In secondary education, solutions that promote living together through dialogue have been crucial. Teachers at these schools realize that their pupils are able to use their intellects to solve problems and that they can be relied on for other school tasks.

Today's high schools were conceived at the beginning of the twentieth century to prepare students for work in an industrial economy that was very different from the economy we have today. We do not know what jobs will exist in the coming years, or what skills or kind of knowledge will be needed to fill them. The health of our democracy depends on a renewed education. Democratic institutions require an educated citizenry that is knowledgeable, reflective, and able to embrace its civic responsibilities. More than ever, the challenges our young people are facing require that all students—not just an elite minority—leave school with a knowledgeable point of view, knowledge of the world, a capacity to grapple with complex problems, and a willingness and an ability to engage with people different from themselves. Good high schools not only provide students with these skills, preparing them for colleges that further develop those skills—they also celebrate the diversity of their student populations and create authentic knowledge.

Notes

1. P.L. Thomas, "The cult of prescription-Or, a student ain't no slobbering dog," in Shirley R. Steinberg & Joe L. Kincheloe, *What you don't know about schools*, Palgrave MacMillan, New York, 2006.
2. Michel Rocard (Chair), *Science education now: A renewed pedagogy for the future of Europe*, in http://ec.europa.eu/research/science-society/document_library/pdf_06/report-rocard-on-science-education_en.pdf
3. "Usos, usuarios y algunas paradojas," *Cuadernos de pedagogía*, 352, December 2005.
4. Monserrat del Pozo Rosselló, "Instantáneas históricas," *Cuadernos de Pedagogía*, 355, March 2006.
5. Interview for *El País*, May 15, 2006. A more developed version of these ideas can be found in Jonathan Osborne, *¿Qué ciencia necesitan los ciudadanos?*, in *La enseñanza de las ciencias y la evaluación PISA 2006*, Fundación Santillana, Madrid, 2006 (http://www.fundacion-santillana.com/upload/ficheros/paginas/200906/seminario_de_primavera_2006.pdf retrieved on March,25, 2011).

References

Barth, P. (2004). A common core curriculum for the new century. *Journal for Vocational Special Needs Education, 26*(1), 17–35.

Etcheverry, G. (2006, April 9). La otra inseguridad. *La Nacion.* Retrieved on 25 March 2011 from http://www.lanacion.com.ar/795229-la-otra-inseguridad

Fanfani, E. (2010, January–June). *La escuela y la educación de los sentimientos. Revista Electrónica Iberoamericana sobre Calidad, Eficacia y Cambio en Educación, 2*(1). Retrieved on January 1, 2011 from http://recursos.cepindalo.es/file.php/161/la_escuela_y_la_educacion_de_los_sentimientos.pdf

Gardner, H. (2004). *Mentes flexibles. El arte y la ciencia de saber cambiar nuestra opinión y la de los demás.* Barcelona: Paidós.

Gates, B., & Gates, M. (2010). High schools for the new millenium: Imagine the possibilities. Retrieved on September 7, 2007 from http://www.gatesfoundation.org/nr/downloads/ed/edwhitepaper.pdf

Gimeno Sacristán, J. (Ed.). (2006). *La reforma necesaria: Entre la política educativa y la práctica escolar.* Madrid: Morata.

Johnson, D., & Johnson, R. (1999). *Aprender juntos y solos. Aprendizaje cooperativo, competitivo e individualista.* São Paulo: Aique.

Miret, I. (2005). "Usos, usuarios y algunas paradojas," *Cuadernos de pedagogía, 352.*

Osborne, J. (2006). *¿Qué ciencia necesitan los ciudadanos?*, in *La enseñanza de las ciencias y la evaluación PISA 2006*, Fundación Santillana, Madrid, 2006 (http://www.fundacionsantillana.

com/upload/ficheros/paginas/200906/seminario_de_primavera_2006.pdf retrieved on March, 25th 2011).

Pozo Rosselló, M. (2006). "Instantáneas históricas," *Cuadernos de Pedagogía*, 355.

Rocard, M. (Chair) (2008). Science education now: a renewed pedagogy for the future of Europe, en http://ec.europa.eu/research/science-society/document_library/pdf_06/report-rocard-on-science-education_en.pdf

Seibel, C. (1996). Genèses et consequences de l'échec scolaire: Vers une politique de prévention. *Revue Française de Pédagogie*, *67*, 7–28.

Thomas, P.L. (2006). "The cult of prescription-Or, a student ain't no slobbering dog," in Shirley R. Steinberg & Joe L. Kincheloe, *What you don't know about schools*, Palgrave MacMillan, New York.

Vera, J., & Esteve, J. (Eds.). (2001). *Un examen a la cultura escolar. ¿Sería usted capaz de aprobar un examen de secundaria?* Barcelona: Octaedro.

Zweig, S. (2001). *El mundo de ayer. Memorias de un europeo.* Barcelona: Acantilado.

· 3 ·

Democratic Governance of Public Mass Schools in Portugal

João Formoshino & Joaquim Machado

The eighteenth-century Age of Enlightenment and its political ideal of "enlightened despotism" inspired the legislation that created the first primary school in Portugal in 1772. Only sixty years later, in 1835, the government decreed that all public primary school was free of charge for all citizens. At the same time, it imposed on parents the moral duty of sending their children to school; this moral commitment was made a legal requirement in 1844.

The Slow Building Up of Public School for All in Portugal

As the social motivation for sending children to public primary school was low, subsequent laws frequently reasserted this moral commitment and specified punishments for failure to comply with the laws. Despite these various laws, when the Portuguese monarchy was overthrown in 1910 the country's illiteracy rate was very high. The Republican regime (1910–1926) based its policy for national development on the generalization of primary education. It promoted two educational reforms, in 1911 and 1919, that extended compulsory education from three to five years. However, these generous ideas saw little practical implementation.

During the first decades of the dictatorship under Antonio Salazar (who held power from 1926–1974 in the so-called New State) the situation remained stable (see Table 1). Not until the late 1950s and 1960s did the authoritarian regime's education policy change. Prior to 1959, all children attended three years of primary school. Leite Pinto, the minister of education, extended compulsory primary schooling from three to four years for boys in 1956, and for girls in 1960. In 1959 four years of schooling became the minimum requirement to become a civil servant.

In 1964 primary school was extended to six years, thus extending compulsory education. The idea of single school track for all children was abandoned when Minister Leite Pinto was replaced. The next minister launched a tripartite system creating three formal school paths:

1. the fifth and sixth year of primary school (*ciclo complementar do ensino primário*) was created for the rural areas;
2. the first cycle of the grammar school (*liceu*) and the first cycle of technical education (*escola técnica*) were combined into a single preparatory cycle for secondary education (*ciclo preparatório do ensino secundário*), which was the academic path created in cities and large towns;
3. the third formal school path or track was created in 1965 for isolated rural areas—the televised school (*telescola*), a system of teaching through television. With *telescola*, the lessons were prepared and delivered by highly qualified teachers through an educational television channel, which were followed up in the schools by local monitors, often primary school teachers.[1]

This compartmentalized system created specific school paths for specific social groups. During the last years of the New State regime (1970–1974), these education ideas were abandoned. The political regime (now led by Caetano, who succeeded Salazar in 1968) launched a comprehensive democratic reform led by Minister of Education Veiga Simão, who recognized the urgent need to create a democratic system of mass education. This reform was approved in 1973, but it was not implemented before the dictatorial regime was overthrown by a military coup d'état in April 1974, which was followed by a revolutionary government. The revolutionary regime maintained compulsory universal schooling of six years and the same permissible school-leaving age, but in 1978, the level of education required to be a civil servant was upgraded from four to five years.

Table 1. The Building Up of Compulsory Schooling: 1844–2009

Date	Number of Years of Compulsory Schooling		Compulsory Attendance Years
	Boys	Girls	
1844	4		7–...
1870	4	4	7–...
1880	4	4	6–12
1894	3	3	6–12
1911	3	3	7–14
1919	5	5	7–14
1927	3	3	7–13
1952	3	3	7–13
1956	4	3	7–14
1960	4	4	7–14
1964	6	6	7–14
1974	6	6	7–14
1979	6	6	6–14
1986	9	9	6–15
2009	13	13	5–18

In 1986 the new regime that followed the April revolution formulated and implemented a comprehensive reform of the educational system via the Lei de Bases do Sistema Educativo (Law 48/86, October 14). This reform extended compulsory schooling to nine years. Basic education was structured into a first cycle of four years (primary education was nominally transformed into the "first cycle of basic education"), a second cycle of two years (the preparatory cycle of secondary education became the "second cycle of basic education"), and a new, additional third cycle (the previous first cycle of secondary school was transformed into the "third cycle of basic education"). It took a long time for both semantic and substantial changes to be internalized.

During the 1980s successive laws extended the benefits of public basic education to a broader public. In 1987 the law guaranteed the right of access to free education to children with special needs; in 1989 it decreed access to free compulsory schooling for the children of immigrant workers from member countries of what was then called the Economic European Community.

In the mid-1990s the government guaranteed de facto basic schooling for all children and adolescents up to age 15. However, among those recently given access to the education system, academic success in the third cycle of basic education was low and the dropout rate was high. In 2007 a debate began about the advantages of promoting basic education through age 18, thus making secondary education compulsory. The need to make the last year of preschool education obligatory was also discussed. In 2009 compulsory education was expanded to thirteen years (Law 85/2009, August 27). Table 1 synthesizes this information.

The Conceptualization of Social Diversity as Academic Heterogeneity

Since 1967, the universal character of the post-primary school has produced important quantitative and qualitative transformations in Portugal's education system. Quantitative changes include an increase in the number of students, teachers, and school units; qualitative transformations are largely the result of the diversity of students and teachers in communities where the schools are integrated.

Special needs children represent one new student population that has specific requirements and demands. Children and adolescents from different geographic origins (rural and suburban), different socioeconomic groups (children of peasants and workers), and different national, linguistic, and ethnic groups (immigrants, ethnic and linguistic minorities) are also new to state post-primary schools. This social and cultural diversity encompasses academic diversity, since these new students generally come from families with less formal education who are not well acquainted with the values, norms, and processes of formal education. These populations also tend to be less motivated to participate in formal instruction and may even be resistant to school culture.

This new social and cultural diversity was initially perceived by the school system (central educational administrators, directors, and teachers) as problematic, since teaching homogeneous academic groups had been the cornerstone of grammar school pedagogy; social and cultural diversity was considered the kind of heterogeneity that broke the mold of traditional teaching practices. Reinforcing homogeneous grouping practices was viewed as the only answer to the "problems" of mass schooling.[2]

The first way of dealing with this diversity was based on the assumption that extending grammar school education to these new populations was the natural democratic response, since it provided access for all children to what until then had been only for middle-class children. The enforcement of curricular and pedagogic uniformity based on homogeneous ability grouping was perceived as the way forward (Formosinho, 1987). This meant blending the ideological concept of equality as uniformity with the centralized bureaucratic tradition of governing the education system from the top.

Due to the social and cultural diversity of public schools, uniformity no longer flowed naturally within the tradition of grammar schools based on homogeneity; it had to be reinforced by centrally defined bureaucratic norms. This "bureaucratic pedagogy" was enforced in terms of classroom pedagogy and curriculum management. Uniformity in classroom practice was enforced by bureaucratic control of all details of school management. Curricular and pedagogical uniformity was obtained by planning for the "average able student" taught by an "average teacher" in an "average school." Thus, this "one-size-fits-all curriculum" (Formosinho, 1987, 2006) was taught to all students, regardless of their learning, ability, motivation, interests, or expectations; in all classrooms, regardless of level of tracking; and at all schools, regardless of the population of the communities they served.

Policy Changes to Adapt Basic Schooling to New Populations

Applying the traditional recipe for homogeneity to the culturally diverse schools led to massive failure among the new population of students. As a Portuguese academic said in 1988, "It is morally wrong to compel these new populations to attend a school which is structurally organized for their failure."[3] The Commission for the Reform of the Educational System (Comissão de Reforma do Sistema Educativo) tried to raise awareness of the dangers of normalizing a high level of school failure. The commission organized an important national seminar to discuss the problem and published a report on the topic; one chapter carried the ironic title, "How to Organize a School for Educational Failure" (Formosinho, 1988). This massive failure led the government to promote reforms in the areas of teacher education and school curriculum and to launch specific national programs to combat school failure.

Policy Changes in Teacher Education: From the Creation of New Professional Courses to Continuous Education

In order to educate all these new students, the school system had to recruit many new teachers. In the 1970s and 1980s, the sudden need for thousands of new teachers on short notice could only be achieved by lowering the standards of access to the profession and the academic and professional qualifications of the teaching staff. This short-term solution for enlarging the teaching corps was accompanied by policy changes that committed the universities to improve teacher training in order to produce qualified professionals who were prepared to teach in the new, more diverse schools. This meant creating courses aimed at the teaching profession from the very first year of college, rather than offering them as an add-on to the existing academic qualifications. These new courses were called *modelo integrado* (integrated model courses) because they integrated subject knowledge, educational science, and teaching practice within the same curriculum.

If the primary concern in the 1970s and 1980s was centered on restructuring the initial training of teachers, the main concern in the 1990s was the need to provide ongoing training for these teachers, as it soon became clear that the initial training was not enough to prepare teaching professionals for the difficulties of educating students in diverse schools. In 1989, under the new statutes for a career in teaching, in-service training became essentially compulsory—all advancement in the teaching career depended on attending a minimum of twenty-five hours of training sessions (courses, workshops, projects, internships, study circles) per school year. To promote this system of continuous teacher education, a decentralized system was set up through the creation of Centros de Formação de Associação de Escolas (in-service centers), which were based on the association of neighboring schools: The schools within a specific geographical area created a teacher in-service center and elected a pedagogic commission that selected the director of the center. In the first stage, these in-service activities were very much schoolified; that is, they copied formal teaching processes like structured courses, formal lectures and the like. In the late 1990s, school-based teacher education projects that blended (mainly through workshops and study circles) professional and organizational development emerged as an alternative to the in-service centers. In 2005 continuing teacher education became centralized and was based on national programs focused on specific subjects, such as the Portuguese language, mathematics, and experimental teaching of science.

In the mid-1990s, a specialized system of teacher training (*formação especializada*) was created to qualify teachers for specific roles in schools, such as school management, leading sociocultural activities, special education, guidance, curriculum development, student teaching supervision, in-service training, and information and communication technology. This system remains decentralized.

Policy Changes in Curriculum: Toward a More Flexible Management of the Centralized National Curriculum

During the 1990s, awareness of the massive educational failure among the new student populations led the government to change the paradigm of school reform, thereby accepting the need to diversify the curriculum and differentiate classroom pedagogy. The first reform of the curriculum under this new paradigm led to a revised syllabus and programs, along with important changes in the evaluation system that emphasized formative rather than summative assessment (Decree-Law 286/96, August 26, 1989). The government also set up a curricular area to be used by the school (*área-escola*) in order to promote interdisciplinary, collaborative practices among the teachers. As there was no change in the pedagogical organization of the schools or in teachers' professional work patterns, this reform failed to achieve its purpose. However, it served as a safety valve for the system because it allowed a channel for the innovators:

> [It was] the answer to all those who wished for a different school—with autonomy, decentralised, with local participation, with a less academic curriculum not restricted to academic classroom centred activities and accepting the need for sociomoral education of all children. (Formosinho, 1991, p. xi)

There was another important contribution to this new school paradigm: the government's decision to accept the Declaration of Salamanca (1994), which decreed that all special needs children would be allowed to attend regular schools. This political decision led to new initiatives for curricular adaptation and the establishment in 1996 of alternative curricula (Decree-Law 319/91, August 23, 1996).

In 2002 there was the second comprehensive reform of the curriculum under this new paradigm. In 2001 the main guidelines for a new form of organization and management of the curriculum for compulsory education and for learning assessment were defined (Decree-Law No. 6/01, January 18). The reorganization of compulsory education contributed to the creation of a national curriculum based on a common benchmark that coordinated content knowledge with the development of skills acquired.

The national curriculum established a set of learning competencies, along with differentiated and appropriate responses to the needs and characteristics of each pupil, school, or region, in terms of ability to learn. Within the limits of the national curriculum, each school may organize and manage the teaching/learning process autonomously, adapting it to its own pupils by bringing in local and regional components and building its own curricular project.

This *gestão flexível do currículo* (flexible local management of the national curriculum) was considered an important instrument of school autonomy and of the adaptation of mass schooling to the new population of basic schools. This flexible management operated through the school and the classroom curricular projects. The *projecto curricular de escola* (school curricular project) is an organizational document that contains the strategies for developing the national curriculum by adapting it to the school context. The school curricular project became an important instrument of school autonomy. The *projecto curricular de turma* (classroom curricular project) is an organizational document that contains strategies for adapting the national curriculum and the school curricular project to the context of each class.

The creation in 2001 of the nondisciplinary curricular areas of *estudo acompanhado* (classroom curricular project) and *área de projecto* (project work area) created new instruments for the flexible management of the national curriculum, and for the support of the new school population. However, the lack of change in the pedagogical organization of schools and the very slow change in teachers' professional working patterns have greatly limited the schools' use of this flexibility.

Policy Changes Regarding Educational Success: The Creation of National Programs

Between 1987 and 2010, successive national programs tried to adapt mass basic schooling to the new populations and new social contexts, with innovations such as curricular programs, multicultural programs, and socioeducational programs to combat school failure and school dropout. This eventually led to the establishment of national programs specifically focused on reducing the number of dropouts and promoting academic success in school.

In 1987 an interministerial program, Programa Interministerial de Promoção do Sucesso Escolar, was created to promote success in primary education (Leite, 2000). In 1991 Programa de Educação para Todos (Education for All Program) was established to emphasize the work of teachers in order to promote school success and create "school/community" and "school/economy" partnerships.

In 1991 Secretariado Coordenador dos Programas de Educação Multicultural, a national program for multicultural education, was created and coordinated by a central agency to answer the specific needs of heterogeneous communities and schools. Plano Nacional de Prevenção do Abandono Escolar, a new national plan, was launched in 2004 to prevent school failure, with the specific aim of reducing dropout rates by 50% in six years. The 2004 report of the Conselho Nacional de Educação (National Advisory Board for Education) refers to the main bias of the program: its focus on the individual student who fails or drops out ("I will not give up" was one important motto of the program), which minimized the mobilization of the school and the communities.

Policy Changes Regarding Educational Success: The Creation of Educational Priority Areas

Another important mechanism developed to combat educational failure was the allocation of more resources to specific schools located in priority areas. The idea was to set up a mechanism of affirmative action for the deprived schools and communities. The first use of this concept was in 1988. It prioritized intervention in schools serving deprived and immigrant or minority groups (e.g., gypsy communities). These schools were given more teaching staff to carry on their socioeducative mission.

In 1996 another program was launched based on the same priority area concept—Território Educativo de Intervenção Prioritári (Priority Area Educational Territory)—in order to promote equality of access and success in basic schooling, making the school the pilot for the promotion of school success. Schools benefiting from this program were located in areas where there were serious social, economic, and cultural problems; a large number of pupils enrolled in special educational support programmes; and /or students with multiple intervention needs. This renewed the idea of partnership between the school and the local community. This program was abandoned in 1998, but reinstated in 2008. The program renewed in 2008 created flexible modes of managing the central curriculum and created new vocational courses in many secondary schools, even some that had a strong grammar school tradition. This idea of educational priority areas was first launched in 1988, reviewed in 1996, abandoned in 1998, and again renewed in 2008. This is a typical pattern of Portuguese educational public policy—an ideas is thrown at a difficult problem, abandoned, and reinstated without a formal reevaluation of its impact.

The Governance of the New Basic School

All these changes in basic schooling had implications for both the government and the management of schools. The new school populations demanded better representation of the stakeholders, and the new pedagogical challenges required more professional autonomy for teachers.

The "Democratic Management" of Schools: 1974–1987

In 1974 the revolutionary movement set up democratic management committees[4] of schools (*comissões de gestão*) consisting of elected teachers. Democratic management was viewed by most of the teachers as the absence of close control and the creation of a flat hierarchy, since the existence of hierarchic rules was identified with the previous dictatorial regime.

During the 1980s the central administration of education was slowly recovering hierarchic control over schools, so democratic management over time became more compatible with top-down normative rule. The school managers were contained on one side by the teaching staff, and on the other by the educational administration (Central Administration until 1980, Central and Regional Administration from 1987). The school manager's job was to work between two straight lines—the will of the teachers who elected them and the will of Central Administration who ruled over them. There was no apparent space in this kind of management for significant parental participation.

From 1974 to 1998 the Central Administration used so-called democratic management to sustain the initial impact on the constant growth of the school system. In the 1970s and 1980s the education system (both Central Administration and the schools) concentrated on survival—setting up enough classrooms to accommodate the new students, recruiting enough teachers for these new classes, appointing these new teachers on time, and doing all this before the new school years began.

Before 1987, the Portuguese school was regarded by the state as an administrative unit of the Central Educational Administration; although managed by elected teachers, schools had no autonomy and were governed by central rules and directives. This can be seen as an objective compromise reached in the revolutionary years between an administration that wanted to continue appointing school managers and teachers who wanted to control state schools.

The Proposal of the Commission for the Reform of the Educational System: 1987–1988

The concept of an autonomous school was first discussed in the 1987 report by a government commission created to plan the implementation of the Comissão de Reforma do Sistema Educativo (Formosinho, Fernandes & Lima, 1988). The distinctions between the government (*direcção*) and the management (*gestão*) of schools, school autonomy, parental participation, and decentralization were discussed extensively in the national debate conducted by the commission in 1987 and 1988.[5]

After this debate, many academics, parent associations, and some teachers supported the strong belief that emerged about the need for state schools to be more than mere administrative units of the Educational Administration. This resulted in the conceptualization of the state school as an "educational community." This was also influenced by the inadequacy of state schools that were fully governed and managed by teachers, without the participation of parents and community representatives.

Developments, 1989–1996

In 1989 the government established the principles for an autonomous school (excluding primary and preschool) (Decree-Law 48/49). Initially considered more a rhetorical declaration of principles than a working document, it allowed for a slow internalization of the need for autonomy and gave rise to the timid exercise of school autonomy.

Two years later, the government applied a new law for school governance to all levels of education (Decree-Law n° 172/91). This model set up a participative framework for the participation of parents and the community, creating a Conselho de Escola (School Governing Body) that selected and appointed the head teacher. The model was applied in thirty schools on an experimental basis and was properly assessed, but it was not widely adopted (Conselho de Acompanhamento & Avaliação, 1996).

A New Model for the Governance of Schools: 1996–2007

In 1996 a newly elected government launched a program for the consolidation of school autonomy. It commissioned a report from an academic specialist, João Barroso, who defended the idea that autonomy should start from what schools already had and really wanted, in the form of a contract (Barroso, 1996). In 1998 the government passed legislation establishing a new model for the autonomy, governance, and management of schools (Decree-Law 115-A/98).

This government attempted to reconcile the different positions on school participation and autonomy that had been discussed since 1988. One opinion, originating with the Commission for the Reform of the Educational System report and supported by many academics and parents associations, highlighted the need to overcome the governing of state schools solely by teachers. Consequently, it emphasized the need to create proper governing bodies that included parents and community representatives and had the power to select the school director. The other position, defended by teachers unions and the majority of teachers, emphasized the need for state schools to continue being managed by teachers who elected their own head teachers. As of 1991, the law was closer to the first position and the teachers unions did not support it. The 1998 law included elements from both positions in an attempt to produce a norm that could be accepted by both teachers unions and parents associations.

The new 1998 law for school autonomy, administration, and management determined the following governing and management bodies: *assembleia de escola* (school assembly), *conselho executivo* (executive council), and *conselho pedagógico* (pedagogical council). The school assembly consists of an equal number of teacher representatives and other representatives. The school assembly is limited to twenty members and must ensure the representation of several stakeholders: teachers, parents and guardians, students, nonteaching staff, local authorities, and representatives of social, economic, cultural, artistic, scientific, and environmental interests. The *assembleia de escola* is the body responsible for defining guidelines for school activities and the participation and representation of the educational community, but it has no power to select the management.

Although the executive body is responsible for drawing up the educational project, it must be submitted to the school assembly for approval. Thus, this body is responsible for approving, monitoring, and assessing the educational project and its implementation. An innovation in this 1998 law is the creation of a new position in the school structure—the chairman of the school assembly.

The executive body is responsible for managing the school. It is composed exclusively of teachers elected to serve; all the school bodies participate in this election. The president of the executive body attends the meetings of the school assembly, although he/she is not entitled to vote.[6] Because the chairman is a teacher elected by the assembly, and a different electoral college elects the president of the executive body, there appears to be a dual authority in the school. In fact, the chairman of the school assembly is primarily an honorific position, as the power remains with the executive body.

This 1998 law was the precursor of the "autonomy contract" between the school and the regional authority, but the main instrument of school autonomy remained the educational project. Each school was required to have an educational project that established its educational framework by defining its educational orientation and laying out its principles, values, goals, and strategies.

The Contract for Autonomy and Development: 2006–2010

Although foreseen in the 1998 law, only one contract for school autonomy had been signed by 2006. In the 2006–2007 school year there was a serious government effort to establish a new relationship between the educational administration authorities and the schools, using the autonomy contract. This new instrument for school autonomy was piloted in 24 schools selected from the 136 that volunteered for this project. The process was based on five stages: (1) initiative of the school; (2) examination of the contract by a national committee; (3) open discussion of the contract in a meeting between the school representatives and the national committee; (4) negotiation between the school and the Educational Regional Administration about specific demands regarding equipment and facilities; and (5) signing of the "autonomy and development contract" by the school and the Educational Regional Administration. Thus, the contract was not a document, but the working product of a process that included self-evaluation, writing, discussing, rewriting, and negotiating.

Another New Model for the Governance of Schools: 2008–2010

In 2008 a new model was devised for the governance of schools (Decree-Lawi 75/2008, April 22), the sixth from 1974 to 2010.[7] The new governing bodies are composed of the General Board (*Conselho Geral*), which resulted in fewer teachers serving as representatives than the previous School Assembly model, and the director, who is selected by the General Board after a local competition for the position.

Grouping Basic Schools in Organizational Clusters

An important policy measure for the governance of basic schools was the redefinition of the concept of the school as an organizational unit, which is created by grouping several scattered schools located in the same area under one governing and management body—the so-called schools cluster (*agrupamento de escolas*). The schools cluster is an organizational unit that has its own governing and management bodies, integrating classes from preschool through the three cycles of compulsory education (*ensino básico*).

Grouping Basic Schools by Affinity: 1996–2002

This idea of grouping several schools serving the first levels of education (preschool and primary school) into one organizational unit began in

1996–1997. The idea was to overcome the organizational and pedagogical mismatch between preschool and primary school and to address the isolation caused by the scattering of small preschools and primary schools. This process, which was based on continuity of levels of education, lasted for six years.

Vertical Grouping of Basic Schools by Affinity: 2002–2007

The same idea was subsequently applied to the process called the "vertical grouping of schools," which involved grouping schools from preschool through the three cycles of compulsory education, thus putting all compulsory education under the same management. This vertical process began in 2002 and was completed five years later.

There were various reasons for this vertical grouping of schools:

- School network reasons (restructuring of the educational network, elimination of situations of isolation and the scattering of small schools, expansion of preschool education)
- Organizational reasons (the creation of larger administrative units,which provided access to more resources, and better leaders and managers)
- Pedagogical reasons (better pedagogical continuity across the different educational levels, promotion of common pedagogical projects across cycles, interaction across educational levels and cycles)
- Social reasons (better integration of pupils' paths, better dropout prevention).

Grouping Basic and Secondary Schools: The "Mega-clusters," 2010

The extension of basic education to the secondary school level led to the extension of the grouping concept to all compulsory school units in the same area. This process of creating the so-called *mega-agrupamentos* (mega-clusters) is now advancing, and has reduced the number of school organizational units by almost one-third.[8] This grouping process means a progressive concentration of power, which may increase the bureaucratic pattern of educational administration—social and cultural diversity in a territory may become more a rhetorical argument than an inspiration for innovative pedagogical practices to serve the diverse students receiving their basic education.

The Building of a Mass Education Model for the Governance of Basic Schools

The discussion about the most appropriate model for governing basic mass schools has been centered primarily on questions of power rather than on how to better serve the new populations who needed basic schooling. The questions of power, discussed for thirty-six years (1974–2010), include the role of teachers versus parents on school boards; the power of teachers to select the school director; the authority of the school director; the role of the municipality in the supervision of schools; and the autonomy of the school versus the hierarchic authority of the state—that is, the balance between school autonomy and hierarchic bureaucratic control. No discussions addressed two other important dimensions of adapting basic schooling to the new populations—pedagogical management and the professional teaching culture.

Teachers and educational managers should discuss the pedagogical management of schools; they should discuss new models of teaching culturally diverse and mixed-ability groups of students, instead of maintaining traditional homogeneous grouping practices. Teachers and educational managers should discuss the professional culture and question the traditional individualist working patterns. Moreover, teachers should develop new collaborative practices as a means of dealing with social and cultural diversity. These two issues—pedagogical management and teachers' professional culture—are the main factors that determine whether students fail in school or achieve academic success in school and eventually in life.

Notes

1. This innovation was aimed at extending the six years of compulsory schooling to isolated rural areas; later, the same system was used in suburban peripheral areas, when local junior preparatory schools were overpopulated. This system lasted for almost forty years. It began to decline in the 1980s, and in 2003 it was declared extinct, since all schooling was delivered via direct contact teaching.
2. Grouping practices, especially tracking, often have the effect of reducing equity. Research generally shows that tracking and between-class ability grouping benefit students who are placed in high-end tracks or groups, while having a detrimental effect on students placed in low-end tracks or groups. Tracking based on the student's ability determines course-effective content and often the career path that a student chooses. In summation, students in low-ability tracks tend to receive lower quality instruction (see, for example, Attinasi, 1994; Secada, 1992).
3. I am quoting from memory an oral intervention of Lemos Pires in a seminar promoted by

the Comissão de Reforma do Sistema Educativo in 1987 about the educational success in compulsory schooling.

4. The initial *comissões de gestão* designation (1974–1976) was later changed to *conselho directivo* (directive board, 1976–1998).

5. It is evident that a school with parent and community representation can be more self-directed in relation to the Central Educational Authorities than a school managed by teacher civil servants. Therefore, it is essential in an autonomous school to have a governing body with parents and community representatives differentiated from the management body.

6. The president of the executive council should be a fully qualified teacher of that school with a minimum of five years' experience; he/she must be qualified in school administration and management, having acquired these qualifications through a specialized course, or must have working experience in a position of school administration and management.

7. There were created models for the management and government of schools in 1974 (May), 1974 (December), 1976, 1991, 1998, and 2008.

8. In 1996 there were around 12,000 to 13,000 school units; in 2007 there were approximately 1,200 units.

References

Attinasi, J. (1994). Academic achievement, culture, and literacy: An introduction. In B. Bowman (Ed.), *Cultural diversity and academic achievement*. Oak Brook, IL: North Central Regional Educational Laboratory, 23–47.

Barroso, J. (1996). *Autonomia e gestão das escolas*. Lisbon: Ministério da Educação.

Carvalho, R. (1995). *História do ensino em Portugal. Desde a fundação da nacionalidade até ao fim do regime de Salazar-Caetano* (2nd ed.). Lisbon: Fundação Calouste Gulbenkian.

Clímaco, M. (1995). *Observatório da qualidade da escola. Guião organizativo*. Lisbon: Ministério da Educação, Programa Educação Para Todos (PEPT).

Conselho de Acompanhamento e Avaliação. (1996). *Relatório final*. Lisbon: Ministério da Educação.

Formosinho, J. (1987). O currículo uniforme pronto a vestir de tamanho único. In E. L. Pires et al. (Eds.), *O insucesso escolar em questão*. Braga, Portugal: Universidade do Minho, 41–50.

Formosinho, J. (1991). Concepções de escola na reforma educativa. In Sociedade Portuguesa de Ciências da Educação (Ed.), *Ciências da educação em Portugal: Situação actual e perspectivas* (pp. 31–51). Porto, Portugal: Afrontamento.

Formosinho, J. (1992). O dilema organizacional da escola de massas. *Revista Portuguesa de Educação, 5*(3), 23–48.

Formosinho, J. (2007). School autonomy in Portugal—1987–2007. In Inspecção-Geral da Educação (Ed.), *As escolas face a novos desafios / Schools facing up to new challenges* (pp. 69–89). Lisbon: Author.

Formosinho, J. (Ed.) (2009). *Formação de professores. Aprendizagem profissional e acção docente*. Porto, Portugal: Porto Editora.

Formosinho, J., Fernandes, A. S., & Lima, L. (1988). Organização e administração das escolas dos ensinos básico e secundário. In Comissão de Reforma do Sistema Educativo, *Documentos preparatórios II* (pp. 141–263). Lisbon: Ministério da Educação.

Formosinho, J., & Machado, J. (2005). A administração da escola de interesse público em Portugal—políticas recentes. In J. Formosinho, A. S. Fernandes, J. Machado, & F. I. Ferreira (Eds.), *Administração da educação. Lógicas burocráticas e lógicas de mediação* (pp. 115–162). Porto, Portugal: Edições ASA.

Formosinho, J., Sousa-Fernandes, A., & Machado, J. (2007). Contratos de autonomia para o desenvolvimento das escolas portuguesas. *Administração Educacional*, 4, 7–32.

Leite, C. (2000). Uma análise da dimensão multicultural do currículo. *Revista Educação*, IX (1), 20–26.

Secada, W. (1992). Race, ethnicity, social class, language, and achievement in mathematics. In D. Grouws (Ed.), *Handbook of research on mathematics teaching and learning*. Reston, VA: National Council of Teachers of Mathematics.

· 4 ·

Crisis and Trends in Spanish Universities

The Bologna Process, Year Zero

Gloria Braga Blanco & José Luis San Fabián Maroto

University Government

Spain's 1978 constitution transferred management of the country from a cen-tralized government to the autonomous communities. On the one hand, this has allowed universities to operate in an environment of freedom and to govern themselves; on the other hand, often it has allowed internal groups to prioritize their own interests over the demands of public service (Pereyra, Luzón & Sevilla, 2006).

In fact, the autonomy of Spanish universities is a fiction, given that they are financially dependent on public subsidies, "so their autonomy in this area only really exists in the tight framework defined by the size of these subsidies" (Salaburu, 2007, pp. 212–213). In other words, their autonomy depends on the economic capacity of each autonomous community and the political priorities of its government. This creates big differences between universities: Investment per student may vary by up to 200% (Pereyra, Luzón & Sevilla, 2006).

The university government is based on a formal democratic model in choosing heads of department or deans. The 2001 Ley Orgánica de Universidades (Organic University Law) introduced some changes in this area, among them the direct election of the rector[1] and the transfer of power for making fundamental decisions to the governing council. This has resulted in a tendency to concentrate decision-making power, and to reduce the space for discussing university policies. The right to participate in the election of a rector every four years has been exchanged for the right to participate in the daily running of the university.

Furthermore, the debate today centers on whether people should be democratically elected to management positions or appointed to them. The Estrategia Universidad 2015,[2] published in 2010 for the Ministry of Science and Innovation, proposes that the rector (agreed with the governing council) directly designate the department heads or deans, because this is the most effective way to implement the strategic plan. In theory, this would do away with personal "fiefdoms" and allow for a strategic plan more in accordance with the general interests of the institution.

The aim is to incorporate some elements of the Anglo-Saxon university model into a policy that unites governance, management, and organization, giving a greater role to individual government organs over collective ones and creating a greater role for participants from outside the university. This type of structure facilitates agile and flexible decision-making. This model also favors accountability, whereas the collegial model dilutes responsibility among the various members of the community. The fact that the governing council includes members from outside the university makes it more likely that the university's relations with the broader society will be taken into account.[3] The pendulum of authority in higher education has swung away from academics in favor of managers and bureaucrats (Altbach et al., 2009). In fact, the Spanish system differs greatly from the American one. Among its peculiarities is the "bureaucratic tangle of national, autonomous community and university regulations," which makes higher education one of the most regulated areas of activity in the country. In spite of this, the world of Spanish universities is frequently chaotic; it may be said that "everyone has competence but no one is responsible" (Salaburu, 2007, p. 210).

Meanwhile, the universities remain fertile ground for micropolitics, where internal conflicts usually end up as fights between clans, though with some ideological coloring, and decisions are made to suit the special interests. [4]

The Universities and Social Responsibility

In principle, the contributions universities make to society are well known. La Ley Orgánica de Universidades describes itself as "a law of society for the university, linking university autonomy with accountability to the society that promotes and finances it" (I. 10). The key question is, therefore, what is understood by *society*? The European Higher Education Area (EHEA) tries to generate synergy between the business-economic system and the university with the purpose of producing a competitive advantage for Europe. In this case, the meaning of *society* would appear to be the same for both entities. But, as Dias Sobrinho (2009) points out, the social responsibility of higher education should be radically different from the social responsibility of businesses:

> The quality of higher education is directly related to its capacity to contribute to personal and societal development...which requires higher increases in the schooling of the population, in terms of coverage and quality, strong reinforcement of policies to increase equity and reduce poverty, strategies for the exploitation of natural resources, and the application of knowledge to ensure sustainable development. (Dias Sobrinho, 2009, p. 109)

The social responsibility of universities demands increased public funding. Paradoxically, however, public funding is declining while funding from businesses and students is on the rise. "Zero cost" is the current refrain of university managers, and the cutbacks have had the most significant impact on human resource policies, especially as concerns the hiring of academic staff. In recent years, innovative education projects have been funded initially, only to be cut off just as they are beginning to take root. In Spain, public funding of higher education is much lower than the European average—a tendency that the current economic crisis is exacerbating—and the proposal to raise it to 1.5% of GDP by 2015 will be difficult to achieve. The resources necessary to ensure the mobility of academic staff and students are not being provided. Teaching is once again the area that suffers most. Reductions in class size have been stopped, and teachers have been moved from one area of knowledge to another solely to reduce costs, without considering the consequences for teaching quality. These developments coincide with the implementation of the EHEA.

Diversification and Inequality

A basic criterion for evaluating the social contribution of universities is that they do not generate inequality. However, access to post-compulsory secondary education is distorted by class, which occurs mainly in terms of access to and the ability to continue university studies. "Education for all" has not become a reality in the Spanish universities—those from lower social classes, immigrants, ethnic minorities, and people with disabilities are generally underrepresented, as are women in certain subject areas and in teaching and administrative roles.

Inequality has increased in recent decades, both between national higher education systems and within individual countries. International classifications favor universities that use English as their main language of research and instruction, which teach a great number of disciplines and have access to significant research funds (Altbach et al., 2009). The demands of globalization—such as mobility, versatile qualifications, business-university cooperation, and promoting competition—increase inequality, not only between universities, but also within them. Increases in fees, reform of the student loan system, and the privatization of higher education all may exacerbate disparity in access to learning opportunities between students who travel and students who do not, and between those who earn degrees that will lead to well-paid employment and those who do not (Bjarnason et al., 2009).

Campaigns that boast of the high rates of employment among those who do professional training courses discourage an ever greater number of students from going to university. Short-term work opportunities are valued to the detriment of employability, and training to meet an immediate need works to the detriment of lifelong education. However, in an epoch of crisis such as the current one, it is young people who are not university graduates who suffer the worst unemployment. Employability refers not only to choice of professions, but also mobility between professional spheres. It is not a matter of choosing between generic and specific competencies. The world of work, which demands training to fill specific needs that may not last long, cannot be the only reference point for the development of university policies (García Manjón, 2009).

Civic Education: The Absent Citizenship

Despite the fact that educating citizens to be critical thinkers is essential in our epoch, efforts to do so have been largely abandoned by the universities. In Spain, the introduction of civic education in the primary and secondary school curriculum aroused great controversy, and it was associated with the risk of indoctrination. In higher education, few are concerned about this risk, perhaps because university students are seen as being fully developed as citizens.

The guidelines for the development of new degree areas in the framework of the EHEA demand that issues such as human rights, gender equality, and multiculturalism be addressed. However, this demand does not identify specific subjects, and as a result treatment of these issues is spread among all the subjects; this method already has been shown to be ineffective in nonuniversity teaching contexts.

The idea of European citizenship is still a vague utopian concept, as is the idea of a Europe consisting of fully cooperating and socially aware nations. According to the EHEA, "a good education" leads to the development of technoscientific and other "leadership" fields, including physics, information technology, biotechnology, mathematics, business, languages, marketing, etc. (Carreras, Sevilla & Urbán, 2006).

Higher education has become a competitive business, questioning the view that higher education is a public good "benefiting not only the individuals but also the whole society" (Tilak, 2009, p. 16). Students must compete for the degrees most in demand, and the universities must compete for the best position in evaluations and for funding from public or private sources. Although competition has always been a factor in the academic world and can help to promote excellence, it also can contribute to the deterioration of the academic community, mission, and values (Altbach et al., 2009).

Students: At the Center of Education?

UNESCO's "World Declaration on Higher Education in the 21st Century: Vision and Action" states that students and their needs must be at the center of our consciousness, and that we must regard them as essential and responsible protagonists in the renovation of higher education (UNESCO, 1998, art. 10). However, it fails to explain how this can be done in practice. The current system of representation is not able to integrate students into the life and governance of the university.

In his incisive analysis of the media image of the various actors participating in the Bologna debate, Fernández Barbudo (2010) argues that students are being delegitimized by their immaturity, lack of information, and demagogy, and he offers two dominant images: the "manipulated student" and the "anti-system student." The youth-maturity dichotomy offers a simple and automatic explanation for the lack of information; that is, it achieves two objectives at the same time, delegitimizing both the group making the argument and the argument itself. The current representative mechanisms have not failed because of students' lack of interest. On the contrary, the actions taken by students were key to initiating debate on the EHEA. The lack of adequate channels for dialogue between students and policy-makers at all levels highlights some of the problems associated with the design and implementation of the EHEA. Did no one consider how students could effectively participate in an informed manner in the Bologna Process? The really worrying thing is that no one pays attention to students until they take to the streets with placards and get the attention of the media, and no one appears to be concerned about what prompts them to do this (Michavila & Parejo, 2008).

Unfortunately, most teachers show deep-seated ignorance of their students as participants in university life. They tend to treat them as academic or political objects; the former when they are needed to justify employing a teacher, and the latter when their votes are needed. Through his or her vote, a student can participate in the election of the rector and can rate the quality of teachers from 1 to 5. However, the student is not allowed to express an opinion, or is simply not listened to, because nobody really wants to hear what he or she has to say.

Teaching, Research and the Evaluation of Quality

It is usually said that the European Academic Credit (ECTS) is not only a measure of a student's workload but also an indication of the need to focus on new teaching methods. The development of the student competencies demands that their teachers develop new, coherent, and appropriate pedagogic strategies (De la Cruz Tomé, 2003; Colás & de Pablos, 2005; Miguel, 2006). However, no proof of training or competence in teaching is demanded of academics when they are employed by universities.

The development of teaching guides based on the ECTS and competencies does not guarantee much. The "comparability" between different higher education systems sought by the Bologna reform through the development of common formal structures (degree length, the European credit, etc.) is purely imaginary. The ECTS credits will have the same number of hours as the rest of Europe, but "what is done within those hours is what is important and that is exactly what we are going to ignore" (Laporta, 2009).

From the point of view of what is learned and what competencies are produced by the various degrees, these structures do not guarantee common results for education processes across Europe. In fact, these results are very diverse, even within individual countries that have a shared academic culture, study plans, and management structures.

Any political reform, and especially educational reform, implies a new pedagogy, regardless of how bad it might be. The EHEA reform has given new life to the Manichean debate over whether subject contents or pedagogical techniques should have primacy (Iraberri & Almendro, 2009). In fact, the "army of pedagogues" that is supposedly behind this reform is nowhere to be seen. What is known is that there are schools of thought in pedagogy that are being ignored, and the bad (technicist) pedagogy of many who support the implementation of the EHEA is provoking aversion to the reform among academic staff, instead of stimulating the pedagogical reflection that is a necessary part of the teacher's job.

As Carreras, Sevilla, and Urbán (2006) have suggested, the discourse of the "pedagogical revolution" seems like an excuse to implant a "business spirit" (European Commission, 10/01/2003) and to privatize the university. Those who work in universities today know that what dominates is the short term: budget problems, competition between faculties, employment of graduates, and so on (Sousa, 2005). If all these issues are not taken into account, the new conception of university education is going to have, at best, a secondary influence.

Spain's research budget is one of the lowest in the EU, despite the fact that in recent years, research has increased its significance over teaching. What is important for the promotion of academic staff is research, the quality of which is demonstrated by publishing in prestigious journals, attending scientific events and congresses, carrying out research projects, strengthening networks, and creating and funding new patented innovations. Teaching takes second place and merits are assigned automatically, in contrast to the more rigorous evaluation applied to research. The contradictions in the functions of the university are again apparent. The prestige of the academic staff comes from research, but the continued existence of the faculties depends on the number of students enrolled. Degree programmes are classified in terms of their productivity in research and are funded in the same way; however, few students aspire to become researchers.

Yet, as Tilak (2009) has pointed out, the ministers of education also speak about public responsibility. This has led to the development of complex systems to evaluate research and teaching, and of a new academic caste that specializes in the new procedures. The National Evaluation and Quality Plans implemented since 1995 have revealed important areas for improvement, but have had barely an effect on "quality." Later, the National Center for the Evaluation of Quality and Accreditation (ANECA) was created to make external evaluations, and in the future, it will permit the competitive financing of universities.

The assurance of quality is frequently considered to be compliance with certain earlier requisites that are not connected to the public service aspects of education. Moreover, the "systems of internal quality control" require a culture and practice of self-evaluation that usually does not exist in the universities. Internal evaluation barely exists, and what does exist tends to be bureaucratic. Furthermore, external evaluation depends excessively on the university administration. Despite the introduction of agencies that assess quality, significant black holes remain in the evaluation of university teaching and management. The programs aimed at ensuring quality, which constitute a fundamental part of new higher education, have proved difficult to implement effectively.

And in the Middle of the Crisis...the Train to Bologna Arrives

Between Skepticism and the Formal Change

The EHEA reform is being implemented late in Spain in comparison with other European countries, and within a context of disorientation, lack of debate, and a low level of participation by the university community. The few, weak opportunities for participation, institutional inertia, and erratic policies of successive education ministers have caused this lack of motivation. Information campaigns organized by the Ministry of Education have concentrated on how to implement the reform and have avoided discussing the basic principles, which are considered irrevocable (Carreras, Sevilla & Urbán, 2006). Moreover, there has been little coordination among the universities about the design of new degree programs. This lack of coordination will limit the recognition of academic credits, a mistake that it will be difficult for ANECA to solve later.

It has been said that the Bologna reform was born at the margin of the institutions of the European Union. In fact, there is no common document that obliges EU member states to participate in the field of higher education. The absence of a legal framework for the EHEA is justified on the basis that it does not seek to homogenize higher education, but to harmonize it.[5]

In any case, it remains doubtful whether the explicit objectives of the Bologna reform are being achieved, at least in Spanish universities. These objectives include the following: adoption of a system that allows qualifications to be compared, thus favoring the employability of European citizens; a two-stage teaching system, in which successful completion of the first stage provides access to the labor market; promotion of student mobility; quality control through comparable design criteria and methodology; and promotion of the European dimension of teaching.

ECTS credits do not guarantee that qualifications will be recognized, and the definition of competencies in the teacher guides does not ensure that teaching methods will be renewed. The European academic credit is based on the average student, but all students are different, each with their own focus and speed of learning. Although successful completion of the new degrees (four years) in theory does allow students to practice the relevant profession, there are serious doubts whether an undergraduate qualification will provide favorable entry into the labor market.

To judge by the recent report by the European University Association (Sursock & Hanne Smidt, 2010), this situation is not much different in other European countries than it is in Spain. The Bologna Declaration (1999) and the meetings of ministers of education every two years have not ended resistance from Germany, France, the U.K., Italy, and also Spain.

Bologna: Solution or Problem?

It would be an error to attribute all the resistance to Bologna to an attachment to old ways or a clinging to comfort (Sendín & Espinosa, 2009). Compared to northern European countries, the resistance of countries such as Spain is not due so much to the dominant teaching methodologies as to the existence of different cultures and organizational structures, things that are difficult to change by merely issuing norms. Spanish universities suffer from rigidity, compartmentalized qualifications, lack of state planning, low funding, lack of teacher mobility, and low student mobility.

Above all, however, there is disagreement about the direction the EHEA has taken. Paradoxically, the countries that signed the Declaration of the Sorbonne (1998) are among those most resistant to the later reforms. The Magna Charta of European Universities (1988) includes, for good reason, principles such as "the university as a meeting place, based on humanism and dialogue"—exactly the values that have lost ground in the successive agreements arising from the meetings at Lisbon, Bologna, Prague, and so on. The structural objectives of the Prague Strategy (2000) are prevailing: deregulation of the labor market, increased private funding in higher education, an exclusively work-oriented function of higher education, a business spirit, and mobility for workers and students. The Estrategia Universidad 2015 includes among its strategic outlines competitive funding, governance along business management lines, and the transfer of results from public research to the private sector ("technology parks," "clusters of excellence"), all in a globally competitive environment.

Many see Bologna as a project to commercialize education and scientific knowledge that is inseparable from the transnational liberalization of the universities that is occurring under the direction of the World Trade Organization in the context of the General Agreement on Trade in Services. Education is one of the twelve services covered by the latter agreement, which aims to promote the liberalization of trade in services through the progressive elimination of trade barriers. According to Sousa Santos (2005), the EU strategy is to help its universities to be more competitive globally, thus it proposes a new relationship between universities and the world of business and, in the last analysis, the transformation of the universities into businesses.

All this leads to various forms of externalization of the *res publica* of the universities (García & Navarrete, 2009). These include the outsourcing of public services to private businesses, the introduction of private-sector management techniques, provision of services to the private sector, and collaborative agreements with businesses, all of which make the administration of the university into just another actor in the market.[6]

Bologna ought to make us somewhat self-critical. We agree with Laporta (2009), who says, "We are Bologna." We should stop seeing Bologna as either the cause of or the cure for all the problems Spanish universities suffer from, and instead look at what matters of interest it raises for us. These include revising teaching methods and the professional competencies of degrees, and improving student welfare and encouraging mobility without allowing reflection to be directed by bureaucracy. If we want to improve our universities, we ought not to give Bologna excessive attention because if we do, we run the risk of failing to pay attention to the present problems of Spanish universities, including endogamy, social isolation, bureaucratization, and lack of attention to teaching and civic education (San Fabián, 2009).

It is possible that Bologna lacks both the virtues its defenders claim and the ills its detractors have assigned to it. There are undoubtedly general tendencies that Bologna could accentuate, but the most basic problems are inside the universities—the threat does not come just from the outside. "A university in social ostracism due to its elitism and protection of special interests, and paralyzed by its inability to question itself…is easy prey for advocates of neoliberal globalization" (Sousa Santos, 2005).

What would have happened if, instead of Bologna or the Lisbon Convention, UNESCO's "World Declaration on Higher Education in the 21st Century" (1988) had been taken as a framework for change?[7] We argue that the mission of the universities is to prepare highly qualified graduates who are also responsible citizens. The World Declaration also holds that institutions of higher education should defend and raise awareness of universal values such as peace, justice, liberty, equality, and solidarity. Why have the contents of this text not been included in the Bologna process so that they can function as both objectives and guides?

Perhaps the strangest thing is that for those who look at them from outside, Spanish universities seem to be doing fine. However, if we take the universities' inscrutability into account, it is really no wonder.

Notes

1. Currently, each university can decide how it elects its rector—either by a vote of the whole university community, or, as was done previously, by a vote of only a representative group of all the university colectives.
2. This document was drawn up by a foundation related to a bank (Fundación CYD) and the Conferencia de Rectores de las Universidades Españolas (CRUE) on the basis of a number of different studies, especially those coordinated by Samoilovoch (2008) and Eurydice (2008), as well as the *Informe Bricall* (2000).
3. Introducing such a change would require an amendment to the Ley Orgánica de Universidades. The Governing Council, with a majority of members from outside the university, would substitute the current Social Council.
4. Boni et al. (2009), in a study of the University of Valencia, show how decisions relating to the Bologna Process are being taken in a context of a low level of participation and power imbalance.
5. The methodology adopted by the EU to deal with this problem is called the Open Coordination Method. It was designed as an instrument to develop the Lisbon Strategy in those areas where the EU lacks transferred competencies.
6. Faced with the closure of humanities and social science faculties, the ministry said, "If a faculty closes, it won't be because of Bologna but rather because of the market."
7. At the World Conference on Higher Education in 1998, 182 countries participated, with education ministers leading their delegations in many cases; there is no document that demonstrates a greater degree of consensus. It is said that 46 countries support the Bologna process.

References

Altbach, P. G., Reisberg, L., & Rumbley, L.E. (2009). Tras la pista de una revolución académica: Informe sobre las tendencias actuales. Abstract for the World Conference on Higher Education, July 5–8, 2009, UNESCO, Paris.

Bjarnason, S., Cheng, K., Fielden, J., Lemaitre, M., Levy, D. & Varghese, N.V. (2009). A new dynamic: Private higher education. Paper presented at the World Conference on Higher Education, July 5–8, 2009, UNESCO, Paris.

Boni, A., Peris, J., López, E., & Hueso, A. (2009). Scrutinizing the process of adaptation to the European higher education area in a Spanish university degree using power analysis. *Power and Education, 1*(3), 319–332.

Bricall, J. M. (2000). Informe "Universidad 2000." Paper presented at Conferencia de Rectores de las Universidades españolas (CRUE), Barcelona.

Carreras, J., Sevilla, C., & Urbán, M. (2006). €uro-universidad. *Mito y realidad del proceso de Bolonia*. Barcelona: Icaria.

Colás, P., & De Pablos, J. (Eds.). (2005). *La universidad en la Unión Europea*. Málaga, Spain: Aljibe.

De la Cruz Tomé, A. (2003). El proceso de convergencia europea: Ocasión de modernizar la universidad española si se produce un cambio de mentalidad en gestores, profesores y estudiantes. *Aula Abierta, 82*, 191–216.

De Miguel Díaz, M. (Ed.) (2006). *Metodologías de enseñanza y aprendizaje para el desarrollo de competencias. Orientaciones para el profesorado universitario ante el espacio europeo de educación superior*. Madrid: Alianza Editorial.

Dias Sobrinho, J. (2009). Higher education: A public good, a state duty. In S. Bergan et al. (Eds.), *Public responsibility for higher education* (pp. 99–120). Paris: UNESCO.

Estrategia Universidad 2015. (2010). *La gobernanza de la universidad y sus entidades de investigación e innovación*. Fundación Conocimiento y Desarrollo (Fundación CYD) y Conferencia de Rectores de las Universidades Españolas (CRUE). Borrador. Ministerio de Ciencia e Innovación.

Eurydice. (2008). *Higher education governance in Europe. Policies, structures, funding and academic staff*. Paris: Author.

Fernández Barbudo, C. (2010). Los estudiantes y Bolonia. Intersticios. *Revista Sociológica de Pensamiento Crítico, 4*(1), 201–229.

García Manjón, J.V. (2009). La empleabilidad de los universitarios en el marco del espacio europeo de educación superior. In J. V. García Manjón (Ed.), *Hacia el espacio europeo de educación superior* (pp. 140–157). La Coruña, Spain: Netbiblo.

García, P., & Navarrete, M. (2009). Bolonia: Un análisis sobre la privatización de los servicios públicos y su relación con el proceso de Bolonia. *Cultura para la Esperanza: Instrumento de Análisis de la Realidad, 74*, 36–38. Retrieved from http://www.eurosur.org/acc/html/revista/r74/74bolo.pdf.

Iraberri, D., & Almendro, A. (2009). Bolonia y la pedagogía. El controvertido papel de la pedagogía como bisagra imprescindible en el desmantelamiento neoliberal de la educación pública. In L. Alegre & V. Moreno (Eds.), *Bolonia no existe. La destrucción de la universidad europea* (pp. 41–63). Hondarribia, Spain: HIRU.

Planas, J. (2004). Querían recursos humanos y llegaron ciudadanos. Reflexiones sobre el proceso de construcción del Espacio Europeo de Educación. *Revista de la Educación Superior, 33*(2), 130.

Laporta, F. J. (2009, May 28). Bolonia somos nosotros. *El País*. Retrieved from http://www.elpais.com/articulo/opinion/Bolonia/somos/elpepuopi/20090528elpepiopi_4/Tes.

Michavila, F., & Parejo, J. L. (2008). Políticas de participación estudiantil en el Proceso de Bolonia. *Revista de Educación*, número extraordinario, 85–118.

Pereyra, M. A., Luzón, A., & Sevilla, D. (2006). Las universidades españolas y el proceso de construcción del espacio europeo de educación superior. Limitaciones y perspectivas de cambio. *Revista Española de Educación Comparada*, *12*, 113–143.

Salaburu, P. (2007). *La universidad en la encrucijada. Europa y EEUU.* Madrid: Academia Europea de Ciencias y Artes.

Samoilovoch, D. (2008). Alternativas y propuestas para la gobernabilidad de las universidades españolas. Paper presented at the conference Alternativas y propuestas para la gobernalidad de las universidades organized by Fundación CYD and CRUE. September 4–5, 2008, Santander.

San Fabián Maroto, J. L. (2009). Bolonia: ¿el problema, la solución, o ninguna de las dos cosas? *Organización y Gestión Educativa, 5.* 16–17.

Sendín García, M. A., & Espinosa Martín, M. T. (2009). Una visión histórica-normativa del EEEE. De la Declaración de Bolonia a la oferta de los nuevos títulos universitarios. In J. V. García Manjón (Ed.), *Hacia el espacio europeo de educación superior* (pp. 2–21). La Coruña, Spain: Netbiblo.

Sousa Santos, B. de. (2005). La Universidad en el Siglo XXI. *Para una reforma democrática y emancipadora de la universidad.* Mexico City: Centro de Investigaciones Interdisciplinarias en Ciencias y Humanidades Coordinación de Humanidades.

Sursock, A., & Hanne Smidt, H. (2010). *Trends 2010: A decade of change in European higher education 2010.* Brussels: European University Association.

Tilak, J. B. G. (2009). Higher education: A public good or a commodity for trade? Commitment *to* higher education or commitment *of* higher education to trade. In S. Bergan et al. (Eds.), *Public responsibility for higher education* (pp. 15–42). Paris: UNESCO.

UNESCO. (1998). Declaración mundial sobre la educación superior en el siglo XXI. Visión y acción. Retrieved from http://www.unesco.org/education/educprog/wche/declaration _spa.htm.

· 5 ·

Bologna Process(ors)

Knowing Very Well What They Are Doing, but Still Doing It[1]

João Menelau Paraskeva

In memory of my mother

Globalization involves the "intensification, and [the] acceleration of social exchange and activities [that do] not occur merely on an objective material level[, and which involve] the subjective plane of human consciousness" (Steger, 2009, p. 12). Understanding neoliberal globalization policies (Sousa Santos, 2005a, 2006; cf. also ch. 1) involves an accurate set of critical hermeneutical processes that digs extensively into the very marrow of the cultural, economic, and political origins of these policies. Neoliberal globalization in its multiple forms does not happen in a social vacuum. In fact, "it is precisely in its oppression of non-market forces that we see how neoliberalism operates not only as an economic system, but as a political and cultural system as well" (McChesney, 1999, p. 7; Olssen, 2004); this creates endless intricate tensions between cultural homogenization and cultural heterogenization (Appadurai, 1996). Thus, accurately examining the forms of neoliberal globalization (Sousa Santos, 2005a) implies a cautious consideration of the emergence of Reaganism and the legacies of Bush in the United States and Thatcher and Major in the United Kingdom. These leaders were responsible for society's turn to the right, a cultural revolution that initiated a frenetic attack not only on the state apparatus but also on the very idea of the welfare state, and highlighted the market as not just *a* solution for the crisis but *the* solution (cf. Hall, 1988: Harvey, 2005; House, 1988). This "rightist turn" needs to be understood as a nonmonolithic bloc that has been able to edify an intricate and powerful coalition of seemingly antagonistic groups—neoliberals, neoconservatives, authoritarian populists, and a fraction of a new middle class (Apple, 2000). As Sousa Santos (2005b, p. vii) claims, "neoliberalism, contrary to what is commonly maintained, is not a new form of liberalism, but rather a new form of conservatism" in which subtly specific yet powerful religious groups are steadily assuming prominent positions. In fact, the current role played by O[cto]pus Dei, of a Vatican within the Vatican (Hutchison, 2006) and a kind of sophisticated expression of Christian-fascism "lite" (Kincheloe & Steinberg, 2007), threatens our examinination of the hegemonic forces behind neoliberal globalization that have been developing and upgrading their strategies.

In analyzing the latest metamorphosis of new rightist policies, Mouffe (2000, p. 108) stresses that both Tony Blair and Bill Clinton were able to construct a "radical center." Unlike traditional political groupings, the radical center is a new coalition that "transcends the traditional left/right division by articulating themes and values from both sides in a new synthesis" (Mouffe, 2000, p. 108). Fairclough (2000), in contrast to Mouffe, stresses that the radical center strategy does not consist only of "bringing together elements from these [Left and Right] political discourses," but also in its ability to "reconcile themes which have been seen as irreconcilable beyond such contrary themes, transcending them" (Fairclough, 2000, pp. 44–45). Fairclough also argues that this strategy is not based on a dialogic stance. In other words, the radical center achieved consent within the governed sphere "not through political [democratic] dialogue, but through managerial methods of promotion and forms of consultation with the public; [that is,] the government tends to act like a corporation treating the public as its consumers rather than citizens" (2000, p. 129). While such radical centrism targets the state, neoliberal forces actually need a strong state to promote their interests, especially in areas such as education and training—fields that are closely related to the formation of an ideologically submissive labor force (Brown & Lauder, 2006; Hill, 2003). The state actually has been paving the way for the market (Macrine, 2003; Paraskeva, 2003, 2004, 2007, 2008, 2010a; Sommers, 2000). Recent bailouts of banks, insurance companies, and car industries bear testimony to our claim that such a state actually fosters "new privatized legal regimes [and is] a state that has itself undergone transformation and participated in legitimizing a new doctrine about the role of the state in the economy" (Sassen, 2000, p. 59).

We are not claiming that there is no alternative to such neoliberal hegemonic forms of globalization. We concur with Sousa Santos's (2006) insightful analysis that "the idea of globalization, as a linear, homogenizing and irreversible phenomenon [is] false [and is based] on a determinist fallacy [that] consists of inculcating the idea that globalization is a spontaneous, automatic, unavoidable and irreversible process which intensifies and advances according to an inner logic and dynamism strong enough to impose themselves on any external interferences" (p. 395). Despite its disastrous impact on the oppressed all over the world, this hegemonic power bloc managed to produce a large consensus "of the liberal (or rather, neoliberal) economy; (2) of the weak state; (3) of liberal democracy; and (4) of the primacy of the rule of law and the judicial system" (Sousa Santos, 2006, p. 394). That said, I now turn to a desconstruction of the latest metamorphosis of a state within the context of hegemonic neoliberal globalization.

As Appadurai (1996) and Olssen (2004) both claim, albeit from different angles, state sovereignty has never been in jeopardy within the contemporary global cultural flows. In essence, the neoliberal imprimatur is a result of non-stop struggles between the state and market forces. Such intricate tensions are the fuel needed for the neoliberal intellectual engines (Paraskeva, 2001, 2005, 2006a, 2009, 2010a). In fact, such radical centrism, while searching for the dissolution of old contradictions between "right" and "left" (Fergusson, 2001), was able to lay a solid foundation for the gradual emergence of a new concept of the state, especially with regards to its role, anchored in a need to modernize government at almost at any cost. Democratic forces have been colonized by managerial insights in such a way that governments end up being weak executives of what Ball (2007) calls *Res plc*, which operates with the passive blessing of an anemic popular vote (Fergusson, 2001).

We argue that such mercantilist neofundamentalism has paved the way for what Agamben (2005) called a "state of exception"—the embryo of what I have called neoradical centrism. Whereas radical centrism claims to offer a broad managerial concept for the public good by demonstrating new managerial dynamics in and of itself (Newman, 2001, p. 46), *neo*radical centrism actually refines the entire common-sense cartography edified and stitched together by radical centrism (cf. Hall, 1988). What is currently at stake for the neoradical centrists—who are profoundly influenced by the menacing aims of Opus Dei— is not the need for modernizing forms of governments, but the unbalanced tension between force and law. In short, force paradoxically transcends law in the so-called democratic nations. Marx was not far off when he argued in his *Theses on Feuerbach* that religious frameworks are ingenuous ideas and concepts that are edified by individuals in reaction to their complex material milieu. In fact, neoliberal globalization "is having pronounced effects on the exclusive territoriality of the nation state; that is, its effects are not on territory as such but on its institutional encasements" (Sassen, 2000, p. 50).

The issue today is so complex that it goes well beyond Clarke and Newman's brilliant analysis in *The Managerial State* (1997) in which they challenge, among other things, the tensions of welfare without a state. Nowadays, as Clarke, Gewirtz, and McLaughlin (2001) accurately argue, the issue goes well beyond the creation of mixed economies that served the common good, or the emergence of a new form of public management, of transforming citizens into consumers, or even new forms of entrepreneurial government.

The state is stumbling before the tyranny of transformation in a way already identified by Clarke and Newman (1997). In the midst of today's policy of "welfarecide," which has been orchestrated by the so-called radical center, neoradical centrism emerges as an answer to a complete framework of needs that are the consequence of this policy. Whereas radical centrism cannot be seen as a crisis but as an answer to the crisis (Apple, 2000), neoradical centrism cannot be seen as a need but as the only answer to address ever more pressing needs. As Agamben (2005) argues, "the necessities transcend the law" (p. 1). Taking Agamben's approach a step further, neoradical centrism is able to overcome the multifarious tensions prompted by "state of exception vs. state sovereignty" and edifies a "point of imbalance between public law and political fact" (p. 1). In fact, Agamben claims that the state of exception "appears as the legal form of what cannot have legal form" (p. 1). The layout of neoradical centrism is "ambiguous, uncertain, borderline fringe, at the intersection of the legal and the political" (pp. 1–2), making it conveniently well situated in a coded no-man's land and quite ripe for marketers.

If we view recent events such as corruption in the oil industry, recalls in the food industry, and biodiesel policies as the dangerous costs of democratic numbness, we will be able to recognize how the state of exception "tends increasingly to appear as the dominant paradigm of government in contemporary politics, [a] threshold of indeterminacy between democracy and absolutism" (Agamben, 2005, pp. 2–3).

Based on the need to defend the values that support an insolent Western culture, the state of exception, which is a state of necessities, has legitimized the conditions to justify the common use of torture and genocide, thereby allowing mass imprisonments, the extermination of particular categories of evil individuals, and the fabrication of new identities. For instance, it has become commonplace to refer to those at Guantanamo Bay as "detainees" rather than POWs who should be treated in accordance with the Geneva Conventions. Meanwhile, the state of exception simultaneously reinforces the conditions that reduce societal development to a pale economic equation. In fact, "the state of exception is not a special kind of law (like the law of war), it is suspension…of the juridical order itself" (Agamben, 2005, p. 4; see also Todorov, 2003). Falk (1999) claims that territorial sovereignty "is being diminished on a spectrum of issues in such a serious manner as to subvert the capacity of states to govern the internal life of society, and non-state actors hold an increasing proportion of power and influence in shaping [the] world order" (p. 35).

In essence, such neoradical centrism wins the consensus of the vast majority of the population, assuming neofundamentalistic perspectives (Todorov, 2003, p. 20). Todorov writes that, odd as it might seem, such a political platform gathers disparate political entities, including Maoists and Trotskyists. Unfortunately, some of the best Marxists are politically to the right of center (Paraskeva, 2006b; 2010a). Paradoxically, "the Marxist account of the relation between economical and political power seems persuasive only after Marxism has lost its capacity to win adherents to its world view" (Falk, 1999, p. 46). Welcome to what Žižek (2008) calls liberal communists—the new Porto Davos elite generation.

Neoliberal globalization "has intermingled our categories of thought, discouraged the projection of 'imagined communities' on a global scale, and eclipsed the image of global governance by way of a society of states" (Falk, 1999, p. 47). We are experiencing a process that entails

> much "creative destruction," not only of prior institutional frameworks and powers (even challenging traditional forms of state sovereignty) but also divisions of labour, social relations, welfare provisions, technological mixes, ways of life and thought, reproductive activities, attachments to the land and habits of the hearth. (Harvey, 2005, p. 3)

Why then, despite almost three decades of having a distressing effect on society and attacking "the even more localized rest" (Bauman, 2004, p. 3), does a hegemonic bloc continue to dominate? As we are reminded (Jessop, Bonnett, Bromley, & Ling, 1984; Apple, 2000, p. 23), one must ask, "How is such an ideological vision legitimated and accepted?" It is undeniable that neoradical centrism is not exactly a direct detour from the orthodoxies laid out by the radical centrists. In some ways, it is a platform that, as Hall (1992) puts it, goes toward radical centrism by taking advantage of a particular kind of contradiction within the very marrow of neoliberal globalization. Neoradical centrism should be seen as the latest capitalist metamorphosis of "righting" the Left. This deterioration cannot be detached from the politics of common sense and the role the media plays in building a particular web of meanings.

This state of exception (Agamben, 2005), together with the irreversible need to create new markets "by state action if necessary" (Harvey, 2005, p. 2) in areas that never existed before, are two sides of the same coin, a devastating currency for sectors such as public education, especially in semi-peripheral nations such as Portugal.

A Final Blessing to Portugal's Public Higher Education

Higher education in Portugal is in crisis; in fact, it is not an exaggeration to say that it is bankrupt (cf. Araújo, 2007; Rodrigues, 2007; 2008). The entire Portuguese higher education system—both public and private—is penniless and on the brink of collapse (Nóvoa, 2006).

Myriad researchers point out that the strategic disinvestment in public institutions, which has been led by neoliberal policies over the last four decades, has pushed higher education in Portugal and many other nations into a moribund state (cf. Apple, 2010; Aranowitz, 2000; Giroux, 2007; Nóvoa, 2006; Paraskeva, 2010b). Economic decline is a crucial card in the neoliberal global approach, and as mentioned before, it creates the conditions for the totalitarian market solution. As Harvey (2005) claims, it is "the role of the state to create and preserve an institutional framework appropriate" (p. 2) for market mechanisms. Thus, it is an intentional crisis—a premeditated disaster that allows marketers to put their strategy in place (cf. Klein, 2007).

At the end of the second millennium the Portuguese higher educational system clearly deteriorated into an unsustainable and indefensible condition, propelled by an intricate set of neoradical centrist strategies. Those strategies include (a) asphyxiating financial policies for public institutions, (b) "mistreatment" of the EU's cohesive structural funds, (c) lack of a strong, clear public policy for education in general and higher education in particular, and (d) the EU's nonstop project of incorporating new territories, thus gaining newer (and bigger) markets.

Today in Portugal the vast majority accept fairly passively that public higher education's days are justifiably numbered, and that the solution is to follow the recommendations made by the OECD (2006) and ENQA (2006)—in a nutshell, that higher education must adapt to market mechanisms. As Gewirtz puts it (2002, p. 13), higher education in Portugal has embraced a process of re-acculturation. Much of this neosocial sense is achieved by giving particular social concepts and aims a positive semantic twist, thus giving birth to a new discourse that has the force to justify the unjustifiable, to say the unsayable, and to present this discourse as a perfect representation of reality (Gee, Hull & Lankshear, 1996, p. 29; Macedo, Dendrinos & Gounari, 2003). Marketers were able to build acquiescence to the destruction of what they dared to call a "state monopoly" in higher education in Portugal, thus perverting the very idea of the public good.

As I have discussed in great detail elsewhere (Paraskeva, 2010b), the OECD (2006) and ENQA (2006) reports claim that the Portuguese higher educational system is dated, incapable of addressing national and EU needs, and in desperate need of a total overhaul. Despite millions of euros flowing into Portugal from the EU structural cohesion fund for over a decade, the country's higher educational system shows unbalanced and uncontrolled growth that affects "the quality of the education and compromised the credibility of the system" (ENQA, 2006, p. 19), as well as irrational development of programmatic diversity (OECE, 2006, p. 23). Unfortunately, and shamefully, the EU funds had nothing to do with social convergence—one of the European Union's top priorities (cf. Duff, Pinder & Pryce, 1994). The EU's cohesion structural funds, such as the European Regional Development Fund, provide a pertinent example of Europe's inconsequence in creating a more just higher educational system. The very fact that "the expansion of higher education was mainly seen in the private sector" (ENQA, 2006, p. 19) supports this undisputable claim.

OECD (2006) and ENQA (2006) both outline the challenges for Portuguese higher education at a systemic level, namely, specialization, improvement of education and research quality, clarification of the roles of universities and polytechnics, rationalization of human resources, incorporation of market needs, connection with the knowledge-based economy, managerialism and autonomy, and so on. OECD's recommendations for an overhaul of the Portuguese higher education system aim to reform secondary education; to connect the higher education system to developments in the labor market; and to establish a symbiosis between the state, markets, and academia that is anchored in the so-called knowledge-based economy (2006, p. 29).

OECD also makes a call to follow the Lisbon Strategy (LS, 2000) and the Bologna Declaration (BD, 1999). The Portuguese academic establishment reacted strongly against this recommendation because the catastrophe in Portuguese higher education reached crisis level precisely because of the LS and the BD, which repeat some of the major issues that structured the Bologna Magna Charta Universitatum (1988).

Higher education in the European Union reached a crucial turning point with the creation of a Common European Higher Education Area, in which both the LS (2000) and the BD (1998) have dictated the construction of the EU's knowledge-based economy—an issue to which we will return.

According to the BD (1999), higher education in the European Union needed to be radically transformed. This transformation was intended to lead to the construction of a completely different higher education platform based on three pillars that would facilitate conditions (1) for mobility, (2) for employability within the EU for students and teachers, and for researchers and administrative staff, and (3) to guarantee that competition would occur not only within European higher education, but also with international higher education systems (Lourtie, 2001).

While mobility implies issues such as trust and flexibility, employability becomes the "most elusive of the three main goals of the [BD, since it implies] quality assurance, relevance of programmes, clear information on objectives and learning outcomes of the programmes, and accreditation" (Lourtie, 2001, p. 7). In short, an intricate complex of new technicalities was created. The BD, as Amaral and Veiga (2008; 2009) adamantly state, is much more about form than substance.

The BD (1999) is, in fact, a political attempt to deconstruct nation-states and higher education systems, and to simultaneously create a common transstate "Higher Education Union" platform. Transnational education "is growing and challenging traditional education [and policies] geared towards transparency and quality of qualifications should contemplate the transnational offer" (Lourtie, 2001, p. 3). Moreover, it "is part of the equation when discussing international competitiveness. The global educational services market is growing fast. It challenges the traditional institutions and can no longer be ignored" (Lourtie, 2001, p. 10). Transnational education, therefore, "is the most obvious manifestation of globalization in higher education [and] is flourishing in almost every country" (Hoffman, 2001, p. 25).

Needless to say, the vast majority of higher education institutions in the EU are not ready for such a step. In Portugal, for example, almost every higher education and/or college department was unprepared for this transformation. Amaral and Rosa (2008) argue that borderless or transnational higher education shows a lack of transparency, raises the problem of students' protection, and is a green light for the emergence of several rogue providers.

The BD (1999) must be seen as an intricate process that is now moving toward a competency-based system, one that will create a common path, regardless of the different rhythms of each nation-state's higher education system. It is unnecessary to mention the interface between the BD (1999) and the EU's transnational educational policies and politics (cf. Adams, 2001).

The BD (1999) has provided a pathway for downsizing the Portuguese higher education system and legitimizing revised funding policies. Under the BD (1999), Portugal's higher education system's undergraduate courses were reduced from five to three years. This raises serious concerns about quality, credibility, lack of autonomy, and employment, as well as the quasi end of the tenure system. It also is noteworthy that this reduction did not occur in professional courses such as medicine, which immediately created different academic castes.

The financial asphyxiation of the public higher education system opens the door for the mercantilization of Portuguese higher education. The lucky few who were able to escape the cutbacks promoted by the BD (1999) now need to justify their salaries and are forced to compete in a tight race for funds (Molnar, 2006). This raises some concerns about the loss of academic freedom, because "faculties and schools are completely in the hands of the market, a market that determines what counts as legitimate" (Levine, 2003, p. 33). Academic freedom fosters "an open and public debate" about social issues, facilitates research that deals with tough issues, creates a strong university, allows the emergence of cutting-edge thinking, and encourages powerful discussion (Altbach & Peterson, 2007, p. 72). Academic freedom is viscerally intertwined with institutional autonomy, and there can be no social cohesion in the face of intellectual repression. A repressive system is a clear obstacle to public engagement and opens the door not only for the emergence of pseudo-universities, as Altbach (2005) puts it, but also for the conversion of existing universities into pseudo-universities.

The subordination of higher education institutions must be contextualized within the realm of neoliberal strategy—a strategy that pursues an ideology of control while suppressing certain inconvenient truths—which is forcing these institutions to engage in a business ideology. Barrow (1990) accurately claimed that the interplay between hegemony and the relative autonomy of intellectuals must be understood at any given time as "the result of a historical balance of power between intellectuals, administrators, and economic and political elites" (p. 247). Duke University provides a pertinent example. Ranked the world's third most prestigious university, Duke experiences the daily conflict between the compulsory needs and wants of the market and what professors understand is providing the best education for the students (Bradshaw, 2008). We are experiencing a powerful "academicide."

The move to three-year undergraduate courses hides another strategy, which is to adopt an EU core curriculum in higher education. This strategy is likely to be approved by EU members without much effort. We are experiencing a process of establishing selective traditions (Williams, 1961) in an attempt to preserve an obsessive cognitive and epistemological diet (Steinberg, 2006) and promote the cult of the pedagogy of the big lies (Macedo, 2006), which includes a cognitive decapitation (Kozol, 2005) and a process of historical engineering (Chomsky, 1992, 2002), all of which raise serious concerns over whose knowledge is in and whose is out (Apple, 2000; Giroux, 1981). Issues such as mobility, employability, and competition actually expose the intention of the BD (1999)—the consolidation of a "two-speed" European Union, rather than social cohesion. In other words, students and teachers from peripheral countries such as Portugal will be encouraged to migrate to the European Union's "locomotive" state members—England, France, and Germany. In fact, this is already happening. In return, only a tiny percentage of English, French, and German students will use this mobility to attend a Portuguese higher education institution.

These policies will have a lethal impact on teacher education, as teacher education programs openly engage in the selective production of deskilled teachers (Apple, 1986; Giroux, 1981), thereby legitimizing cognitive passivity and reinforcing the "technification" of teacher education (Kincheloe, 1993, pp. 1–16).

Another puzzling concern is the way the Portuguese higher education system is surrendering in the face of what Macedo, Dendrinos, and Gounari (2003) call the hegemony of the English language. It now openly defends the belief that what counts as good research has to be published not only in English, but also in particular peer-reviewed English-language journals or by well-known English-language publishing houses—that is, certain U.S. and U.K. publishers. Through academia and deeply anchored to economic logic, the English language is becoming what Esperanto tried and failed to become—a global language. According to Giroux (2007), this is not education, "it is a flight from self and society" (p. 184). As Phillipson (2003) argues, the role the English language has been playing within the so-called hegemonic globalization project is a threat to other languages, identities, cultures, and ideological apparatuses within the European Union.

At my own University of Minho at Braga—and in the midst of these dev-astating new policies—the Full Professors Council (2005) had the temerity to draw up the Reference Internal Act, a list of requirements—what those who opposed it called a grocery list—that determine whether a faculty member maintains his or her position or gets promoted. Needless to say, the majority of the members of that council did not meet the grocery list. Based on an odd sci-entific argument of "disciplinary areas," these stewards of epistemology overt-ly prohibit anyone but themselves from thinking, debating, interacting, inviting, or organizing events dealing with issues of public education, educa-tional policies and politics, or of gender, class, race, and ethnicity within the educational institutional premises. As Marx would put it, welcome to the mis-ery of pedagogy—or to update that, the misery of mediocrity.

The problem of the Portuguese higher education system "is not one of bureaucracy in the sense given by Max Weber, but rather a problem of the lack of it" (Jacquinet, 2008, p. 7). In other words, as Jacquinet (2008) argues, "too many employment-related decisions are determined by personal relatioshps and friendships, which reveals a complex mechanism of institutionalized favoritism" (p. 7). Those interactions include endogamy, and locally, *amizade* (friendship, *cunha* (nepotism), and *caciquismo* (bossism).

The transformations in the Portuguese higher education system bring to the fore a complicated issue—the very mission of public higher education. "What is a university for, and what must it consequently be?" (Ortega y Gasset, 1944, p. 28) are questions fundamental to understanding the mission of the univer-sity. Universities need to assume a holistic mission (Ortega y Gasset, 1944), one that is related to basic questions such as who can get into college, and what will they be taught when they arrive? (Aronowitz, 2000, p. 126).

Research data shows that Portuguese higher education is deeply segregated—racially, economically, culturally—and it also reveals a puzzling fact: While it is undeniable that the majority of students cannot make it into higher education, it is also true that a substantial number who have completed a higher education cannot find a job. This segregation would not be reduced under the policies of the BD (1999; Teixeira, Rosa, & Amaral, 2006). The commodification of post-secondary education has brought to the fore issues such as uniformity-raising stan-dards, blind audit policies, and practices that will create more obstacles for the vast majority of the population or, as neoliberals claim, for the deserving poor. Although "the university represents a privilege difficult to justify or defend" (Ortega y Gasset, 1944, p. 33), in a way we are facing a strategy that promotes the sense that higher education is not for everybody (Aronowitz, 2000, p. 108).

Promoting this idea is now in the hands of a market-driven university led by a particular group of political commissars, or new cultural managers, as Chomsky (2003) puts it, who are willing to act like CEOs. Veblen (1918) earlier anticipated this dangerous reality. Today's cultural managers are actually building new social formations in which the future of universities will rely heavily on the number of enrolled students and material investment figures such as buildings, all while neglecting scholarship issues. In a system already fueled by what Jacquinet (2008) calls ceremonial adequacy—a mechanism of academic and social regulation in universities that imposes rules of nomination and progression in the professional careers, namely, that of professors—this is a social catastrophe.

The BD, by claiming the need to edify a common educational area, provides clear evidence of how neoradical centrist hegemonic movements are using higher education as a powerful space in which to foster the process of fabricating a Europe (Nóvoa & Lawn, 2002) fundamentally guided by Western values. In a letter addressed to Lionel Jospin, Michel Rocard, Jacques Delors, and all French socialists, Touraine (1996, p. 27) expresses his perplexity over the way the so-called contemporaneous or modern socialists dare to submit all universities to the same rules, dismantling any chance for elaboration and fostering their own policies. It is obvious that what the European Union's higher education institutions are being guided to transmit is deeply linked to the need to reinforce a particular kind of Western culture. We are, in fact, facing an economic and cultural device that will help shift the European Union into a new dimension. This process not only needs to be contextualized within what Gewirtz (2002) calls the postwelfarism epoch—one in which education becomes a commodity driven by visions of competition, efficiency, effectiveness, freedom, and blind results—but also must be perceived as a strategy to westernize the West. Unfortunately, in the European Union, the Common European Higher Education Area has nothing to do with Sadiki's understanding (2001) of the internationalization of higher education, an understanding that fosters a real global community and engages in a curricular plurality that does not minimize non-Western epistemologies.

The BD (1999) cannot be dissociated from the LS (2000). As Simão, Santos, and Costa (2002) argue, the LS anchored its objectives quite clearly in a triangular relationship between a sustainable economy, knowledge and competition, and social cohesion. Simão et al. claim that it is a remarkable achievement of EU policies to have constructed a knowledge-based society, a goal that relies heavily on social cohesion—that is, investing in people to fight social exclusion—and in a new education that foresees a new economic architecture. Both the BD and the LS impose a new mission for a higher education system, one that is anchored in four pillars: citizenship, culture, science, and innovation (Simão et al., 2002). It is impossible not to notice the economic card that is being subtly but undeniably played in the LS (2000). More than half of the twenty-four guidelines listed in LIG (2005) are anchored or driven by an economic leitmotiv.

Such economic architectural fundamentalism has been seen as the best way for Portugal and the rest of EU members to participate dynamically in the knowledge-based economy. Echoing Naisbitt and Aburdene's (1999) 1980s' perspective, the LS (2000) overtly reveals the EU member states' need to transform the EU economy into a knowledge-based economy by 2015. The aim is to build the world's best, most vibrant, and most competitive economy capable of securing sustainable economic growth, thereby ensuring better jobs and social cohesion—an ambition overtly defended by OECD (1996) reports as well. The importance of a knowledge-driven society is not minimized by the BD (1999).

A Europe of knowledge is now widely recognized as an irreplaceable element of social and human growth, and as an indispensable component in consolidating and enriching the European citizenry, capable of giving its citizens the necessary competence to face the challenges of the new millennium, together with an awareness of shared values and a common social and cultural space (BD, 1999, p.5).

We do not claim that the Portuguese higher educational system is not in need of extensive reform. However, it is one thing to need reform, and quite another to mindlessly follow OECD's and ENQA's compulsory policies, which are basically the final blessing on an already moribund system. We do have serious concerns over the implications of the BD (1999) for semi-peripheral countries such as Portugal. Some of the crucial effects of the BD are already visible and perfectly palpable in Portugal, namely (a) consolidation of defunding policies, (b) the mercantilization of the higher education system, (c) the emergence and crystallization of an English-only movement, (d) the legitimation of a "two speed" EU, and (e) a relegitimizing of particular kinds of knowledge that universities should transmit—intricate issues we discuss in the next section.

Welcome to the neoliberal euthanasia of the Portuguese public higher education system. Welcome to the inaugural attempt to legitimize an unaccomplished, noteworthy, and noble utopia—the right to dream and to maintain a full free public higher education that will allow the oppressed masses to hold on to their rights and fight for the transformation of the very conception and practice of power.

Academic Capitalism

Slaughter and Rhoades (2004) argue that the continuous reduction of state funds, "marked by periodic, intense fiscal crises, has played an important part in legitimating academic capitalism" (p. 14). The BD (1999) must be perceived as a trump card within the theory of academic capitalism (Slaughter & Rhoades, 2004) that claims the need to mercantilize higher education systems, and in doing so, ends up reinforcing higher education institutions as powerful devices of an economic and cultural westernization of the West, which is precisely the case in Portugal.

Slaughter and Rhoades (2004, p. 1) bluntly identify the effects of the theory of academic capitalism in higher education: (a) a shift from a public good knowledge and learning regime to an academic capitalist knowledge and learning regime; (b) knowledge as raw material; (c) networks of actors who link universities to each other, to corporations, and to various state agencies; (d) a reshaping of students' identities and higher education borders; and (e) the standardization of teaching.

It is precisely this set of new relations between higher education institutions and agents and society at large (local and global)—in which higher education assumes a core business-oriented curriculum—that presents quite a frightening situation, especially when one thinks of peripheral nations such as Portugal.

When considering cases such as the Missyplicity project described by Slaughter and Rhoades (2004), in which the American businessman John Sperling used his fortune to clone his pet dog Missy, what comes to mind is MIT's colonization of the Portuguese higher education system. The Portuguese government paid over 63 million euros to MIT to provide oversight of specific university departments and centers. Unsurprisingly, that money was taken from the higher education budget, driving higher education institutions into an even more chaotic situation. If, as Slaughter and Rhoades (2004) argue, "the Missyplicity project captures many of the promises, pitfalls, ironies, and contradictions that characterize the changing relations of colleges and universities to the new economy" (p. 2), what would we say about MIT's predatory relation with the Portuguese higher education system? Like Missyplicity, MIT's interface with Portuguese higher education institutions leads one to question the government's use of taxpayers' money and "raises questions about the terms of the academy's engagement with the new economy" (p. 7). Finding out what is amiss(y) will be the new mission for the Portuguese higher education system. The "siliconization" of higher education, as Washburn (2005) demonstrates, raises serious concerns over "one of the central missions of the university, [which is] to nurture and protect the information commons, the pool of knowledge and ideas unencumbered by ownership claims that [it] is freely available to researchers and the public at large" (p. 143).

The theory of academic capitalism must undeniably be contextualized within one of the primordial strategies of a state (of exception) that is surrendering "to corporations to construct the new economy" (Slaughter & Rhoades, 2004, pp. 20–21). The question is how one rescues the state and public institutions, such as universities, from such neoradical centrist hegemonic threads.

Democratizing Democracy: Final Thoughts

Despite the fact that we are facing a global context powerfully dominated by neoliberal forms of globalization, Sousa Santos (2008) argues that this does not mean there are no spaces for alternative articulations, both nationally and internationally, to challenge such hegemony. In fact, the "current regime of neoliberalism and the incursion of corporate power into higher education . . . demand a profoundly committed sense of collective resistance" (Giroux, 2002, p. 457). Thus, "a creative, democratic and emancipatory reform of public university" (Sousa Santos, 2008, p. 50) needs to be situated in such a context. This reform should be seen within the vast counter-hegemonic globalization movement, which is the best way to challenge neoliberal globalization (Sousa Santos, 2008; see also ch. 1 of this volume).

Nations' reform of their public university systems should generate projects focused on policy choices that qualify the inclusion of each country in the contexts of production and distribution of knowledge. These factors are increasingly transnationalized and polarized between contradictory processes of transnationalization—neoliberal globalization and counter-hegemonic globalization. This country project therefore must express a broad political and social contract and allow the emergence of several subsequent contracts, one being the educational contract, and within it, the university contract as a public good (Sousa Santos, 2008, p. 51).

The new university contract starts from the premise that the university has a crucial role in building a country's place in the contradictory and polarized world of globalizations, and thus is fighting to define the crisis hegemonically and reconquer its own legitimacy (Sousa Santos, 2008). The struggle for its own legitimacy, Sousa Santos stresses, will be increasingly demanding, and university reform should focus on crucial areas. One of those areas, Sousa Santos argues, is the ecology of knowledge, which implies an epistemological revolution within the university, and as such cannot be decreed by law. The task is to promote dialogue between scientific or humanistic knowledge produced by the university and lay, popular, traditional, urban, rural knowledge that comes not from Western cultures, but from non-Western perspectives (indigenous, African, Oriental, etc.) circulating in society. By specializing in scientific knowledge and by considering scientific knowledge to be the only valid form of knowledge, the dominant academic tradition actively contributed to the disqualification and even destruction of much nonscientific knowledge, and thereby contributed to the marginalization of social groups that depended upon that knowledge (Sousa Santos, 2008, p. 69).

Thus, as Sousa Santos (2008) stresses, there is no social injustice without cognitive injustice. Universities have to play a leading role in addressing one of the most challenging issues that we have before us—democratizing democracy. It is undeniable, Vavi (2004) claims, that democracy bypasses the poor. Democracy is in danger—you could say that democracy is in need of democracy. In order to democratize democracy, Sousa Santos (2003) suggests, "we need to reinvent social emancipation since traditional modern social emancipation has been pushed into a kind of dead end by neoliberal globalization" (p. 26).

Thus, the struggle for democracy, as Shivji (2003) argues, "is primarily a political struggle of the form of governance, thus involving the reconstitution of the state and creating conditions for the emancipatory project" (p. 1). We need, as Sousa Santos (1998) notes, to fight for the state as a spotless new social movement—that is, "a more vast political organization in which the democratic forces will struggle for a distributive democracy, thus transforming the state in a new—yet powerful—social and political entity" (p. 61). Such a state is "even much more directly involved in redistribution criteria, and profoundly committed with economic and cultural inclusive policies" (Sousa Santos, 1998, p. 60). It is just such a state—a spotless new social movement—"that will reawaken . . . the tension between capitalism and [real] democracy, and this can only be achieved if democracy is conceived and plasticized as redistributive democracy" (p. 61). The struggle for a redistributive democracy is the first crucial step in reinforcing the state's role in a more just society and converting it into a spotless new social movement (Shivji, 2003; Sousa Santos, 1998). It is time to recapture higher education as a new public sphere (Giroux, 1995, p. 239). The task is to reinvent daily how to democratize democracy, to challenge "eugenic processes of nullification" (Memmi, 2000), and to not merely bracket, but to eliminate social inequality (Fraser, 1997, p. 92). What we are claiming here is the need to fight for a new public community university that will engage in a collective task "of developing a politics that extends beyond the nation-state and reclaiming the academy as a democratic public sphere" (Giroux, 2007, p. 203). As the Mozambican writer Couto (2005) claims, this is the best way that we have "to challenge a past that was portrayed in a deformed way, a present dressed with borrowed clothes, and a future ordered already by foreign interests" (p. 10).

Despite neoliberal globalization's hegemonic position, a counter-hegemonic globalization—what Sousa Santos (2006) terms insurgent cosmopolitanism—has propelled a myriad of social movements and transformations neoliberal globalization. It is exactly within the very marrow of such counter-hegemonic forms of globalization and their clashes with the neoliberal hegemonic globalization that new itineraries of social emancipation are developing. It is these clashes—economic, political, and cultural quarrels that Sousa Santos (2003) calls "clashes between North and South" (p. 26)—that would bring to the fore "the wrangle between representative and participatory democracy" (p. 26).

Public universities have a key role in the transformative processes of democratizing democracy, something that, painfully, not only the ENQA (2006) and OECD (2006) but also the BD (1999), LS (2000), and the Common European Higher Education Area seem to neglect.

Note

1. An earlier version of this paper appears in *Policy Futures in Education* and in Paraskeva, J. (2010) *Unaccomplished Utopia*. Rotterdam: Sense Publishers.

References

Adam, S. (2001). Transnational education project report and recommendations. Paper presented at the Confederation of European Union Rector's conferences, March 2001, Salamanca.

Agamben, G. (2005). *The state of exception*. Chicago: University of Chicago Press.

Altbach, P. (2005). The rise of the pseudouniversity. In P. Altbach & D. Levy (Eds.), *Private higher education*). Rotterdam: Sense Publishers.

Altbach, P., & Peterson, P. (Eds.). (2007). *Higher education in the new century: Global challenges and inovative ideas*. Rotterdam: Sense Publishers.

Amaral, A., & Rosa, M. J. (2008). Internationalisation, trans-nationalisation and globalisation: Can quality mechanisms be an adequate regulation tool?" In A. Amaral, A. Rovio-Johansson, M. J. Rosa, & D. Westerheijden (Eds.), *Essays in supportive peer review* (pp. 203–220). New York: Nova Science Publishers.

Amaral, A., & Veiga, A. (2008). How does the Bologna Process challenge national traditions of higher education institutions? In J. Välimaa & O.-H. Ylijoki (Eds.), *Cultural perspectives on higher education* (pp. 238–256). Dordrecht: Springer.

Amaral, A., & Veiga, A. (2009). Survey on the implementation of the Bologna Process in Portugal. *Higher Education, 57*(1), 57–69.

Appadurai, A. (1996). *Modernity at large: Cultural dimensions of globalization.* Minneapolis: University of Minnesota Press.

Apple, M. (1986). *Teachers and texts. A political economy of class and gender relations in education.* New York: Routledge.

Apple, M. (2000). *Official knowledge. Democratic education in a conservative age.* New York: Routledge.

Araújo, J. (2007). Interview. Lisbon: Radio Televisão Portuguesa.

Aronowitz, S. (2000). *The knowledge factory: Dismantling the corporate university and creating true higher education.* Boston: Beacon Press.

Ball, S. (2007). *Education PLC.* London: Routledge.

Bauman, Z. (2004). *Globalization: The human consequences.* London: Polity Press.

Bradshaw, D. (2008, May 12). Business education. *Financial Times* Special Report.

Brown, P. H., & Lauder, H. (2006). Globalization, knowledge and the myth of the magnet economy. In H. Lauder, P. H. Brown, J.-A. Dillabough, & A. Halsey (Eds.), *Education, globalization and social change* (pp. 317–340). Oxford, UK: Oxford University Press.

Chomsky, N. (1992). *Chronicles of dissent: Interviews with David Barsamian—Noam Chomsky.* Monroe, ME: Common Courage Press.

Chomsky, N. (2002). Legitimacy in history. In P. Mitchell & J. Schoeffel (Eds.), *Understanding power: The indispensable Chomsky* (pp. 135–137). New York: New Press.

Chomsky, N. (2003). Language, politics and composition. In C. P. Otero (Ed.), *Noam Chomsky on democracy and education* (pp. 374–436). New York: RoutledgeFalmer.

Clarke, J., Gewirtz, S., & McLaughlin, E. (2001). Reinventing the welfare state. In J. Clarke, S. Gewirtz, & E. McLaughlin (Eds.), *New managerialism: New welfare?* (pp. 1–26). London: Open University Press.

Clarke, J., & Newman, J. (1997). *The managerial state.* London: Sage.

Couto, M. (2005). *Pensatempos.* Lisbon: Caminho.

Deem, R. (2004). Globalization, new managerialism, academic capitalism and entrepreneurialism in universities. In M. Tight (Ed.), *The RoutledgeFalmer reader in higher education* (pp. 287–302). London: RoutledgeFalmer.

European Ministers of Education. (1999). Joint declaration of the European ministers of education. Retrieved from http://www.bologna-berlin2003.de/pdf/bologna_declaration.pdf

European Network for Quality Assurance in Higher Education—ENQA. (2006). *European association for quality assurance in higher education 2006.* Helsinki: Author.

Fairclough, N. (2000). *New labor, new language?* London: Routledge.

Fergusson, R. (2001). Modernizing manegerialism in education. In J. Clarke, S. Gewirtz, & E. McLaughlin (Eds.), *New managerialism: New welfare?* (pp. 202–221). London: Open University Press.

Fraser, N. (1997). *Justice interrupts: Critical reflections on the 'postsocialist' condition.* New York: Routledge.

Full Professors Council. (2005). *References internal act.* Braga, Portugal: Universidade do Minho.

Gabbard, D. (2003). Education is enforcement: The centrality of compulsory schooling in market societies. In K. Saltman & D. Gabbard (Eds.), *Education as enforcement: The militarization and corporatization of schools* (pp. 61–78). New York: Routledge.

Gee, J., Hull, G., & Lankshear, C. (1996). *The new work order: Behind the language of the new capitalism.* Boulder, CO: Westview Press.

Gewirtz, S. (2002). *The managerial school: Post-welfarism and social justice in education.* London: Routledge.

Giroux, H. (1995). Beyond the ivory tower: Public intellectuals and the crisis of higher education. In M. Bérubé & C. Nelson (Eds.), *Higher education under fire: Politics, economics, and the crisis of the humanities* (pp. 238–258). New York: Routledge.

Giroux, H. (2002). Neoliberalism, corporate culture, and the promise of higher education: The university as a democratic sphere. *Harvard Educational Review, 72*(4), 425–463.

Giroux, H. (2007). *The university in chains: Confronting the military-industrial-academica complex.* Boulder, CO: Paradigm Publishers.

Hall, S. (1988). The toad in the garden: Thatcherism among theorists. In C. Nelson & L. Grossberg (Eds.), *Marxism and the interpretation of culture* (pp. 35–57). Urbana: University of Illinois Press.

Hall, S. (1992). Cultural studies and its theoretical legacies. In L. Grossberg, C. Nelson, & P. Treichler (Eds.), *Cultural studies* (pp. 277–294). New York: Routledge.

Harvey, D. (2005). *A brief history of neoliberalism.* Oxford, UK: Oxford University Press.

Hill, D. (2003). O neo-liberalismo global, a resistência e a deformação da educação. *Revista Currículo sem Fronteiras, 3*(2), 24–59. Retrieved from www.curriculosemfronteiras.org

Hoffman, R. (2001). *International seminar on transnational education.* Malmo, Sweden.

House, E. (1988). *Schools for $sale: Why free markets won't improve America's schools, and what will.* New York: Teachers College Columbia University.

Hutchison, R. (2006). *Their kingdom come: Inside the secret world of Opus Dei.* New York: St. Martin's Press.

Jacquinet, M. (2008). *Higher learning in Portugal. A Veblenian approach to the evolution of organizations and hierarchies.* Lisbon: Universidade Aberta.

Jessop, B., Bonnett, K., Bromley, S., & Ling, T. (1984). Authoritarian populism, two nations and Thatcherism. *New Left Review, 147*, 33–60.

Kincheloe, J. (1993). *Toward a critical politics of teacher thinking: Mapping the postmodern.* Wesport, CT: Bergin & Garvey.

Kincheloe, J., & Steinberg, S. H. (2007). Cutting class in a dangerous era: A critical pedagogy of class awareness. In J. Kincheloe & S. H. Steinberg (Eds.), *Cutting class: Socioeconomic status and education* (pp. 3–69). Lanham, MD: Rowman & Littlefield.

Kozol, J. (2005). *The shame of the nation: The restoration of apartheid schooling in America.* New York: Crown.

Levine, A. (2003). Educación superior: Una revolución externa, una evolución interna. In M. S. Pittinsky (Ed.), *La universidad conectada. Perspectivas del impacto de internet en la educación superior* (pp. 25–42). Anadaluzia, Spain: Ediciones Aljibe.

Lisbon Integrated Guidelines. (2005). Lisbon: Presidência do conselho de ministros. Lisbon Strategy. (2000). Lisbon: Conselho de Ministros.

Lourtie, P. (2001). Furthering the Bologna process—Report to the ministers of education of the signatory countries. Prague, May 2001.

Macedo, D. (2006). *Literacies of power: What Americans are not allowed to know.* Boulder, CO: Westview Press.

Macedo, D., Dendrinos, B., & Gounari, P. (2003). *The Hegemony of English.* Boulder, CO: Paradigm Publishers.

Macrine, S. H. (2003). Imprisoning minds: The violence of neoliberal education or "I am not for sale." In K. Saltman & D. Gabbard (Eds.), *Education as enforcement: The militarization and corporatization of schools* (pp. 205–211). New York: Routledge.

Marx, K. (1986). Theses on Feuerbach. In C. J. Arthur (Ed.), *The German ideology.* New York: International Publishers. (Original work published 1888).

McChesney, R. (1999). *Profit over people: Neoliberalism and global order.* New York: Seven Stories Press.

Memmi, A. (2000). *Racism.* Minneapolis: University of Minnesota Press.

Molnar, A. (2006). Public intellectuals and the university. In G. Ladsson-Billings & W. F. Tate (Eds.), *Education research in the public interest* (pp. 64–80). New York: Teachers College Press.

Mouffe, C. (2000). *The democratic paradox.* London: Verso.

Naisbitt, J., & Aburdene, P. (1999). *Megatrends 2000.* New York: Avon.

Newman, J. (2001). Beyond new public mangement? Modernizing public services. In J. Clarke, S. Gewirtz & E. McLaughlin (Eds.), *New managerialism: New welfare?* (pp. 45–61). London: Open University Press.

Nóvoa, A. (2006). *Prós e contras.* Lisbon: Rádio Televisão Portuguesa.

Nóvoa, A., & Lawn, M. (2002). *Fabricating Europe: The formation of an education space.* London: Kluwer Academic Publishers.

Olssen, M. (2004). Neoliberalism, globalization, democracy: Challenges for education. *Globalization, Societies and Education, 2*(2), 238–273.

Organisation for Economic Co-operation and Development (OECD). (1996). *Knowledge-based economy.* Paris: OECD.

Organisation for Economic Co-operation and Development (OECD). (2006). Education and Training Policy Division, Directorate for Education. Paris: OECD

Ortega y Gasset, J. (1944). *The mission of the university.* New York: W. W. Norton.

Paraskeva, J. (2001). *As dinamicas dos conflitos ideologicos e culturais na fundamentacao do curriculo.* Porto, Portugal: ASA.

Paraskeva, J. (2003). [Des]escolarização: Genotexto e fenotexto das políticas curriculares neoliberais. In J. T. Santomé, J. Paraskeva, & M. Apple (Eds.), *Ventos de desescolarização. A nova ameaça à escolarização pública* (pp. 57–115). Lisbon: Edições Plátano.

Paraskeva, J. (2004). *Here I stand: A long revolution: Ideology, culture and curriculum. Michael Apple and critical progressive studies.* Braga, Portugal: University of Minho.

Paraskeva, J. (2005). Da mente como músculo ao rapto (e não ao repto) da escola pública. In J. Paraskeva (Ed.), *Um século de estudos curriculares* (pp. 97–140). Lisbon: Edições Plátano.

Paraskeva, J. (2006a). Portugal will always be an African nation: A Caliban prosperity of a prospering Caliban? In D. Macedo & P. Gounari (Eds.), *The globalization of racism* (pp. 241–268). Boulder, CO: Paradigm Publishers.

Paraskeva, J. (2006b). Neo-Marxismo com garantias. Hegemonia, cultura e senso comum. In J.

Paraskeva, E. Ross & D. Hursh (Eds.), *Marxismo e educação*,vol. 1 (pp. 59–90). Porto, Portugal: Profedições.

Paraskeva, J. (2007). Kidnapping public schooling: Perversion and normalization of the discursive bases within the epicenter of New Right educational policies. *Policy Futures in Education*, 5(2), 137–159.

Paraskeva, J. (2008). *Ideologia, cultura e curriculo*. Porto: Didactica Editora.

Paraskeva, João (2009). Mozambique: Remasculimization of Democracy. In Dave Hill and Ellen Rosskam (Eds.) (Vol. 3) *The Developing World and State Education: Neo-liberal Depredation and Egalitarian Alternatives*. New York: Routledge, 197–215.

Paraskeva, Joao (2010a). Hijacking public schooling. The epicenter of neoradical centrism. In S. Macrine, P. McLaren & D. Hill (Eds.) Revolutionizing Pedagogy. Education for social justice within and beyond neoliberalism. New York: Palgrave, 167–186.

Paraskeva, Joao (2010b). Introduction. Unaccomplished utopia. In J. Paraskeva (Ed.) *Unaccomplished utopia. Neoconservative dismantling of public hgher education in the European Union*. Rotterdam: Sense, xi–xiv.

Phillipson, R. (2003). *English-only Europe? Challenging language policy*. London: Routledge.

Rodrigues, A. (2007). UMinho sem orçamento de estado para funcionar em 2007. *UMDicas*, 4, Braga: Universidade do Minho. (21 de Janeiro).

Rodrigues, A. (2008). *Report from the rector of the University of Minho*. Braga, Portugal: Universidade do Minho.

Ross, E., Kesson, K., Gabbard, D., Mathison, S., & Vinson, K. (2005). Saving public education, saving democracy. In D. Gabbard & E. Ross (Eds.), *Defending Public Schools* (p. xi). Westport, CT: Praeger.

Sadiki, L. (2001). *Internationalizing the curriculum in the 21st century*. Canberra: Centre for Education Development and Academic Methods, Australia National University.

Shivji, I. (2003). The struggle for democracy. Retrieved from http://www.marxists.org/subject/africa/shivji/struggle-democracy.htm

Simão, J., Santos, S., & Costa, A. (2002). *Ensino superior: Uma visão para a próxima década*. Lisbon: Gradiva.

Slaughter, S., & Rhoades, G. (2004). *Academic capitalism and the new economy*. Baltimore: Johns Hopkins University Press.

Somers, M. (2001). Romancing the market, reviling the state: The politics and knowledge of civil society and the public sphere. A. E. Havens Center for the Study of Social Structure and Social Change. Madison: University of Wisconsin.

Sousa Santos, B. de. (1998). *Reinventar a democracia*. Lisbon: Gradiva.

Sousa Santos, B. de. (2003). Prefácio. In B. de Sousa Santos (Ed.), *Democarizar a democracia— Os caminhos da democracia participativa* (pp. 25–33). Porto, Portugal: Edições Afrontamento.

Sousa Santos, B. de. (2005a). A critica da goverrnacao liberal: O forum social mundial como politica e legalidade cosmopolita subalterna. *Revista Critica de Ciencias Sociais*, 72, 7–44.

Sousa Santos, B. de. (2005b). *Another knowledge is possible*. London: Verso.

Sousa Santos, B. de. (2006). Globalizations. *Theory, Culture and Society*, 23, 393.

Sousa Santos, B. de. (2008). A universidade no seculo XXI. Para uma reforma democratica e emancipatoria da universidade. In B. Sousa Santos & N. de Almeida Filho (Eds.), *A universidade no seculo XXI. Para uma universidade nova* (pp. 13–106). Coimbra, Portugal: Centro de Estudos Sociais.

Steinberg, S. (2006). Bebate. In J. Kincheloe & S. Steinberg (Eds.), *F Scale Redux: Empire building in the new millennium*, Key Note Address, III Third International Conference on Education, Labor, and Emancipation Teaching for Global Community: Overcoming the Divide and Conquer Strategies of the Oppressor. El Paso, Texas and Ciudad de Juaréz, Chihuahua, México.

Teixeira, P., Rosa, M. J., & Amaral, A. (2008). *Cost-sharing and accessibility in higher education: A fairer deal?* Dordrecht, Netherlands: Springer.

Todorov, T. (2003). *A nova ordem mundial*. Porto, Portugal: ASA.

Touraine, A. (1996). *Carta aos socialistas. Carta para Lionel (Jospin), Michel (Rocard), Jacques (Delors) e todos os socialistas freanceses (e não só . . .)*. Lisbon: Terramar.

Vavi, Z. (2004, January 13). Democracy has by-passed the poor. *Sowetan*. Retrieved from http://www.marxists.org/subject/africa/vavi/poor-bypassed.htm

Veblen, T. (1918). *The higher learning in America*. New York: B. W. Huesch.

Williams, R. (1961). *The long revolution*. New York: Columbia University Press.

Žižek, S. (2008). *Violence: Six sideways reflections*. New York: Picador.

· 6 ·

The Professional
Career for Teachers

José Gimeno Sacristán

The Teaching Career: A Central Point
for Policy Concerning Teachers

To a great extent, improving education depends on whether one has competent, motivated, and socially considerate teachers who are well prepared to innovate. The conviction that a fair and quality education requires committed professionals who are willing to perfect their practice is pure common sense. Nevertheless, it is increasingly clear that the teaching profession is losing its appeal; that teachers are not prepared to the degree they should be; that the selection of candidates is not as rigorous as it should be; and that large sectors of the teaching population who enjoy the professional stability and job security characteristic of civil servants are nonetheless lacking in incentives to improve in terms of performance—a circumstance that can easily paralyze even the most dedicated of teachers. Moreover, if we take into account the fact that wages have fallen in recent years—at least in those countries belonging to the Organisation for Economic Co-operation and Development (OECD)—we could be faced with a truly worrisome decline in the quality of teaching.

There is also concern about the declining relevance and social image of teachers, both of which are directly related to the fact that, increasingly, culturally undercapitalized groups are entering the profession. What is more, teacher education institutions lack academic prestige, which can be both cause or product of the fact that future teachers seem to be receiving insufficient training where understanding young people and their problems is concerned. Those who teach marginalized student populations, for example, are often ill-equipped to deal with the cultural diversity in their classrooms. This situation can lead to conflict, as such students expect and deserve the improved social status education promises them and reject a system that renders them as outsiders, failures, and repeaters, or as backward, disinterested, and violent youth.

The OECD has been developing a global project to meet the challenges posed to teaching policies. This project addresses the following political aims: turning teaching into an attractive career, preparing teachers to the fullest extent possible, selecting and contracting the most highly qualified teachers, retaining the most efficient teachers, and developing and applying policies affecting teachers in active service. Table 1 summarizes the measures developed by the OECD (2005) for each of these aims.

Although various aspects presented in Table 1 are relevant to the subject of this chapter and clearly reflect a strategy for making teaching a more attractive career—one capable of retaining the best of teachers—we believe that the subject is much more complex than this.

A Broad Sense of Professionalism in Teaching

We never stop experiencing change—biological, psychological, cognitive—in our own lives, in our relations with others, in our connections to the environment, or in the ways we engage in significant activities, such as those related to our professions—changes due mainly to influences external to ourselves. We may or may not notice changes as they arise in numerous and unpredictable ways and at varying rates in our everyday and professional activities. They may be experienced as positive or negative; they can move us, or we can move ourselves in response to them. Even individuals who are most resistant to change often feel compelled to "go with the flow," while simultaneously experiencing a sense of loss of what had been the basis of their known world.

Such personal and relational dynamics occur in real time: What we do in life consists of whatever we can fit into a lifetime. That is the *career* of life. Experiencing a succession of events, performing certain actions, or dealing with

Table 1. Policy Implications

Policy objective	Directed towards the teaching profession as whole	Targeted to particular types of teachers or schools
Making teaching an attractive career choice	Improving the image and status of teaching Improving teaching's salary competitiveness Improving employment conditions Capitalising on an oversupply of teachers	Expanding the supply pool of potential teachers Making reward mechanisms more flexible Improving entrance conditions for new teachers Rethinking the trade-off between the student-teacher ratio and average teacher salary
Developing teachers' knowledge and skills	Developing teacher profiles Viewing teacher development as a continuum Making teacher education more flexible and responsive Accrediting teacher education programmes Integrating professional development throughout the career	Improving selection into teacher education Improving practical field experiences Certifying new teachers Strengthening induction programmes
Recruiting, selecting and employing teachers	Using more flexible forms of employment Providing schools with more responsibility for teacher personnel management Meeting short-term staffing needs Improving information flows and the monitoring of the teacher labour market	Broadening the criteria for teacher selection Making a probationary period mandatory Encouraging greater teacher mobility
Retaining effective teachers in schools	Evaluating and rewarding effective teaching Providing more opportunities for career variety and diversification Improving leadership and school climate Improving working conditions	Responding to ineffective teachers Providing more support for beginning teachers Providing more flexible working hours and conditions
Developing and implementing teacher policy	Engaging teachers in policy development and implementation Developing professional learning communities Improving the knowledge base to support teacher policy	

Note. Reprinted from Teachers matter: Attracting, developing and retaining effective teachers (p. 10), by Organisation for Economic Co-operation and Development (OECD), 2005, Paris: Author. Copyright 2005 by OECD. Reprinted with permission.

given situations all leave traces on our memories that are loaded to a greater or lesser extent with feelings and emotions—a magma from which we choose references to create memory and, in this way, weave our identities. The most noteworthy aspects act as signals that make sense of the passing of time in one's life. Milestone events signaled at different moments in life turn into reference points from which to construct credible narrations about oneself and how one has come to be. The narration of that marked time represents identity in its diachronic dimension. We are what we remember we have done, thought, and felt. For others we will be, and will not stop being, just that, depending on the extent and intensity of our shared experience. Thus, we do not plan the course or career of life and identity; we construct it through a process in which, to paraphrase the words of the poet Antonio Machado, everything moves and everything stays, but our thing is moving, moving and making paths. This happens in life in general, and can therefore be applied to many of its facets such as professional practice, but only inasmuch as such practice is not narrowly construed as the mere application of techniques to, and by, inert beings devoid of their own subjectivities.

We try to understand the complexity of real change, and we seek to simplify the chaotic world of personal experience by using various strategies that put order to such chaos. First, we tend to believe that what we do and what happens to us is due to some conscious decision. We see changes as logical or as adapting to a model, as guided by personal will. For us, changes do not happen by pure chance; they come about through the personal initiative of human subjectivity as well. However, although this perception of change may condition some of the actions teachers perform, a good share of their actions are quasi-automatic. Lack of awareness about how such automated mechanisms are rooted in habit can therefore lead those who engage in them to feel insecure, and understandably so, when someone from the outside undermines, criticizes, or seeks to change them.

Second, some may think that movements (initiatives, changes) and their effects occur naturally, that they are in keeping with a certain order, as if guided by some outside control. For instance, the idea of development, so critical to education, is an example of how we make sense of reality—as dispersed and dynamic as it is—by trying to understand and explain it as if it were the result of implementing some law or observing some logic. Development suggests a succession of transformations or changes that follow a clear sequence over time and are ordered in a certain way. Development is postulated such that it includes ordered stages carried out in sequence, one built into or from the other. Progress in development thus involves reaching ever-higher levels of responsibility, complexity, richness, or ability of achievement through a sequential process. Time frames, construed as linear or cyclical, are established to explain what happens, or should happen, at a particular point in time or within a given period. Underlying the idea of development is the assumption that there is a cumulative process of "gains," or growth in knowledge, skills, relationships, expressive abilities, and so on.

And, finally, the changes occurring over the course or *career* of a lifetime can be understood as always taking place in a context controlled by institutions, whose demands we adapt to or resist. Changes are ordered from the inherent logic of this assumption, not in response to the will of individuals, but as a result of adaptation to social rules, which allow for more or less significant deviations from what is considered normal and acceptable.

Having established these premises, we will now consider their relevance to professionalism and the teaching career.

If we start from the idea that teachers were people before they became teachers, we assume that many of the changes they experience emerge from interactions between their personal and professional lives. To be a better or worse teacher, to change one's ways of thinking and educating—such traits are not independent from other personal qualities and social relations. It is hard to establish a model for the teaching career based on people's personal progress, on the idiosyncrasies of each individual at any one time. Given that education has a moral component and takes place in the heart of complex social processes in which personality is clearly involved, it is hard to imagine only one clearly shaped and stable form of teacher professionalism because there are numerous ways of envisioning, feeling, and acting on such professionalism. Aphorisms such as "Every master has his book" ("Cada maestrillo tiene su librillo") and "A bad person might be a teacher, but a good teacher can never be a bad person" ("Puede haber alguna mala persona que sea maestro, pero no puede ser que haya buenos maestros que no sean buenas personas") draw our attention to the intersection between professionalism and the idiosyncrasies of the teacher's personal being—that is, the interaction between professionalism and other dimensions of the person. Students know the singularity of their teachers; thus, when students value their teachers, that assessment holds a special significance over teachers valuing their students.

If by *career* one understands the configuration, evolution, and maintenance of the specific abilities that help the teacher achieve an acceptable level of teaching quality, and if professionalism is radically tied to the personal and vital dynamics unique to each individual, teacher professionalism can only be understood as an aggregation of such special characteristics. If each person has his or her own life and own career, then *the* teaching career does not exist. The critical landmarks along the road to becoming a teacher consist of those experiences, both personal and professional, that are most noteworthy. The career cannot be standardized; it cannot be internally measured along scales; it does not allow for the classification and hierarchy of professionals. It does, however, allow the professional to be understood.

Given these considerations, it should not surprise us that those who attempt to establish typologies, grades, or levels in the teaching career frequently encounter difficulties. This is not because the activities teachers engage in are highly standardized or similar in type, but because, on the contrary, and as seen from our standpoint, there is an infinite variety of ways of developing, along the subjective, experiential plain, into a teacher. A teacher identifies as such based on who he or she is as a person. Have we not all on occasion thought someone should not be in a certain profession because of his or her personality? That said, such subjective and personal dimensions of teaching must not be used to invalidate attempts to control or improve teaching practice, for there clearly must be some form of performance assessment and clarification where good practices are concerned.

Each teacher's personal history and overall approach to his or her individuality help determine what it means to be a teacher: how one understands oneself as such; the commitment one has to the profession; one's attitude in the classroom; how one understands his or her social function; the implicit assumptions or theories that sustain one's perception of students, the value of education, and so on. From this perspective, professionalism is a way of being, thinking, and feeling about the world of education. Of course, understanding professional development in this way does not mean it cannot be assessed at some of the stages of the professional career. For example, in-depth interviews can be used to decide who will be selected for initial training. This would be a far more rigorous and objective procedure than the simple assessment of applicants' academic curricula.

While it would exceed the scope of this chapter to address the various teaching career models and policies developed for educational systems around the world, it would make even less sense to focus on the author's country of origin (Spain) because, despite more than thirty years of discussion, little has been accomplished there to establish a career for teachers that both articulates the various teaching corps or levels and offers a system of incentives for a profession that is losing the social presence it deserves (see OECD, 2009). Rather, what follows is an account of some fundamental issues affecting the teaching career, as well as some of its most debatable points, followed by suggestions for the future in the field.

The Order of Issues Posed
by the Teaching Career

A professional career system for teachers must establish a structure that is justifiable on three levels: the discursive, the methodological, and the practical—that is, the *why*, *how*, and *for what* of the career should be clear, contrasted, and acknowledged (see Figure 1).

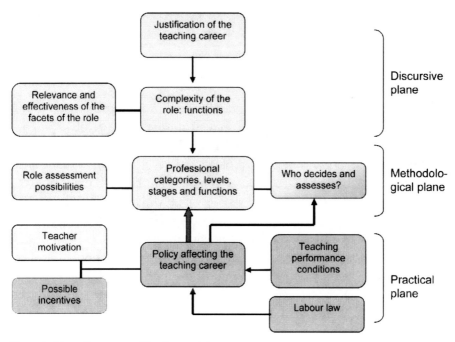

Figure 1. Map of issues posed by the teaching career.

On the first level, the discursive, we believe that the philosophy sustaining the teaching career should be sincerely embraced by its practitioners; the complexity of the role or functions of today's teachers appreciated; and the relevance of those functions accepted and valued. There should also be an acknowledgement that such functions are often carried out under conditions that greatly determine teaching outcomes, even as they are beyond teachers' control.

The second level, the methodological plane, reflects the various options for structuring the teaching career according to the perceived functions it fulfills. This involves specification and adoption of a system of professional categories, levels, stages, and functions, around which the course of the career is shaped. This level represents those aspects that the proposed progression of the career is meant to achieve, considering the complexity of functions involved, and the purpose that guides it. The options chosen here will determine what information will be used; if and how such information can be obtained; whether it is viable; and, most significantly, who will design and conduct the teaching assessment system.

Finally, on the third level we encounter the practical problem of how the teaching career is to be carried out: what policies are needed, and with what other policies they must be combined or compatible, all while respecting teachers' rights and motivations, especially where incentives are concerned.

Justification of the Teaching Career

We often assume that as one's teaching develops over the years through professional practice, this process of development automatically involves progressive growth in the quality of one's pedagogical practice. This assumption is somehow implied in the notion of "professional development," which essentially means growth according to a certain model—an approach that makes the improvement of teachers' competencies equivalent with time. The idiosyncratic nature of such experience suggests that teachers have diverse repertoires for making the most of others' experiences in educating students. However, what is important is not a teacher's experience, but his or her reflections on it. Don Quijote told Sancho Panza that experience is the mother of all sciences; Oscar Wilde warned that experience is simply the name we give to our mistakes. Positive practical knowledge can be drawn from experience, but it is also an acknowledgment of our errors.

Educational practices, therefore, must be subject to some form of valuation criteria and norms of a technical character. This, in turn, raises the question of what type of assessment should be used and what consequences it might have. On the one hand, teachers are encouraged to adapt to the most acceptable standards of good practice and to contribute to some extent to achieving the values of justice, equality, and respect for learners' rights. On the other hand, these practices can and must be justified from a technical point of view in order to determine which teaching abilities are more effective in achieving the best quality teaching-learning processes and outcomes—an assessment process based on a broad sense of what "outcomes" refer to, as we shall explore further on.

Reference to "best practices" tacitly implies that not all practices are good practices. That is, in the idea that "not everything is of the same worth" we find the main point of reference for establishing distinctions between teachers, and for comparing ourselves to others throughout our professional career. The methodological freedom that teachers are afforded as experts of course cannot be interpreted as freedom to do anything they please. In this sense, there needs to be consensus around the role of knowledge: how to update the curriculum and methodologies; how to make use of current material resources; and how best to apply the most reasonable assessments. Such demands are not derived from teachers' rights, but rather from the students' right to a quality education under equal conditions.

If this third, practical plane of development of the teaching career, involving the processes and products of learning and education, is not sufficiently acknowledged—that is, if we do not improve teaching-learning practices more or less directly, or recognize that some practices are more worthwhile than others—then it becomes hard to justify everything else based on the argument that the teaching career, in and of itself, will necessarily improve the quality of education. Developing higher quality education can mean many things, including more resources; improved media for learning; a lower student-teacher ratio; more specialists; or better working conditions. Many other, less obvious aspects can also be improved—conditioning factors that we believe can strengthen the more direct determinants of a quality education.

These conditioning factors are constantly at work in the real-world learning process. For instance, those that influence educational outcomes in terms of school success or failure include family origin, students' personal circumstances, the school environment, and acquisition of the necessary basic skills, among others. Ample educational research conducted on both small and large scales has repeatedly identified the influence of such factors on learning outcomes. In reference to the oft-cited findings from the Programme for International Student Assessment (PISA), while the 2001 report offered a comparative analysis of more than thirty variables ranked by the value of their correlation with math scores from students in compulsory secondary education, all variables related to teachers were placed in the second half of the report—a decision that raises doubt about how much attention the study actually paid to teaching (OECD, 2001, p. 229).

In other words, when a lack of quality in educational systems is detected and denounced, direct appeal must be made to the very processes that contribute to such outcomes, with the due attention such processes deserve. For example, when an alarm is inevitably sounded by low reading scores, factors such as teaching methods, common practices at school, the ability to motivate learners, the quality of materials used in teacher education, and other conditioning factors simply are not taken into account. The activation of the learning process in students is what determines outcomes: how well that process is adapted to learners' needs and interests; learners' perceptions of its relevance; the amount of time dedicated to the learning process; amount and quality of motivational input and individualized attention; and so on.

Other less obvious factors that condition the learning process—family cultural origin, for example—may not be directly detectable, strictly speaking, in learning activities, but they can serve to strengthen or weaken the learner's potential for learning; that is, they represent previous conditions that operate through learners in ways that teachers can either make good use of or compensate.

In sum, establishing a professional teaching career requires starting with several assumptions:

- Although teaching, and all that concerns teachers, are not the only factors that determine the differences in student outcomes, they are undoubtedly important to learning. Teachers do have responsibility for the results of their teaching.
- It is essential to clarify and assess the different functions teachers perform, and to distinguish between required functions and those taken on voluntarily.
- The differentiation of functions, including the limitations noted above, can be established and can give cause for the adoption of scales of degrees that reflect teachers' personal or team merit. Treating all teachers equally despite differences in their levels of dedication, commitment, and desire to improve, demoralizes the best and unreasonably affirms those who do just the minimum.
- Teacher professionalism, understood as an element of each individual teacher's identity, does not in itself guarantee the desire or the will to develop the best possible practice. Although it is important to encourage teachers by using external incentives—improved working conditions, increased salary, and so on—a teacher's internal motivation is much more influential.
- Merely fulfilling basic work responsibilities should not be considered a merit.
- It is important to support the best teachers so they do not abandon teaching and help recruit new teacher candidates.
- Most teaching career systems make it clear that the establishment of levels serves the purposes, fundamentally, of differentiated wage policies, sectorial promotion, and improved working conditions. Less tangible and nonmaterial incentives of a personal, intellectual, and social nature are also worthy of consideration.
- A successful teaching career must be accompanied by other policies and actions, especially those related to selection, initial immersion in the job, development, wage policy, inspection, external assessments, and innovation programs.
- The increasing use of assessment policies and practices in the entire educational system gives the impression that any problem

can be solved by assessment. If students' academic progress is assessed by external standardized tests, and if individual schools, curricula, and the school system itself are assessed as well, teachers can expect the same. Pressure to submit an entire school system to external assessments is intense, and teachers are key figures in this scheme. The pressure grows with the demand for competition, which in turn has given rise to policies proceeding from neoliberal ideologies such as the privatization of public services, including education. Furthermore, there is growing alarm due to the coverage given to the perceived endemic school failure of universalized schooling—supposed proof of its inefficiency.

- Investing more money in education is seen as "giving more of the same," while education keeps getting more expensive. Figure 2, which covers a considerable period of time, shows how the cost per student in the United States has been following an almost exponential trend, while student assessment scores in reading, for example, remain practically constant.

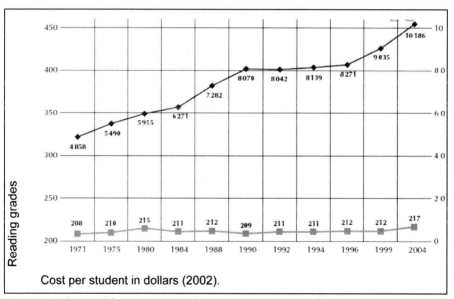

Figure 2. Evolution of the rising cost of education vis-à-vis stagnated learning outcomes. Grades in reading according to the National Scale (4th grade, 1971–2004) of the U.S. National Center for Education Statistics. Data compiled from statistics reported in the *Digest of Education Statistics*, 2005 (NCES, 2006).

In conclusion: Does the improvement of teachers' well-being correspond to improvement in learner outcomes? Not necessarily. Might this awareness serve to justify establishing some form of quality control of teachers? Indeed, we find that teacher salaries absorb the largest portion of resources invested in education.

Although it may be easy to accept that in theory, teachers and their teaching methods impact student learning and education in general, it is not so easy to answer questions of a more practical nature, such as: Which qualities, actions, or relationships are the most influential, and which most valuable teaching practices can be extracted from this knowledge? Do teachers' competencies improve over time? Is seniority necessarily a merit, and can it ever work to the detriment of learners? Does professional development stop at some point in the course of experience? Is it possible to establish a consensus on the use of ethical and technical criteria in evaluating teacher performance?

The Complexity of the Role and Relevance of Teaching Functions

The job of a teacher is complex; it is not always easy to translate teaching into a regular job profile;[1] nor can teacher education be neatly packaged into a fixed protocol of pre-established, prescriptive actions that anybody can follow. As suggested, the issues raised on the methodological plane of the diagram in Figure 1 are transcendental, and thus pose three challenges:

1. Specifying the criteria for good teaching and clearly expressing what teachers' functions are—the actions and tasks they are to perform—speaks to the kind of information needed to set levels in the teaching career. These criteria should help determine whether a teacher fulfills the requirements, and to what extent.

2. Quality standards must be established around what are considered good practices and what teachers should and should not do. Teachers should be subject to controls that ensure they meet their obligations. Merely fulfilling obligations is not a merit, but it can be a merit, to perform quality tasks such as going beyond the call of duty, working in especially adverse conditions, improving oneself, collaborating for the improvement of the profession and public education, and so on. All such initiatives should be positively valued, but not so much to "motivate" teachers who now feel helpless as to satisfy the students' right to the best possible educa-

tion. For this same reason, the career would have to be upward moving, not downward.

3. The characteristics that teachers must develop, as well as the functions that the good teaching professional should be able to perform, are numerous. They should be assessed using various methodologies. As discussed above, there are important qualities of professionalism that experts, teachers, assessors, and administrators have underestimated by overusing quantitative analysis for the sake of promoting objectivity, which is confused with the apparent measurability of human observation. In other words, "objective" information gathered through interviews or observation of teaching is more revealing than a whole curriculum embodied in quantifiable hours of improvement.

Different countries have various ways of assessing teachers: according to students' scores on standardized tests; classroom observations; qualifications from colleagues, administrators, and academic authorities; self-assessment; interviews; portfolios; and qualifying exams for teacher credentialing and placement (OECD, 2009).

Table 2 shows the most common functions and activities in the practice of the teaching profession. Some are for permanent practice, others are more temporary in nature; some are compulsory, others are optional. The competencies of a teaching job-profile are not developed in a vacuum or without support; they are regulated by the availability of resources, the context, the external environment, and the specific circumstances of the exercise. Such circumstances must be considered when assessing teachers.

Table 2. Competencies for the Teacher Job Profile

THE TEACHER SHOULD:

1. Possess remote cultural preparation.
2. Interpret reality, its dynamics and needs: ongoing professional development.
3. Employ strategies that educate citizens and transmit democratic values.
4. Maintain adequate interpersonal relations in communication with all educational agents.
5. Plan the curriculum.
6. Develop materials.

7. Understand the nature of teaching activities and the character-istics of teaching development and difficulties, depending on lev-els and system specialties.
8. Integrate new technologies into education and other functions.
9. Assess students.
10. Be familiar with managerial posts.
11. Perform services in schools: libraries, etc.
12. Offer tutorials.
13. Develop out-of-school activities.
14. Develop strategies for remedial education.
15. Offer advice and help.
16. Address students' special needs.
17. Create relationships with students' families.
18. Mediate in and solve, conflicts, etc.
19. Engage in training and improvement.
20. Engage in research and related activities.

RECENT DEMANDS:

- Engage in coordinated work at school and online with other teachers and centers.
- Be familiar with new tools and resources to practice the assigned functions.
- Interpret situations and take the initiative in solving problems.
- Educate in multicultural societies.
- Work in highly conflictive contexts.
- Operate in learning contexts other than schools.
- Manage the diversity inherent to universal education.

Motives to "Move" Willpower

Taking the initiative or making a difference cannot be reduced to a system of rewards and punishments, to the promise of or lack of incentives, or, most typi-cally, to the recognition of "good" professionals, which keeps everyone else from entering the teaching career. The motives that stimulate proactive teaching do not originate from or maintain a link with wages. In general, human beings devel-op various types of motives. Maslow proposed that all individuals need to satis-fy some basic needs that can be ordered hierarchically in the form of a pyramid (adapted for our purposes here), with basic physiological needs on the bottom followed in ascending order by security and social needs involving the ego and the need for self-actualization. Needs can be infinitely reproduced and extended, one involving the other, or become specialized, among other qualities.

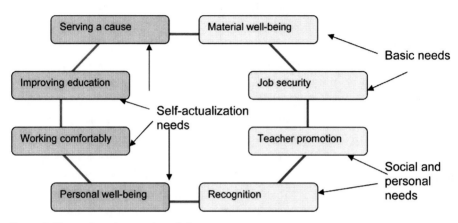

Figure 3. Types of teacher needs and their incentives.

A primary consideration here is that teachers assert their professionalism by fulfilling obligations related to their contract with society. Likewise, but on a more practical level, teachers' responsibility in honoring their teaching-contract demands is not negotiable: Teachers occupy positions and are paid for services rendered, as defined by trade-union regulations, perceptions of progress, standards of professional conduct, and individual decisions. The teacher's responsibilities are a source of satisfaction if they are assumed willingly, and if the career choice is personally motivated, if it does not conflict with other interests outside the profession, and if it is guided by motives on the higher end of the Maslow pyramid. The teaching career should therefore be understood as an obligation that can be practiced with unequaled dedication and quality. This demands changes, modulations, and taking on new tasks, as the teaching contract is immersed in a society that changes with the passing of time.

However, a teaching career cannot be defined only by the conditions of a contract. Tom (1984) notes that teaching is a job of moral character that has significant impact on human subjects. Teachers' professionalism and sense of identity should be enhanced by the satisfaction of knowing that they are supporting the right of all children to an education, and that their actions are guided by aims related to equality, dignity, democracy, high values, and improving society. In this sense, it is hard to separate obligation from receiving honors for "having done well." In fact, anything less than this level of commitment in entering the teaching career might be considered a shortcoming.

Nonetheless, in practice, it does not seem that these criteria for valuing teaching always motivate teachers themselves, when seen from their perspective. In a study of teachers' opinions about the most positive aspects of their job, Egido (2008) found that teaching was attractive to them because of work stability (80%); professional autonomy (71%); holidays (53%); the length of the working day (48%); the possibility of promotion (13%); and the retirement age (10%).

However, if the teaching career is structured according to a scale of bureaucratic categories—without consideration for teaching dimensions that are not strictly contractual, and that we consider to be progressive or constitutive of professional empowerment—it may serve to improve teachers as workers, but not necessarily as teachers. Economic incentives can raise teachers' quality of life and guarantee their well-being and security, but it is doubtful that such incentives motivate them to teach better or increase their desire to study or read more material related to their specialty. It is equally inconceivable, by contrast, to assume that poorly paid teachers would intentionally give students less personal attention. In a recent OECD (2009) report, a review of related research led to the conclusion that improving teachers' wages did not cause any change in the quality of the education they delivered to their students (p. 124). Given this weakness in the teacher wage-practice correlation, it follows that better paid teachers be required to meet specific objectives.

The teaching career must work as a tool to improve education, and teachers in turn must assert their rights and attain a reasonable standard of well-being that is worth demanding. In summary, we cannot expect that teachers will be motivated by a pay raise or recognition of merit; instead, they are motivated by a personal commitment derived from having chosen the field of teaching, from the cultural expansion and professional progress inherent to the job, from the security offered by knowledge of the job, from dynamics encountered both in school and beyond school hours and spaces, from their ability to deal with unpredictable situations, and from acquiring the maturity to handle the personal risks that arise in their professional relationships.

Note

1. The job profile stipulates the level of knowledge, competences, and aptitudes required for the practice of that particular post.

References

Egido, I. (2008, November 7). Condiciones materiales y laborales del trabajo del profesorado (Material and working conditions of the job of teachers). Lecture presented at COFAPA (Confederación de Padres y Madres de Alumnos), Madrid. Retrieved from http://www.cofapa.net/leerart.php?id=174&s=1

National Center for Education Statistics (NCES). (2006). *Digest of Education Statistics, 2005 (NCES 2006–030)*. Tables 25 and 108. Washington: U.S. Department of Education, NCES, National Assessment of Educational Progress (NAEP). Retrieved from the NCES web site at: http://nces.ed.gov/programs/digest/d05/

Organisation for Economic Co-operation and Development (OECD). (2001). *Knowledge and skills for life*. Programme for International Student Assessment (PISA). Paris: Author.

Organisation for Economic Co-operation and Development (OECD). (2005). *Teachers matter: Attracting, developing and retaining effective teachers*. Paris: Author.

Organisation for Economic Co-operation and Development (OECD). (2009). *Assessment and recognition of the quality of teachers*. Paris: Author.

Tom, A. (1984). *Teaching as a moral craft*. New York: Longman.

· 7 ·

Preservice Teacher Education in Portugal

The Transformative Power of Local Reform

Maria Alfredo Moreira & Flávia Vieira

Democracy in Schooling and Teacher Education

If we agree with John Dewey (1916/2007) that school is the primeval institution that sustains the principles of a democratic society and that democracy should be the method through which society is transformed, then learning activities at school, along with the preparation of teachers, should be based on democratic principles and processes.

The demands on schools and teachers are becoming more complex. Society now expects schools to be sensitive to cultural, linguistic, class, and gender issues; to promote tolerance and social cohesion; to respond effectively to disadvantaged students and students with learning or behavioral problems; to use new technologies; and to keep pace with rapidly developing fields of knowledge and approaches to student assessment (OECD, 2005). Accordingly, teachers are expected to have much broader competencies and roles, to work in multidisciplinary teams, and to be accountable to others regarding their work.

Teaching quality is the most important school variable influencing student achievement. However, defining the key competencies required for teaching is a problematic issue because definitions of quality depend on the theories and practices of teacher education institutions and agents, as well as on education-al policies and contexts. Nevertheless, if we defend a democratic, transforma-tive view of education, we may agree that teachers should develop at least four macro-competencies (Jiménez Raya, Lamb, & Vieira, 2007): a critical view of education in terms of its social role; the disposition and ability to promote learn-er autonomy by centering teaching on learning; the capacity to identify and manage constraints to democratic schooling; and the ability to be proactive in a professional community. Developing these competencies in teacher education programs implies the adoption of a reflective, inquiry-based approach to the school experience, as well as the acquisition of critical knowledge of what being a teacher means: "Teachers need to do more than simply implement par-ticular techniques; they need to be able to think pedagogically, reason through dilemmas, investigate problems, and analyze student learning to develop appro-priate curriculum for a diverse group of learners" (Darling-Hammond & Hammerness, 2005, p. 392). This requires a view of teaching as an uncertain professional activity (Schön, 1987), an arena for the problematic that should be extended "beyond the craft and subject matter of teaching to include ethi-cal and/or political considerations" (Tom, 1985, p. 38), a space for interperson-al empowerment with a view to social transformation.

Models of teacher education are often distanced from these views, which require teacher educators to take a critical stance and subvert macro- and micro-politics. As Zeichner argues (1988, p. 27), what happens *inside* teacher education courses defines their contribution to teacher learning. Teacher edu-cators play a decisive role in shaping practices and making the best of adverse conditions by developing a scholarship of teacher education, thus becoming authorized agents of local innovations that respond more effectively to educa-tional and social demands. This has been our experience since 1995, when we set up a supervisory project for the development of reflective teaching and ped-agogy for autonomy in schools, through the use of action research. In the dis-cussion that follows we reflect on problems of preservice teacher education in Portugal and present some aspects of our work as a case of what we call the *trans-formative power of local reform.*

Problems of Preservice Teacher Education in Portugal

Preservice teacher education in Portugal is carried out in universities and in poly-technic schools of education.[1] Before the full adoption of the Bologna Process in

Portugal in 2007, first-cycle education programs (*licenciatura*) took five years, after which students could become full teachers.[2] There were two main types of programs: integrated, as at University of Minho,[3] where students earned educational course units from the first year of their teaching programs, along with subject-specific course units; and sequential, where students could engage in teacher training after completing three years of subject-related education.[4] The teaching practicum in local schools was either condensed into the final year of the degree programs at universities or dispersed for shorter periods of time during the programs at polytechnic schools of education. National and institutional policies did not prescribe any particular approach to teacher education and supervision, and within each institution there were diverse approaches.

Studies of pre-Bologna teacher education practices identified various shortcomings in terms of their quality. Based on a review of research conducted between 1990 and 2000, Estrela, Esteves, and Rodrigues (2002)[5] concluded that even though researchers of teacher education were seldom clear about the prescription of a particular model or paradigm, they tended to recommend the following principles:

- adopting an integrated model of theory-practice integration and interdisciplinarity;
- defining teacher education goals on the basis of prospective teacher roles and their multiple functions and tasks;
- centering teacher education on particular situations of pedagogical practice;
- developing teachers' reflective ability;
- articulating teacher educators' actions and attitudes; and
- increasing teamwork among teacher educators and research on teacher education. (p. 29)

These recommendations are based on the identification of major shortcomings: a technocratic approach to teacher preparation; the divide between content and pedagogical knowledge and between teacher education and school curricula; lack of collaboration among higher education institutions and local schools; lack of an inquiry-based approach to teaching and learning during the practicum; poor preparation of supervisors; and low investment in a scholarship of teacher education on the part of teacher educators, that is, when their work is analyzed and critiqued, becomes public, and is exchanged with other members of the community so they, in turn, can build on it (Shulman, 2000, p. 50). Canário (2002) further points out the low status of experience and research in teacher education and the conservative nature of programs in terms of pedagogical innovation and the transformation of schools, which suggests that preservice teacher education programs were closer to models that "produce conformity" than to models that favor "innovative transgression" (p. 61). In terms of the democratization of schooling, teacher education institutions seem to be incapable of transforming a naturalized view of schooling based on hierarchy and territory, because academic cultures are also based on these two factors (Canário, 2002; Formosinho, 2001).

Problems in teacher preparation have sometimes prompted calls for a reduction of university-based teacher education and the expansion of probationary periods in schools to increase "on-the-job training" (Korthagen & Kessels, 1999). These problems also have incited arguments in favor of postponing the decision to become a teacher until after graduation and qualification in a specific subject. This was the path followed in 2007 after the implementation of the Bologna Process in Portugal.[6] It is still too soon to assess the impact of the new model, but some issues can be raised.

The major change is that there are now two cycles in preservice teacher education: The first is subject-specific and lasts three years; the second cycle, which culminates in a master's degree, lasts two years and allows students to qualify as teachers for different subject areas and different teaching cycles.[7] The impact of this structural change is not yet clear; will second-cycle student teachers take teaching more seriously because they had more time to decide to become teachers, or will they take it less seriously because their training is shorter? And will they be able to integrate subject and pedagogical knowledge now that these curricular components are clearly separated?

Condensing educational training into two years has created tensions in higher education institutions due to the decrease in teaching hours within disciplines, which has resulted in territorial battles for solutions that may not serve the interests of professionalization, primarily in terms of the practicum. There has been a tendency to overemphasize the academic component of the curriculum and reduce teaching time in schools, along with a decrease of responsibilities[8] and worsened working conditions for cooperating teachers[8] in schools. Even though there is now a greater emphasis on educational research in teacher education programs, curricular changes may hamper an inquiry-based approach to teaching, which requires taking practical training seriously (Ponte, 2005). Given the university-school divide and the academic teacher educators' tendency to be detached from students' concerns and school reality, there is danger in adopting academic forms of inquiry that do not serve school interests.

Concerns about the quality of teacher education programs have certainly increased, but the growing emphasis on mechanisms for accountability and quality control may reduce the autonomy of institutions and induce them to pay lip service to external requirements, and to invest their time and effort in the bureaucratic tasks needed to fulfil them. In the near future, an external, nationwide exam will be administered to teaching graduates after they complete the second cycle of studies, and they can enter the teaching system only if they pass it.[9] It is difficult to imagine how complex teaching competencies can be assessed through a paper-and-pencil test. It is easy to imagine, however, how the national exam could cause a backlash for teacher education programs, making them less critical and more instrumental in order to comply with specific requirements such as planning a course unit or writing an essay on a school subject. We agree with Ponte (2005), who contends that we may be replacing a bad system with an even worse one, which clearly does not represent progress.

This recent reform calls for taking a critical stance toward its potential implications for the quality of current and future teacher education. We may be distancing ourselves more than ever from interdisciplinarity, theory-practice integration, experiential learning, and inquiry-oriented practice, which could reduce the opportunities for teacher empowerment and school transformation. However, as we have pointed out, teacher educators can play a decisive role in enacting local reform by developing a scholarship of teacher education. We now turn to our experience of how this has been done.

Developing a Scholarship of Teacher Education: The Transformative Power of Local Reform

The integration of research and pedagogy is an essential component of a scholarship of teacher education. From our perspective, major goals of the scholarship of teacher education are to develop a critical vision for pedagogy and teacher education, to disclose the forces that impinge on teaching and teacher education, and to envision possibilities for alternative practices. These goals have oriented our choices and action as university supervisors of future language teachers.[10]

Developing a Critical Vision for Pedagogy and Teacher Education

A scholarship of teacher education should integrate a scholarship of school pedagogy based on the development of teacher and learner autonomy. We believe that we cannot let our educational choices be guided by *any* theory. In teacher education, theory has to become a "healing place" (hooks, 1994, p. 61) for teachers and learners and help them make sense out of what is happening—a place where they can imagine possible futures and where life can be lived differently. In our quest to make teacher education theory a "healing place," we have found the concept of autonomy a powerful one worth pursuing and fighting for. We define it as "the competence to develop as a self-determined, socially responsible and critically aware participant in (and beyond) educational environments, within a vision of education as (inter)personal empowerment and social transformation" (Jiménez Raya, Lamb, & Vieira, 2007, p. 1).

We agree with Little (2004) that the pursuit of learner autonomy and the pursuit of democracy in education are one and the same, for "by developing learner autonomy we are equipping learners to engage critically yet responsibly in the social processes they encounter inside but also outside the classroom, and thus contributing to the survival and further development of democracy as a political process" (p. 124). We also believe that teacher autonomy is a prerequisite for learner autonomy, since we recognize that teachers interpret the curriculum and decide whether its development should be open to negotiation with their students, so that it becomes a liberating, enriching growth experience (Little, 1995).

Teacher education for teacher and learner autonomy can be enhanced through collaborative, small-scale action research projects based on democratic action principles: This has been our choice as supervisors in the practicum year for approximately 300 student teachers and 5,000 secondary school learners over the last fifteen years (see Moreira, 2009; Vieira, 2009a; Vieira, Barbosa, Paiva, & Fernandes, 2008; Vieira & Moreira, 2008; Vieira, Moreira, Barbosa, Paiva, & Fernandes, 2006). Our main role as supervisors has been to support teachers and monitor their projects within a dialogic approach, and to investigate and disseminate our work.

By developing a scholarship of teacher education and becoming agents of local reform, we have come to understand the transformative power of projects that counteract and challenge dominant values and practices in the school and university settings. Most of the criticisms noted above regarding the lack of quality in preservice teacher education do not apply to our practice, which is also true in other locations where teacher educators find spaces to maneuver and make the best of difficult situations. Assessing and disseminating those experiences will help us realize how we can enhance a critical vision for pedagogy and teacher education (Barfield & Brown, 2007; Jiménez Raya & Vieira, 2008; Moreira, 2007; Vieira, 2009b).

Disclosing the Forces that Impinge upon Teaching and Teacher Education and Envisioning Possibilities

The concept of autonomy carries both a political and an ethical struggle. It is pursued by encouraging and supporting teaching modes that will engage learners in cooperative work on common problems, in negotiating learning goals and strategies, in dialogic classroom discourse and co-construction of the rules by which their classroom life will be governed, and in the evaluation and assessment of teaching and learning processes—it is democracy in progress, a mode of life (Dewey, 1916/2007). This ideal does not necessarily reflect current realities in Portuguese schools.[11] As Torres Santomé emphasizes (2006), "it is one thing is to teach the theory of democracy, a very different thing to learn to live in democracy and improve it day after day" (p. 87, translation our own). According to Torres Santomé, promoting democratic citizenship demands educational institutions that live by the following ethical principles: integrity and intellectual honesty, moral courage, respect, humility, tolerance, trust in students, responsibility, justice, sincerity, and solidarity (2006, pp. 88–90). We believe that these principles should apply both in schools and in teacher education contexts, but that is seldom the case.

Table 1 presents some major cultural, methodological, and personal constraints that we have identified in striving to promote pedagogy for autonomy through action research in the practicum context. The left-hand column shows how our approach goes against the grain, but this should also be understood as a positive outcome of a scholarship of teacher education: Only by disclosing the forces that impinge upon teaching and teacher education can we start to envision alternatives and "healing places." The right-hand column indicates possibilities that we have explored to face the perceived constraints.

Given the changes and concerns that emerge from recent reforms in preservice teacher education, we fear that some of the constraints pointed out in Table 1 will become even more evident over time. Educational policies that seem progressive may in fact constrain progressive practices previously established through local reforms in more traditional environments. Now that education research is instigated by reform, it is severely constrained by circumstances, whereas in previous circumstances it was more feasible even though it was not so clearly advocated by official discourses. This is just one of the many paradoxes affecting the practice of teacher educators who develop a scholarship of teacher education inspired by democratic ideals. Nevertheless, we believe that our experience has equipped us to face paradoxes and constraints and to keep struggling for our ideals by making our choic-

Table 1. Constraints to and Strategies for the Development of Action Research with Beginning Teachers

CONSTRAINTS	STRATEGIES
Cultural resistance	• uncovering the cultural forces, constraints, dilemmas
• dominant culture of schooling as transmission	• encouraging an inquisitive, proactive stance
• dominant culture of teacher education as technical instruction	• promoting school-university collaboration
	• valuing and disseminating locally validated practices
• dominant culture of research as production of academic, generalisable knowledge	
Methodological limitations	• sensitizing students to reflective teaching, pedagogy for autonomy and action research before the *practicum*
• no previous teaching/action research experience	
	• encouraging choice and initiative on the basis of personal concerns, interests, and practical theories
• mandatory action research	
• lack of support in schools	• providing ongoing support and encouragement
• diversity of supervisory styles/ agendas	• fostering participatory and context-sensitive evaluation
• time constraints (student teachers' and supervisors')	• involving/training the school supervisors
	• making the best of time (quality vs. quantity)
Personal factors	• accommodating diversity within a common direction
• diverse expectations, beliefs, personalities...	• generating and confronting alternatives
• reality shock	• being supportive, stimulating dialogue and (self-) inquiry
• lack of self-confidence	• providing frames of reference to conceptualize practice
• lack of habits of reflection	• fostering self-regulation as a basis for improvement
• resistance to public exposure	• negotiating final assessment (self-/co-assessment)
• fear of external assessment	

Note. Reprinted from "Reflective Teacher Education Towards Learner Autonomy: Moving Towards a Culture of Possibility," by Flávia Vieira and Maria Alfredo Moreira, in *Pedagogy for Autonomy in Language Education—Theory, Practice and Teacher Education*, edited by Manuel Jiménez Raya and Terry Lamb, 2008, Dublin: Authentik. Reprinted with permission.

es in accordance with them and seeking to enhance what we see as quality in our job.

Berliner (2000) has stated, "If teacher educators are put out of the debate by legislators and business leaders, democracy and education will surely suffer" (p. 367). We agree with this statement in principle, but we also feel that public debate among different stakeholders is not necessarily conducive to greater democracy. Decisions are seldom taken on the basis of democratic discussions and dialogically built stances, as hegemonic positions end up imposing their own models (Vieira, 2005). Moreover, teacher educators frequently avoid direct participation in making decisions about the future of teacher educa-tion—some have no convictions about the direction it should take, some fear confrontation between perspectives and prefer to keep silent, and others just don't care. There are also those who prefer to stand outside powerful decision groups and sacrifice status in favor of the struggle to keep their integrity and faithfulness to their ideas, doing their work in isolation or in small commu-nities. These attitudes make it difficult to develop and expand a scholarship of teacher education. In our case, and even though we have disseminated our supervision project for fifteen years, we do not know the scope of its impact. Local reforms can be transformative, but only to a certain extent, especially when teacher education is not a priority of the political agenda nationwide or within institutions.

Policies deriving from the Bologna Process have been mostly structural and more concerned with solving economic problems than with enhancing the quality of education (Amaral, 2005). Teacher education is not an exception. Our perspective is that structural changes do not ensure that we will be any closer than before to an empowering practice of teacher education that pro-motes educational and social change for greater democracy. Nevertheless, we also believe that a scholarship of teacher education based on democratic prin-ciples can represent a powerful strategy for dealing with constraints, design-ing alternative routes, and affirming teacher educators' voices in the educational community.

Notes

1. Up to 2007, there were fourteen public and sixteen private teacher training colleges of higher education (integrated in polytechnic higher education schools but also in some uni-versities), thirteen public universities, the Open University, the Catholic University, and seven private universities that provided courses in preservice teacher training (European Commission, Eurybase). The high number of teacher training courses proved to be excessive for a schooling population that has been decreasing as a result of demo-graphic changes over the last five years (cf. OECD, 2006a).

2. As regards specialized training for professional teachers, courses for specific teaching functions were (and still are) obtained mainly through postgraduate programs.

3. For an evaluation of the first twenty years of preservice teacher training at the University of Minho see Lima, Castro, Magalhães and Pacheco (1995).

4. The sequential approach was typical of older universities that had to adjust their curric-ula to teacher training needs from the 1970s onwards, whereas universities created in the

1970s, as well as polytechnic schools of education (directed at preschool and lower basic education training), tended to adopt the integrated approach, which was expected to better respond to the composite, interdisciplinary nature of teacher professionalization. It was also in these institutions that greater attention was paid to supervision during the teaching practicum, which resulted in the creation of postgraduate programs directed at cooperating teachers at schools, thus increasing research and publication in this domain. For a description of the several scenarios of teacher education in Portugal, as well as a discussion on the recommendations for the design and accreditation of teacher education programs following the implementation of the Bologna Process, see Cruz et al. (2003), Campos (2003), and Ponte (2004).

5. The authors synthesize research undertaken mainly in MA and PhD dissertations produced in three universities (Aveiro, Lisboa, and Minho).

6. The Bologna Process was introduced in higher education in Portugal through the Decree-Law 74/2006, and in preservice teacher education through the Decree-Law No. 43/2007. In fact, the reform started before 2007 through a series of changes that prepared the ground for more recent policies. For example, in 2005 student teachers lost their status as hired teachers and started teaching in their cooperating teacher's classes, which led to a reduction in teaching time; the five-year teaching degrees were successively revised in recent years until their division into two cycles was fully assumed in 2007.

7. Curricula for preschool and first and second cycles of basic education are still based on a semi-integrated model followed by a masters' degree for each of the several cycles of compulsory education or specialization areas. The rationale behind this decision seems to be that these teachers need more pedagogical training, whereas secondary school teachers need a more solid subject knowledge background. If this is the case, then we may be reinforcing a divide of paradigms between lower cycles of basic education and secondary education with a focus on a content-based approach in the latter, which may also be interpreted as assigning a position of "superiority" to third cycle and secondary school teachers.

8. Cooperating teachers are experienced teachers in primary or secondary schools who take responsibilities in the supervision of student teachers, along with university teachers. They are usually referred to as "cooperating teachers" because they cooperate with preservice teacher training institutions.

9. At the time of writing, the removal of this exam is being negotiated by the teacher unions and the Ministry of Education.

10. Other colleagues who no longer work at University of Minho collaborated with us for many years: Graça Branco, Isabel Barbosa, Madalena Paiva, and Isabel Sandra Fernandes.

11. Portugal still presents concerning levels of student exclusion from upper secondary education. According to the OECD, this situation is due to a "predominant Portuguese approach to teaching as telling, and learning as passive reception of knowledge, rather than interaction, questioning and practical experience, is a principal reason for low rates of educational participation and success. The culture and practice of failing large proportions of students at various stages of the education process, and the inordinate repetition rates, reflects the dominance of a curriculum approach using norm-referenced assessment" (2006b, p. 56).

References

Amaral, A. (2005). Bolonha, ensino superior e a competitividade económica. In J. P. Serralheiro (Ed.), O Processo de Bolonha e a formação dos educadores e professores portugueses (pp. 35–45). Porto, Portugal: ProfEdições.

Barfield, A. & Brown, S. H. (Eds.). (2007). Re-constructing autonomy: International perspectives on transforming learner and teacher autonomy in language education. Houndmills, UK: Palgrave Macmillan.

Berliner, D. C. (2000). A personal response to those who bash teacher education. Journal of Teacher Education, 51(5), 358–371.

Campos, B. P. (2003). Quem pode ensinar. Garantia da qualidade das habilitações para a docência. Porto, Portugal: Porto Editora.

Canário, R. (2002). A prática profissional na formação de professores. In B. P. Campos (Ed.), Formação profissional de professores no ensino superior (pp. 31–45). Porto, Portugal: Porto Editora.

Cruz, I., Branco, A., Leite, C., Ferreira, I., Ponte, J. P., & Trindade, V. (2003). A Declaração de Bolonha e a formação inicial de professores nas universidades portuguesas. Lisbon: CRUP.

Darling-Hammond, L. & Hammerness, K. (2005). The design of teacher education programs. In L. Darling-Hammond & J. Bransford (Eds.), Preparing teachers for a changing world: What teachers should learn and be able to do (pp. 390–441). San Francisco: Jossey-Bass.

Dewey, J. (2007). Democracia e educação. (M. A. Vieira, Trans.). Lisbon: Plátano Editora. (Original work published 1916).

Estrela, M. A., Esteves, M., & Rodrigues, A. (2002). Síntese da investigação sobre formação inicial de professores em Portugal (1990–2000). Porto, Portugal: Porto Editora.

European Commission, Eurybase. (2007). The education system in Portugal (2006/07). Retrieved from http://www.dgert.mtss.gov.pt/refernet/docs/Euridice%20-%200%20sistema%20educativo%20em%20Portugal%202007%20EN.pdf.

Formosinho, J. (2001). A formação prática de professores—Da prática docente na instituição de formação à prática pedagógica nas escolas. In B. P. Campos (Ed.), Formação profissional de professores no ensino superior (pp. 46–64). Porto, Portugal: Porto Editora.

hooks, b. (1994). Teaching to transgress: Education as the practice of freedom. New York: Routledge.

Jiménez Raya, M., & Vieira, F. (2008). Teacher development and learner autonomy: Images and issues from five projects. In M. Jiménez Raya & T. Lamb (Eds.), Pedagogy for autonomy in language education—Theory, practice and teacher education (pp. 283–302). Dublin: Authentik.

Jiménez Raya, M., Lamb, T., & Vieira, F. (2007). Pedagogy for autonomy in language education in Europe: Towards a framework for learner and teacher development. Dublin: Authentik.

Korthagen, F. A. J., & Kessels, J. P. A. M. (1999). Linking theory and practice: Changing the pedagogy of teacher education. Educational Researcher, May, 4–15.

Lima, L. C., Castro, R.V., Magalhães, J., & Pacheco, J. A. (1995). O modelo integrado, 20 anos depois: Contributos para uma avaliação do projecto de Licenciaturas em Ensino na Universidade do Minho. Revista Portuguesa de Educação, 8(2), 147–195.

Little, D. (1995). Learning as dialogue: The dependence of learner autonomy on teacher autonomy. System, 23(2), 175–181.

Little, D. (2004). Democracy, discourse and learner autonomy in the foreign language classroom. *Utbildning & Demokrati*, *13*(3), 105–126.

Moreira, M. A. (2007). On democracy and learner autonomy in initial teacher education: Guerrilla warfare? In A. Barfield & S. Brown (Eds.), *Re-constructing autonomy: International perspectives on transforming learner and teacher autonomy in language education* (pp. 56–70). Houndmills, UK: Palgrave Macmillan.

Moreira, M. A. (2009). Action research as a tool for critical teacher education towards learner autonomy. *Innovation in Language Learning and Teaching*, *3*(3), 255–268.

Organisation for Economic Co-operation and Development (OECD). (2005). Teachers matter: Attracting, developing and retaining effective teachers: Overview. Retrieved from http://www.oecd.org/dataoecd/39/47/34990905.pdf.

Organisation for Economic Co-operation and Development (OECD). (2006a). Education at a Glance. Highlights. Retrieved from http://www.oecd.org/dataoecd/35/11/43619343.pdf.

Organisation for Economic Co-operation and Development (OECD). (2006b). Reviews of national policies for education—Tertiary education in Portugal. Examiners' report. December 13 2006, Centro Cultural de Belém, Lisbon, Portugal.

Ponte, J. P. (2004, July 13). A formação de professores e o Processo de Bolonha. Parecer sobre a implementação do Processo de Bolonha na área de formação de professores. *Diário da República*, *2*, 10579–10580.

Ponte, J. P. (2005). O Processo de Bolonha e a formação inicial de professores em Portugal. In J. P. Serralheiro (Ed.), *O Processo de Bolonha e a formação dos educadores e professores portugueses* (pp. 63–73). Porto, Portugal: ProfEdições.

Schön, D. (1987). *Educating the reflective practitioner*. San Francisco: Jossey-Bass.

Tom, A. R. (1985). Inquiring into inquiry-oriented teacher education. *Journal of Teacher Education*, *36*(5), 35–44.

Torres Santomé, J. (2006). *A desmotivação dos professores*. Mangualde, Portugal: Edições Pedago.

Vieira, F. (2002). Learner autonomy and teacher development: A brief introduction to GT-PA as a learning community. In F. Vieira, M. A. Moreira, I. Barbosa, & M. Paiva (Eds.), *Pedagogy for autonomy and English learning: Proceedings of the 1st conference of the working group-pedagogy for autonomy* (pp. 1–11). Braga, Portugal: Instituto de Educação e Psicologia da Universidade do Minho.

Vieira, F. (2009a). Para uma visão transformadora da supervisão pedagógica. *Educação e Sociedade*, *30*(106), 197–217.

Vieira, F. (Ed.). (2009b). *Struggling for autonomy in language education: Reflecting, acting, and being*. Frankfurt am Main, Germany: Peter Lang.

Vieira, F., Barbosa, I., Paiva, M., & Fernandes, I. S. (2008). Teacher education towards teacher (and learner) autonomy: What can be learnt from teacher development practices? In T. Lamb & H. Reinders (Eds.), *Learner and teacher autonomy: Concepts, realities, and responses* (pp. 217–235). Amsterdam & Philadelphia: John Benjamins.

Vieira, F., & Moreira, M. A. (2008). Reflective teacher education towards learner autonomy: Moving towards a culture of possibility. In M. Jiménez Raya & T. Lamb (Eds.), *Pedagogy for autonomy in language education—Theory, practice and teacher education* (pp. 266–282). Dublin: Authentik.

Vieira, F., Moreira, M. A., Barbosa, I., Paiva, M., & Fernandes, I. S. (2006). *No caleidoscópio da supervisão: Imagens da formação e da pedagogia*. Mangualde, Portugal: Pedago.

Vieira, R. (2005). Os institutos politécnicos, as escolas superiores de educação e a Declaração de Bolonha. In J. P. Serralheiro (Ed.), *O Processo de Bolonha e a formação dos educadores e professores portugueses* (pp. 103–107). Porto, Portugal: ProfEdições.

Zeichner, K. (1988). Understanding the character and quality of the academic and professional components of teacher education. Paper presented at the American Educational Research Association, April 1988, New Orleans.

· 8 ·

ICT as a Discourse of Salvation[1]

José Félix Angulo & César Bernal

"It would be difficult to find another time in which an industry could so aggressively impose their schooling interests on a nation and find such an enthusiastic receptiveness (or such a frightening surrender) from teachers." (Roszak, 1988, p. 81, translation our own)

In the Debate of the State of the Nation held in 2010, the Spanish president José Luís Rodríguez Zapatero made an attractive pledge: A computer would be given to every child in primary school from the fifth grade on—420,000 laptops. Some weeks later the president met Bill Gates, who gave his full support to the proposal. Such decisions, made at a high political level, demonstrate the salvation determinism (Popkewitz, 2007) that information and communication technologies (ICT) have acquired. Technology has a seductive effect on human beings, an intense power that has influenced our future hopes, and sometimes it seems that salvation, whatever it means, will be found in the acquisition of more technology. If this seems dangerous as a worldview, when applied to education the results may be paralyzing, misleading, and enormously expensive, both economically and socially (Noble, 1991). Nevertheless, this view has been pervasive since audiovisual aids and ICT entered the schools.

The idea that technology holds all the answers is a commonly held belief in the majority of education initiatives. Yet, technology projects focused on education have not always had a positive impact (Cuban, 1986, 2001). This paper reviews some assumptions about the value of technology, including its impact on work, on the economy of knowledge, and on student learning.

Apocalittici e Integrati

In 1968 Umberto Eco published one of his most striking books, *Apocalyptic and Integrated Intellectuals*. Although the book focused on mass culture (films, comics, popular music, television)—a theme not highly valued at the time—his ideas also can be applied to arguments about the use of technologies in education. Eco's arguments have been adapted to the technology of the moment and now center on the incorporation of new tools and gadgets into educational practice in schools (Cuban, 1986). In this paper we deal with digital technologies, which follow the same pattern as mass and popular media.

People who are critical of the widespread implementation of technologies are often referred to as apocalyptic. This group believes that digital technologies are not only replacing earlier means of communication but also diminishing and even destroying well-established knowledge systems and, as a peripheral impact, education. The cultural and a fortiori cognitive loss is irreparable, according to this view.

Sartori (1998) is one of the authors behind these ideas. He is critical of television and warns of a future full of digital screens (Siegel, 2008). He asserts that digital technology "generates images and destroys the concepts, atrophying our capacity for abstraction and all our understanding capability" (Siegel, 2008, p. 47). This same concern was expressed by Postman (1991) and by Simone (2001), whose analysis was much less passionate and much more rational. Simone asserted that we are facing a third phase of cultural upheaval (the first two having followed the development of writing and printing, respectively) that centers on television and computers as the dominant media. He says humans are moving back to a domain of nonalphabetical hearing and vision and that the younger generations are in the vanguard of this backward movement (p. 39).

Authors who have explored the meaning of the new technologies included the pioneer Nicholas Negroponte; Don Tapscott, who writes about what he calls the "net generation" (1998); Mark Prensky, who refers to them as "digital natives" (2001a, 2001b); and Ante and Holahan, who call them the

"MySpace generation" (2008). Oppenheimer (2004), only partly right, calls them "techno-evangelists." *Bloomberg* magazine writes that this generation of young people "live online...buy online...[and] play online. Their power is growing" (The MySpace Generation, 2005, p. 36). Those who analyze this generation often are strongly critical, using labels such as the "look-at-me-generation" to call attention to their strong narcissism (Orlet, 2007). The detailed report of the British Library Association (Williams & Rowlands, 2007), applies the concept of the "Google generation," and Kress (2010) suggests the idea of a "screen generation," emphasizing the evolution of the "medium of the book and mode of writing [toward] a new constellation of [the] medium of the screen and mode of image" (p. 6).

The general acceptance of these various labels has been an obstacle to appreciating their relevance as a kind of discursive *meme* or *tantra*, impeding the analysis of what is happening beneath the surface. Why there is so much uncritical enthusiasm among the new generations? The answer may be much simpler than we imagine, as Orlet (2007) explains: "So next time you are stuck on an elevator with a young person who is screaming into his cell phone, try to remember that he isn't just some rude, vacuous millennial, he is rather a new model of bottom-line, free-market capitalism" (n.p.).

We do not suggest that all that is happening at the intersection of the younger generation and the growing digital culture is useless, nor are we trying to avoid the challenges posed to our ways of understanding knowledge, communication, social relationships, and education. Our point is that in order to understand the self-indulgent rhetorical discourse on digital technologies, we need to refocus them into the area of economy—or to use the term most widely used in the European Union, the *knowledge economy*.

ICT and the New Labor Conditions

The information era is characterized primarily by its strong connection between information and the economy. This connection has given rise to what Castells (1977) has identified as informational capitalism. It is not just a question of users having more information at their disposal; the information is a valuable good in its own right. As Perelman (1998) writes, "The real information revolution is not that information is suddenly becoming important. Information has always been important. The revolutionary aspect of the information age is the treatment of information as a commodity in ways that would have been unimaginable only a few decades ago" (p. 4).

At this point, we should mention the unresolved controversies about the influence of new information technologies on economics and labor. According to Jeremy Rifkin (1994), the influence of the new information technologies on economics meant the end of employment and the systematic elimination of the production processes, a thesis adopted, albeit with more critical nuances, by Aronowitz and DiFazio (1994), who write, "High technology still destroys more jobs than it creates" (p. 37).[2]

Carnoy (2000) offers an alternative to this pessimistic view of the influence of information technologies. Although his work shows some contradictions relative to the effect of technologies on work, it also presents a more positive outlook:

> Work transformation has been misunderstood and mythicized by authors who maintain that the New Information Technology means a massive and growing labor shortage...The new technology transfers employees, but simultaneously creates new jobs, increasing the productivity of the existing jobs and making possible wholly new products and processes. (p. 22)

However, he later remarks that, taking into account OECD data from the 1990s, there is not much relation between "technological spreading and the growth of employment or unemployment rate...The impossibility of finding any statistical relation between the spreading of information technology and employment shows coherence with almost any of the surveys carried out in the last decade" (p. 56).

The relevance of this ambiguity is that it (unintentionally) obliges us to deal with the impact of technologies in a different context—the significant changes affecting the cultural forms of work. That is the controversy between employment and technology, which is relevant but also difficult to clarify when applied to various types of work, as it indirectly reveals essential changes in the worker's everyday life. This is Carnoy's (2000) most important contribution.

Carnoy (2000) argues that technological globalization creates employment flexibility, individualization of job conditions, workforce fragmentation, and an increase in temporary employment (p. 20). Sennet (1998) adds several more conditions: discontinuous invention of institutions, flexible specialization, and concentration without centralization (p. 48).

These changed conditions come at a high social cost, "especially when dealing with the higher anxiety level caused to the individuals and the families" (Carnoy, 2000, p. 97). Arronowitz and DiFazio (1994) agree, writing that "these sci-tech transformations of the labor process have disrupted the workplace and workers' community and culture" (p. 3). The situation is cause for concern because links are weakened, everyday life erodes, expectations and future prospects disappear, and life becomes uncertain and unstable. This is the real situation we are heading into; a situation usually hidden by an appeal to hacker ethic (Himanen, 2006) or a new world of nets, nodes, and pretended communities (Castells, 1997). The conditions of the new economy, Sennett (1998) asserts, "are fed by an experience which goes adrift in time, from one place to another, from a job to another" (p. 25). How can a human being develop a sense of identity and create a life history in a society made up of episodes and pieces? (Sennett, 1998).

We argue that this scenario is justified, because instead of an enchanting future created by the intersection of globalization, technologies, and economy, we see worrisome changes in the world of employment and economics. The common argument that more technology brings more and better work or job opportunities has not proved completely true. But the negative sociocultural consequences described above are evident.

ITC and Knowledge Economy

We now shift our analytical focus to what has become an ideological engine driving European Union policies. We refer to the so-called knowledge economy, as it was termed in the Lisbon Strategy. First, a brief history (Angulo, 2010).

The knowledge economy started with the founding of the European Economic Community—which has its origins in the late 1950s with the signing of the Treaties of Rome—and it was greatly promoted during the 1990s (Robertson, 2006). The EU secretaries of education met to discuss the aims of standardizing the curriculum programs in Europe, increasing student mobility between countries, and expanding the field of research. In general, their primary objective was to integrate the EU member nations. The first programs resulting from this meeting had a strong communicative purpose: to increase communication among students, teachers, institutions, educational institutions, and so on. In the late 1990s this approach changed. Three documents signed between 1998 and 2005—the Sorbonne Declaration (1998), the Bologna Declaration (1999), and the Bergen Communiqué (2005; see Wächeter, 2004; Angulo, 2010)—set objectives such as instituting university programs that included common requirements for academic degrees (bachelor's and master's degrees and doctorates); a credit system that enhanced student mobility; common standards of quality; and the promotion of life-long learning. The Berlin Declaration (2003) proposed more economics-based aims such as increasing competitiveness within the field of education.

Competitiveness was endorsed by agreement of the EU members' prime ministers in Lisbon Treaty in March 2007.[3] The teatry asserted that its main objective was to make the EU economy more competitive in the world in order to reach full employment by 2010. This strategy was supported by three pillars: a social pillar aimed at modernizing the European social model; an environmental pillar that focused attention on natural resources and sustainable growth; and, most important, an economic pillar aimed at preparing Europe for the transition into an economy based on knowledge.

Four years later, Kok (2004) published a report that strongly criticized the results of these initial objectives, suggesting that they be reshaped and adding two more: 1) a greater emphasis on the internal EU market and the free circulation of goods and capital to create a single services market[4]; and 2) reinforcement of the labor market.

Within this scenario, the Lisbon European Council helped to reshape the scope of European economical theory from a social or Keynesian policy to a neoliberal policy. Competitiveness, particularly in an economy based on knowledge, is now at the center of the European ideology; this represents a hidden form of neoliberalism (Robertson, 2008).

How does this emphasis on a knowledge-based economy relate to ICT? Actually, one cannot function without the other. As Godin (2006) points out, the concept of a knowledge-based economy is justified by the idea that knowledge and information and communication technologies are key factors in a healthy economy. Kok's report (2004) indicates with absolute clarity that

> the knowledge society is a larger concept than just an increased commitment to R&D. It covers every aspect of the contemporary economy where knowledge is at the heart of value added—from high-tech manufacturing and ICT through knowledge intensive services to the overtly creative industries such as media and architecture....The possibilities for wider economic structures to create the network economy and society and a fundamental re-engineering of business processes are being opened up by ICT. They permit every step in value generation to become smarter. Value is being created less in the simple transformation of inputs into outputs and more in fundamentally enlisting the new capacity and competences created by ICT to meet individualised and complex customer needs—whether business-to-business or business-to-consumer relationships. (p. 19)

This idea is repeated in the Project Europe 2030 report, which explains that one of the priorities of the European education system lies "in the improvement of skills in order to get people ready for labor changes as well as for the usage of the new technologies" (Angulo, 2010, p. 23). The most recent Spanish program on the introduction of ICT in schools equates more computers with a better education. Plan School 2.0 identifies learning through ICT with the implementation of new hardware: "All the classrooms will be equipped with interactive whiteboards and wireless Internet connection; every student will have [his or her] own PC, which will be used as a working tool both at home and at school."[5]

All of these proposals, which tend to hide the huge costs of technologies, are modeling the public policies of European and other well-developed countries.[6] In order to extend the information society, they rely on a formula that, Cuba (1986) notes, has been constant since the beginning of the twentieth century: more and new facilities, better education, and, hence, greater economical development. This formula has no purpose other than to increase the digital and technological market; it is all about selling technology to adults—especially middle-class fathers and mothers—who are concerned about the future of their sons and daughters. Selwyn (2003) remarks on the notion of the child as consumer: "Child computer users are successful scholars, entrepreneurs and playmates....[Adding a lot] of child computer user discourse can be seen as an integral part of the promotion of the information society and as economic, political, cultural and societal matter of fact" (p. 372). It is in this context that the labels discussed above—Digital Natives, Net Generation, and so on—most aptly apply.

ICT and Education in Spain: Programs, Programs, and More Programs

Notwithstanding our analysis, we could accept that these market-oriented policies also contain a serious interest in improving the educational process and a willingness to help the young generation face the challenges of the emerging scene (Castells, 2006). Yet, as Perelman (1998) notes, "If we were seriously preparing ourselves for an information economy, we would be devoting more and more resources to education....Unfortunately, other priorities rank far higher than education in our society" (p. 25).

This leads us to another problematic scenario. While there is funding for the public education system, there are also continuous, costly attempts to implement technologies in education. According to data published by *El País*[7], spending on education in Spain as a percentage of GDP dropped from 4.6% in 1995 to 2.8% in 2003—a reduction that is replicated in all the countries under the OECD. In contrast, data provided by Spain's Ministry of Education show a clear increase in education funding, from 4.26% in 2001 to 5.5% of GDP in 2010 (Ministry of Education, 2010). A problem arises when we disaggregate the actual investment using the OECD data: For secondary schools, funding decreased from 11.700 thousand euros in 1998 to 10.855 in 2007. This indicates a clear decrease, but this decrease disappears when we add together the spending on primary and secondary education, which is 20,080 euros and 30,813 euros, respectively. In any case, it is worth noting that since the approval of the Avanza Program to strengthen the "information society" in various public and social spheres, funding has increased considerably for ITC in education, quadrupling from 2000 to 2009, as shown in Table 1.

Table 1. Annual Average Budget for Society Information Development, Avanza Program (in Thousands of Euros)

Years 2000–2004	Years 2005–2008	Year 2009
447,329	1,268,522	1,516,400

Unless we conflate education needs with selling software and hardware, it seems that improving education is not the focus of the Avanza Program's increased investment. This issue of budget planning arises not just in Spain; it is in fact an important problem in other countries as well. For example, according to data from the World Bank, in India public expenditure per primary student as percentage of GDP per capita is less than 10%, and the percentage of children under 5 who are malnourished is 44%. Nevertheless, the World Bank states that "ICT service exports in India are higher than in many other countries. In the IT sector, exports increased from around US$5.000 million in 2000 to more than US$30.000 in 2006, which means around 42% of all exported services" (World Bank, 2009). Therefore, more technology funding and technology productivity does not necessarily mean social or educational improvements.

Table 2. Most Relevant Institutional ICT Proposals for Education

TIME	PROGRAM
1980s	• ATENEA Projects integrating computer equipment into schools and MERCURIO integrating audiovisual media, in those autonomous communities under the jurisdiction of the Ministry of Education and Science • Implementation of similar projects in other autonomous communities: Plan Alhambra, Zahara XXI (Andalusia); Projects ABRENTE and ESTRELA (Galicia); Plan ÁBACO (Canary Islands); Program Press and School, Computer and Audiovisual Media Program (Catalonia); Basque Plan on Educational Computing (Basque Country); etc. • (1984) Resource centers • (1987) Founding of PNTIC (New ICT Program)
1990s	• (1992–1993) Development and spread of previous projects; DELTA and OLYMPUS European Projects; HISPASAT and Knowledge Adventure • ICT Plan on Teaching and Learning (PLATEA) • (1992) Pilot project on the use of videodiscs (CDI players) • Commitment on CD-ROM technology • (1997) Program Aldea Digital for rural areas
2000s	• (2000) Comprehensive endowment on technological resources in all school centers • Plan *Spain.es* 2004–2005 • Avanza Program1 (2005–2009) and Avanza Program 2 (2010) http://www.planavanza.es/InformacionGeneral/PlanAvanza1/Paginas/PlanAvanza.aspx • *Subprogram Internet in the classroom (2005–2009)* ITE (2009–) "Educational Technologies Institute (ITE)": unit of the Ministry of Education in charge of the integration of ICT into educational stages except universities • *Plan School 2.0* (2009)

Let's now consider the other issue: education reforms and projects for the implementation of ICT in education. Like almost every developed country since the 1980s, Spain has undergone "a constant and continuous reform" relative to ICT. Summaries of the initiatives since the early ATENEA Project in the 1980s are shown in Tables 2 and 3.

Although we cannot carry out a detailed analysis of every initiative, it is possible to show that they follow the dynamic reported by Noble (1996)—that is, that innovation and pedagogy are directed by technologies. From the introduction of computer programming such as BASIC and LOGO[8] in 1983 and 1984, respectively, innovation has revolved around new technological gadgets, both hardware and software. In short, the arguments that supported the intro-

duction of LOGO into schools are still being used, with slight variations, to justify the massive sale of technology in Spain under School Plan 2.0:

> This measure would allow adapting the teaching and learning processes to the twen-
> ty-first century, facilitating our students' knowledge and tools which are fundamental
> for their professional and personal development, encouraging human resources and
> social cohesion, and removing digital gap barriers....Teachers will receive the need-
> ed additional information to adapt to the rhythm laid down by new technologies.
> Likewise, the project would mean the development of the publishing and IT sectors,
> and an opportunity to join the most developed countries in the use of technologies.[9]

This wholesale laudatory discourse on ICT benefits from the confusion over
ICT's real impact on students.

Although a number of studies in specialized magazines provide details on
positive learning achievements relative to the various technologies employed,
there also are surveys that show opposite results. Clark's early works (1985,
1994) advised that "thousands of media research studies conducted over a
period of 70 years...have failed to find compelling causal evidence that media
or media attributes influence learning in any essential and structural way"
(1994, p. 27).

More recent reports, such as those by Angrist and Lavy (2002), Goolsbee
and Guryan (2005), the OECD (2004), the World Bank (Wagner et al., 2005),
Rosado and Bélisle (2007), and Cobo Romani (2009) all suggest either that the
impact of introducing ICT in education is vague, or that access-usage and
learning are not clearly correlated. Goolsbee and Guryan's (2005) conclusions
are especially relevant and revealing:

> We find that despite the strong pre-1998 income gradient of Internet access, E-Rate[10]
> funding went disproportionately to low-Internet schools. We also show evidence that
> the E-Rate subsidy led to significant increases in Internet investment. By 2000, there
> were some 68 percent more classrooms with Internet connections than there would
> have been without the subsidy. Urban schools, predominantly black and Hispanic
> schools and primary schools are disproportionately responsive to the subsidy....Judged
> as a policy to close the digital divide among schools, the program clearly succeeded.
> Judged as a means of improving student performance, however, we fail to find strong
> evidence of success. (pp. 25–26)

Thus, faced with evidence of the low impact of ITC in school curriculum, we
cannot accept that the solution will be found in more technology.
Notwithstanding this, computers and other technological gadgets will continue to sell, and they will also continue to be underused (Cuban, 2001).

Rhetoric about ITC does not lead us to a better place but into a jam with not many exits. We must admit that in order to face the educational challenges posed by the information and communication society (de Kerckhove 1997; Castell, 1997, 2001; Piscitelli, 2002) we will have to change our pedagogic system and our schools—a task that is far more complex and implies a greater political commitment than simply distributing technology. Finally, as we all know, pedagogical practice is a much more complicated issue than approving budgets for new computers, digital boards, or digital agendas.

Notes

1. This paper was funded in part by Junta de Andalucía, Consejería de Innovación, Ciencia y Empresa. Research Project 'Escenarios, tecnologías digitales y juventud en Andalucía.' *Reference:* HUM-02599, and by Ministerio de Ciencia e Innovación. *Research Project* 'El Plagio Académico entre el alumnado de Andalucía.' Reference: EDU2009–14019-C02–02.
2. Pioneering works by Kutscher (1987) and Selby-Smith (1987) support this, too.
3. The Treaty of Lisbon is an international agreement that amends the two treaties which comprise the constitutional basis of the European Union (EU). The Lisbon Treaty was signed by the EU member states on 13 December 2007, and entered into force on 1 December 2009. (See 'Teatry of Lisbon' in Wikipedia.)
4. We must not forget that one of those services is education. See Angulo (2010).
5. From School Plan Web 2.0 webpage: http://www.ite.educacion.es/es/escuela-20 (accessed 15 January 2011).
6. Perelman notes: "Today, computer technology evolves so fast that a five-year-old computer is hopelessly obsolete. Although the parts are modular—even more so than a car—you cannot mix parts easily from different generations of computers as you would in an automobile" (1998, p. 12).
7. See El País (13/10/2006) http://www.elpais.com/articulo/sociedad/Espana/paises/UE/gastan/formacion/ciudadanos/elpepisoc/20061013elpepisoc_6/Tes (accessed 15 January 2011).
8. For a discussion of LOGO and its educational qualities, see Papert (1993, 1996).
9. Plan Web 2.0 webpage: http://www.ite.educacion.es/es/escuela-20 (accessed 15 January 2011).
10. E-rate is an effect of the subsidy on Internet investment in schools.

References

Angrist, J., & Lavy, V. (2002, October). New evidence on classroom computers and pupil learning. *The Economic Journal, 112*, 735–765.

Angulo, J. F. (2010). La educación y el currículum en el espacio europeo: ¿Internacionalizar o globalizar? In J. Gimeno Sacristán (Ed.), *Saberes e incertidumbres sobre el curriculum* (pp. 478–497). Madrid: Morata.

Ante, S. E., & Holahan, C. (2008, February 7). Generation Myspace is getting fed up. *Bloomberg Businessweek*. Retrieved from http://www.businessweek.com/magazine/content/08_07/b4071054390809.htm Aronowitz, S., & DiFazio, W. (1994). *The jobless future: Sci-tech and the dogma of work*. Minneapolis: University of Minnesota Press.

Carnoy, M. (2000). *Sustaining the new economy: Work, family and community in the information age*. New York: Russell Sage Foundation.

Castells, M. (1997). *The information age: Economy, society and culture*. 3 vols. Cambridge, MA: Blackwell.

Castells, M. (2001). *La galaxia Internet. Reflexiones sobre Internet, empresa y sociedad*. Barcelona: Plaza & Janés.

Castells, M. (2006). Informacionalismo, redes y sociedad red: Una propuesta teórica. In M. Castells (Ed.), *La sociedad red: Una visión global* (pp. 27–75). Madrid: Alianza.

Castells, M., & Himanen, P. (2002). *The information society and the welfare state: The Finnish model*. New York: Oxford University Press.

Cuban, L. (1986). *Teachers and machines: The classroom use of technology since 1920*. New York: Teachers College Press.

Cuban, L. (2001). *Oversold & underused: Computers in the classroom*. London: Harvard University Press.

De Kerckhove, D. (1997). *Connected intelligences: The arrival of the web society*. Toronto: Somerville House.

Eco, U. (1968). *Apocalípticos e integrados*. Barcelona: Lumen.

European Council. (2010). *Proyecto Europa 2030. Retos y oportunidades*. Informe al Consejo Europeo del Grupo de Reflexión sobre el futuro de la UE en 2030. Stuttgart, Germany: Author.

Facer, K., Furlong, J., & Furlong, R. (2003). *Screenplay. Children and computing in the home*. London: RoutledgeFalmer.

Godin, B. (2006). The knowledge-based economy: Conceptual framework or buzzword? *Journal of Technology Transfer, 31*, 17–30.

Goolsbee, A., & Guryan, J. (2005). *The impact of Internet subsidies in public schools*. Chicago: University of Chicago Press.

Himanen, P. (2006). La ética hacker como cultura de la era de la información. In M. Castells (Ed.), *La sociedad red: Una visión global* (pp. 505–518). Madrid: Alianza.

Kress, G. (2010). The profound shift of digital literacies. In J. Gillen & D. Barton (Eds.), *Digital literacies*. London: TLR & London Knowledge Lab. Retrieved from http://www.tlrp.org/docs/DigitalLiteracies.pdf

Kutscher, R. (1987). The impact of technology on employment in the United States: Past and future. In G. Burke & R. W. Rumberger (Eds.), *The future impact of technology on work and education* (pp. 33–54). London: Falmer Press.

The MySpace generation. (2005, December 12). *Bloomberg*. Retrieved from http://www.businessweek.com/magazine/content/05_50/b3963001.htm

Negroponte, N. (1995). *Being digital*. New York: Alfred A. Knopf.

Noble, D. D. (1991). *The classroom arsenal: Military research, information technology and public education*. London: Falmer Press.

Noble, D. D. (1996). Mad rushes into the future: The overselling of educational technology. *Educational Leadership, 54*(3), 18–23.

Oppenheimer, T. (2004). *The flickering mind: Saving education from the false promise of technology.* New York: Random House.

Organisation for Economic Co-operation and Development (OECD). (2004). *Completing the foundation for lifelong learning. An OECD survey of upper secondary schools.* Paris: Author.

Orlet, C. (2007, March 2). Look-at-me-generation. *American Spectator.* Retrieved from http://spectator.org/archives/2007/03/02/the-look-at-me-generation

Papert, S. (1993). *The children's machine: Rethinking school in the age of the computer.* New York: Basic Books.

Papert, S. (1996). *The connected family.* Atlanta: Longstreet.

Perelman, M. (1998). *Class warfare in the information age.* New York: St. Martin's Press.

Piscitelli, A. (2002). *Ciberculturas 2.0 en la era de las máquinas inteligentes.* Barcelona: Paidós.

Popkewitz, Thomas S. (2007). *Cosmopolitanism and the Age of School Reform: Science, Education, and Making Society by Making the Child.* Abingdon. UK. Routledge.

Presky, M. (2001a). Digital natives, digital immigrants. *On the Horizon, 9*(5), 1—6. Retrieved from http://www.scribd.com/doc/9799/Prensky-Digital-Natives-Digital-Immigrants-Part1

Prensky, M. (2001b). Digital natives, digital immigrants: Part 2: Do they really *think* differently? *On the Horizon 9*(6), 1–6. Retrieved from http://www.twitchspeed.com/site/Prensky%20-%20Digital%20Natives,%20Digital%20Immigrants%20-%20Part2.htm

Rifkin, J. (1994). *The end of work: The decline of the global labor force and the dawn of the post-market era.* New York: Putnam.

Robertson, S. L. (2006). The politics of constructing (a competitive) Europe(an) through internationalising higher education: Strategy, structures, subjects. *Perspectives in Education, 24*(4), 29–44.

Rosado, E., & Bélisle, C. (2007). *Analysing digital literacy frameworks.* LIRE (Université Lyon 2–CNRS) eLearning Programme 2005–2006.

Roszak, T. (1988). *El culto a la información. El folclore de los ordenadores y el verdadero arte de pensar.* Barcelona: Crítica. (Spanish translation Jordi Beltrán)

Sartori, G. (1998). *Homo videns: La sociedad teledirigida.* Madrid: Taurus.

Selby-Smith, J. (1987). The potential impact of new technologies on the level and composition of employment: An Australian perspective. In G. Burke & R. W. Rumberger (Eds.), *The future impact of technology on work and education* (pp. 55–73). London: Falmer Press.

Selwyn, N. (2003). Doing IT for the kids: Re-examining children, computers and the "information society." *Media, Culture & Society, 25*(3), 351–378.

Sennett, R. (1998). *The corrosion of character: The personal consequences of work in the new capitalism.* New York: W.W. Norton.

Siegel, L. (2008). *Against the machine.* New York: Spiegel & Grau.

Simone, R. (2001). *La tercera fase: Formas de saber que estamos perdiendo.* Madrid: Taurus.

Tapscott, D. (1998). *Growing up digital: The rise of the net generation.* New York: McGraw-Hill.

Wagner, D. A., et al. (2005). *Monitoring and evaluation of ICT in education projects: A handbook for developing countries.* Washington, DC: World Bank. Retrieved from http://www.infodev.org/en/Publication.9.html

Warschauer, M., & Matuchniak, T. (2010). New technology and digital worlds: Analyzing evidence of equity in access, use, and outcomes. *Review of Research in Education, 34,* 179–225.

Williams, P., & Rowlands, I. (2007). *Information behaviour of the researcher of the future.* British Library/JISC Study. Retrieved from http://www.jisc.ac.uk/media/documents/programmes/reppres/ggworkpackageii.pdf

World Bank. (2009). *Indicadores del desarrollo mundial son una pauta de referencia en medio de la crisis. Comunicado de prensa* 2009/316/DEC. Retrieved from http://www.go.worldbank.org/TF9FJ7HHK0

· 9 ·

National Technology Plan for Education and Public Schooling

Myths, Limits, and False Promises

Lia Raquel Oliveira

Oh, who will write the story of what could have been.

(SARAMAGO, 1986, P.18)

A Tarzan-like Resolution of a Ministers Council?

The Technology Plan for Education (TPE) is a legal document issued by the seventeenth constitutional government of Portugal.[1] This document is based on the need for "reinforcing the qualifications and competences of the Portuguese society [and] improving and modernizing schools," and it attempts to develop the "physical conditions which favor academic achievement, [thus consolidating] the role of Communication and Information Technologies (ICT) as a basic tool for learning and teaching" (TPE, 2007, pp. 6563).

This discourse omits, as usual, the nature and substance of the "qualifications and competences" to be developed, as well as their relation to pedagogy by objectives—that is, a pedagogy that is anchored in positivist experimentalism and behavioral psychology. As Sacristán (1982) accurately claims, this form of pedagogy is sustained by the cult of social efficiency that dominates schools and the curriculum; it is actually a secular philosophy that dominates Western educational systems driven by market mechanisms. The movement associated with the discourse of competences and pedagogy by objectives originates in the lap of industrial and military training, transfers the problem of technological rationality into education, and converts it into technicism (idem, 1982). Although this technicism has been quite secular in Portugal, the fact is that during the last three decades, it achieved a puzzling level of complexity, a process that Dale (1989; quoted by Apple, 2003) and others termed "conservative modernization."

This technicism, disguised by the apparel of modernization, progress, and social inclusion, neutralizes the problem of public education by dissipating the theoretical and ideological discussions that should support the formulation of the curriculum. In the historic moment we live in, which is marked by a violent neoliberal globalization (Sousa Santos, 2008; Beck, 2002; Paraskeva, 2011a), this absence of foundations and values serves as a justification for flooding schools with computers and the associated paraphernalia:

> With the technological modernization, the school will give a qualitative jump and will open itself to vast areas of knowledge. School will then be the center of a net of projects directed to what really matters: learn more and better, teachers and students. (TPE, 2007, p. 6564)

This statement introduces the dangerous populist, propagandist tone of the entire document and glorifies the common-sense, which is one of the triumphs of the neoliberal policies—gracefully crafted by the hands of the media—that consists of disrupting and rearticulating "the true meaning of determined concepts and practices" (Paraskeva, 2006, p. 71). In one blow, "what matters" is defined around taken-for-granted key concepts that are never discussed. There is not a word about the meaning of public schools or their political mission in the context of a democratic society—not a word about what content is really critical to learn, or how, and to what end. "What really matters," as depicted in this legal document, is to proclaim a neutral public school that has no social classes, no issues of gender or ethnicity—in essence, no problems at all.

Public schools interest all members of society because they constitute a political project of the community (cf. Torres Santomé, 2003). Public education is one of the biggest industries, one of the highest public services of any given modern economy that, by investing in the public good, places the greatest relevance on the question of who its beneficiaries are, as Connell (1993, p. 18) warns when he proposes the concept of curricular justice.

The modernization of schools and the future success of the Portuguese people briefly reappear in the "vision and objectives" section of the TPE (pp.

6566–6567), which includes mention of a high-speed Internet connection; the number of students per Internet-connected computer (2); and the percentage of teachers with ICT certification (90%). These are the indicators for the evaluation of the plan, and they dictate its political and political party commitment.

In other words, borrowing from Connell, we would say that this plan stands on a discursive logic "in Tarzan style in which a group of hairy-chested individuals jumps out of trees shouting screams of 'efficiency, 'competition' and 'market discipline,' shaking every hut inside out, returning to trees while leaving behind a trail of destruction and crisis" (quoted by Paraskeva, 2003, p. 74).

The TPE involves four key action axes: (1) technology, (2) training, (3) contents, and (4) investment and funding. Several problems can be identified in it, starting with its omission of the function of public schools and culminating in the crucial omission of who will be responsible for producing the digital content to be distributed in the schools, as we later point out.

We begin to articulate some of these problems, starting with a few aspects of critical importance that can help unravel and disrupt this hegemonic common sense, which states that ICT, beyond being neutral, are innocuous from a political and ideological point of view.

Navigating without Knowing How to Swim

Bearing in mind the technology axis and the expected ratio of two students per PC, computers are presently being introduced in the schools, and laptop computers are being sold to students at variable prices according to their socioeconomic status. This new technology is sponsored by computer distribution projects such as Magalhães, e-escolinhas (e-small-schools), and e-escolas (e-schools), that involve basic and secondary education up to the twelfth grade. We are facing a considerable consumption of hardware that will rapidly become obsolete—their prices demonstrate that very fact! The computer industry is essentially forcing us to consume the technology that is in its own interest to sell. The best example is the Magalhães computer (within the Magalhães project mentioned above) aimed at younger students, which is presented as Portuguese technology. In fact, it is an old PC transfigured into a toy that operates with technology dating four years back, and its components are mostly from Asia—in other words, a *ruined* computer with its own operating system and corresponding software, which means that it is no longer a common computer but an infantilized and expensive one (around US$400). Knowing beforehand that these computers are old and that this type of equipment is highly polluting, where is the concern with sustainable development and ecology that is so widespread in the media and emphasized both in political discourses and in the school curriculum?

ICT's problematic issues of energy consumption and disposal of old machines simply are not debated, yet their implications range from using precious resources to controlling energy sources, which play a critical role in the planet's geopolitics.

The computers acquired by students and their families become their responsibility, and so do associated difficulties with Internet access, repairs, and replacements. Therefore, in terms of "info-inclusion," two new burdens are created for students' parents: being responsible for updating informatics, and being responsible for their offsprings' success and learning. In the spirit and letter of this document, owning a computer with access to the Internet means not only gaining skills but also doing so almost automatically. Not being able to learn under these conditions is associated with laziness, thus making the individual responsible for his or her success or failure (see Apple, 1993; Connell, 1993; Torres Santomé, 2003; Bauman, 2001; Beck, 2002). This idea is stated or implied in every paragraph of the TPE.

Examining the technology domain more deeply, beyond the technological projects (computers and add-ons), high-speed Internet bandwidth, and Internet in the classroom (local area networks), the TPE includes two more projects related to safety that are still under analysis. Safety in this context means circulating the student's electronic identification card and implementing internal video-surveillance systems in schools (TPE, 2007, pp. 6568–6572).

The electronic card not only serves to "suppress the circulation of cash…[and] control entries and exits of students…[but also to] consult the administrative process, the academic records and student purchases" (p. 6570). It is important to note that access to administrative processes and academic records is currently restricted. The classroom teacher is the faithful protector of each student's file, and even parents can access it only in his/her presence. Is it possible to keep such information private in a world where personal information of all kinds is becoming accessible online? Is it *educative* to control the permanence of students at school in such a way (supposedly proving the system's efficiency in keeping students *locked* in school) while damaging the safety of their own personal data?

There is still the possibility of allowing financial institutions, "as a counterpart, to commercialize financial services based on the student card to 3rd basic cycle and secondary Education students" (idem, p. 6571). Besides being able to, as a counterpart, "[make] brands evident" they may still add "additional functionalities" such as selling financial services and applications to minors.

The intention of equipping every school with video-surveillance systems is justified by the fact that the increase of the technological park constitutes a "window of opportunity" (idem, p. 6565) for theft and vandalism. Apparently, the physical integrity of people gains notable importance. However, video surveillance does not prevente crime in itself, and the social origins of theft and vandalism are not considered.

To some extent, video surveillance associated with the student identification card throws us back to Foucault panopticons and reminds us of the "nightmare triggered by the information technologies" (Steiner, 2008, p. 272) in which privacy and intimacy are constantly harassed.

Teachers Are Sailors and Do Know How to Navigate

Referring now to the training axis, how will the certification of in-service teachers (decreted one year after the TPE began) be made operational? The main objective of certification is to prepare 90% of teachers to use ICT at various levels of proficiency, but nothing is said about the quality of such training.

We may start by questioning whether this certification is necessary. Teachers have always navigated their classrooms to a great degree by intuition and reflection on experience, navigation being "a type of politics" (Silva in Mendanha, 1994, p. 74), a way of making sense of and managing unpredictable situations. They are adaptable, versatile, and only apparently submissive, because they believe in their power to enact their professional call (Steiner, 2005).

Technical ICT training is mostly unnecessary, as teachers already know how to use computers and they can improve their expertise on their own or with peers, but perhaps they need to reflect further on the educational rationales underlying the uses of ICT. From this perspective, professional development may help teachers develop a critical stance that counteracts common-sense, acritical understandings of ICT. Whatever path they decide to take, "the losses equal the gains. Life is destined to navigate between the two and no sailor can proclaim to have found a safe route, free of risk" (Bauman, 2001, p. 75). Teachers' experience is subjected to uncertainty and "continuous anxiety" (idem, p. 93), and any training program that does not acknowledge this fact will fail to promote significant professional empowerment and educational change.

By not taking into account the complexity of the teaching profession and the role and social value of the teacher, the TPE potentially ensures that teachers will lose their professional character, converting them into manual and digital resource managers, "robots run by publishers of scholarly manuals" (Torres Santomé, 2006, p.145). Furthermore, the introduction of performance evaluation grids to assess teachers' skills also reinforces the growing "intensification" of the profession (Apple, 1986) through increased accountability and perfomativity.

"The World Bank predicts that the power of teachers and the central character of the classroom will firmly decline as the use of online pedagogical technologies becomes more and more generalized" (Sousa Santos, 2008, p. 29): This statement refers to higher education teachers, but with the TPE it can be extended to all teaching levels. Moreover, we argue that online technology and digital content will lead to the growth of homeschooling (Paraskeva, 2003, 2006; Torres Santomé, 2003, 2006; Apple, 2003).

Digital Contents Are Cool and There Are No *Sharks* in the Portuguese Sea

Lastly, and most important, who will produce the "digital content" that will be needed for online learning, and how will it be produced? What is the connection between this massive introduction of computers in schools and the contents of schooling?

As regards the content axis, the TPE states that "the contents and the applications are essential to altering pedagogical practices, by favoring the use of more interactive and constructivist teaching methods, and therefore contributing to create a learning culture throughout life" (TPE, 2007, p. 6572). Constructivism has become an umbrella term under which everything fits and is justified—from typically behaviorist computer-assisted teaching to social constructivist approaches (Sacristán, 1982). The discourse of constructivist methods usually focuses on the teacher-student-knowledge triad, thus assuming that knowledge is something autonomous and pre-existent to the act of knowing. Also, these methods obliterate the fact that socially accepted, official knowledge is ideologically tied to interests determined by ruling minorities (Sacristán, 1982, 2000; Apple, 1986, 1993; Torres Santomé, 2006; Paraskeva, 2005, 2006, 2008).

"Knowledge is a process and conscience is intention directed to the world," according to Paulo Freire (1973, p. 43). In a humanist and liberating education that respects humankind, neither teachers nor students can be treated as objects (idem, p. 14). "Men are educated between themselves while mediated by the world" (idem, p. 18), and from that education stems the knowledge that is by nature shared and changing.

The learning management system Moodle is considered by the TPE to be underused, on the grounds that it is used mainly as a channel of communication and document sharing. This is precisely the great advantage of this kind of electronic systems—subtly designated as collaborative platforms. There resides their transforming potential for education in the sense of increased participation. However, what the TPE really proposes is that they should become distance-teaching platforms: "Minimize info-inclusion, making contents and tools available that make distance-teaching viable" (TPE, 2007, p. 6573).

In order to access distance-teaching via the Internet and benefit from its advantages, it is necessary to be info-included and to have overcome the access barrier. Such distance-based systems can, in fact, serve the public interest in specific situations. However, the statement that the "contents, modules and courses" (TPE, p. 6573) of remote access are "low-cost" is far from true. In other words, the TPE provides the means—to a few—for a shift from public and national teaching systems to private online arrangements, since the preparation and maintenance of online environments and materials are not "low-cost." Only homeschooling clients might have the means to access and afford this teaching system.

When the TPE praises and promotes the online teaching modality, it validates "a parallel education but most of all alternative, expressed through the new escol(@) [e-school]. Homeschooling cannot stop being seen as a hardened process of info-exclusion" (Paraskeva, 2006, p. 84). The fact that only some students will have the possibility of learning at home legitimizes power inequalities regarding the families' right to choose what education they want for their children, accentuates the existing socioeconomic differences, and exacerbates conflicts between various group identities (Paraskeva, 2003, 2006; Torres Santomé, 2003; Apple, 2003). As stated above, the discussion about public school concerns us all, as "education is a political project by which we try to conform to the future of the community in which we live in and society in general" (Torres Santomé, 2003, p. 30).

The teaching-learning contents are presented in the TPE as "exercises, textbooks, scholar manuals, electronic apparatuses, etc." (TPE, 2007, pp. 6572–6573). Clearly, these are not likely to enhance "more interactive and constructivist teaching methods," and their use can be based on the same principles of the so-called traditional methods.

Having identified the "format" of the contents of the teaching-learning system, the question remains of how they might challenge dominant learning practices and who will be responsible for producing them. The TPE does not predict any curricular revision and essentially distorts the potentially transformative power of ICT by inducing the reproduction of current approaches. Neither teachers nor students are seen as "knowledge producers." Knowledge will instead keep coming in the format of the dominant scientific culture in order to be absorbed and "digested" (Freire, 1973, p. 43). Who will prepare study materials that allow for multiple perspectives, from which knowledge can be built and rebuilt in a critical and participative way by every individual?

For decades, textbooks have determined what is taught in schools and how it is taught (Sacristán, 1982, 2000; Apple, 1986, 1993; Torres Santomé, 2006; Paraskeva, 2005, 2006, 2008). The entity that produces these textbooks is the "teaching industry," that is, publishers with whom the Ministry of Education establishes protocols. There are several publishers in Portugal, but textbooks are becoming less varied due to the power exerted by a few publishing groups that dominate the market. It is easy to assume that the publishers who produce electronic textbooks will be favored by the ministry for the implementation of the TPE.

The TPE axis of investment and funding relies on European funds, government budget funds and established partnerships with the private sector, hardware and maintenance subcontractors, communication suppliers, and banking. Partnerships have already been established with "major" mobile technology operators (only three companies), equipment purchases have been made, and supply contracts have been signed for Internet access without any publicly publicized contract being made. Part of the equipment and the access supposedly will be paid for by such operating companies and manufacturers; however, despite such partnerships, which are never clear and involve millions of euros, the state is already in debt with these payments. We do not know who is paying and how, in return for what, and who will ultimately pay in the future for computer replacements or Internet access.

Through What Door Did the TPE Enter Public Education?

The TPE was designed in a historical moment that has been profoundly influenced by neoliberal policies, which are responsible for the World Trade Organization's increased influence on education, and for the evolution of education into a consumer good, rather than the common good it should be.

According to Torres Santomé (2006, p. 33), "we cannot forget that the accomplishment of compulsory and public schooling was a political conquest, not a business cause (…). If we analyze the neoliberal attack against public schools we can note that one of its main actions consists of distorting the purposes of educational systems."

This neoliberal action entails globalization and the economy of knowledge, whose wonders and false promises are well documented by Castells (2004) and Jessop (2003). Pierre Lévy's concept of "collective intelligence" is a beautiful idea that helps us imagine a world of communication, in the sense of "understanding" between individuals and peoples, in which redistribution and recognition policies would complement each other (Fraser, 2001) and allow us to perceive a "non-desertified real" (Žižek, 2006). However, the knowledge economy is sustained by policies of globalization that "seek, definitely, to dismantle the apparatus and tasks of the State, with the goal of developing the mercantilist anarchy utopia of a *minimum* State" (Beck, 2002, p. 17). Globalization also signifies the "absence of a world State and, more specifically, a world society without a world State and without a world government" (idem, p. 32).

The TPE was not designed out of the blue, nor is it as innovative as it assumes itself to be. Through what door did it enter public education? The first modernization of schools occurred in Portugal in the 1980s with the introduction of computers in basic and secondary teaching systems, and it was based on the same arguments as today. The EU's project MINERVA (MInisterial NEtwoRk for Valorising Activities in digitisation), carried out between 1985 and 1994, was the most important technology-promoting endeavor, but it coexisted with and generated several other initiatives that lasted until 2006.

The scientific domain of educational technology emerged at the University of Minho also in the 1980s, and it rapidly expanded to other universities and schools of higher education, both public and private. It quickly gained the status of a PhD specialty within the sciences of education field. Since then, there has been a lot of research on educational technology. Nevertheless, topics such as technology and its relationship with the public schools are not being debated. Technology is considered neutral, and it is assumed that its integration into the curricular process is both inevitable and beneficial. Constructivist pedagogies are employed that define and convey contents with the belief that things are as they are, with no alternatives whatsoever. Investments in ICT in the form of training and equipment are usually extreme, and there is no reported analysis of its impact on the educational system.

As regards the TPE, the first official study of the impact of e-initiatives gives us some important hints. Considering the *e-escolas* program (aimed at the second and third cycles of basic and secondary education):

> The overwhelming majority of the participants, regardless of the initiative, come from aggregates where there were computers before they enrolled in the program. Actually 91,1% of the participants of *e-escola* possessed a computer…It is obvious, however, that such possession of computers corresponded fundamentally to the presence of desktop computers. (ANACOM/KPMG, 2010, p. 20)

It continues:

> In the sample, a statistically significant correlation was found between enrollment in the *e-escola* and the families' socioeconomic status (…) it was found that, except for the lower class, there was a progressive growth of participation in the lowest socio-economic levels. In fact, whereas in high and medium-high classes we have enrollments averaging 30,0% (28,9 % for the highest class and 32,1% for the medium-high class), in the medium and medium-low classes there is an enrollment of 50,0% of participants (51,3 % in the case of medium class and 62,7% in the case of medium-low class). (idem, p.41)

Regarding the lower social class, a footnote explains that there were not sufficient data to draw credible conclusions about student enrollment (idem, p. 42). According to this study, it appears that students who already had a computer and Internet access still have it and are using it. However, those with a less priviledged social background were not even close to getting there.

Final, Not Very Liquid Considerations

Liquid modernity, light and volatile—the loss of consciousness, perennity and strength of human relations and social life—is just one different modernity:

> What makes it so modern as it was more or less a century ago is what distinguishes modernity from all other historic forms of human living: compulsive and obsessive, continuous, unattainable and always incomplete *modernization*; the oppressive and ineradicable, insatiable thirst of creative destruction (or destructive creativity, if that is the case: 'clean the place' in the name of a 'new and perfected' project; of 'dismantling,' 'cutting,' 'reuniting' or 'reducing' all of this in the name of the greater capacity to do the same in the future—in the name of productivity or competitiveness). (Bauman, 2001, p. 36)

The "urgency" of integrating and normalizing ICT in public schools certainly aims at promoting elementary digital and technological literacy. However, it also serves the purpose of domesticating ICT potential to transform society. This potential is more or less unpredictable, but we believe—and this relates to our utopian hope in the human species—that young people who use such technologies today will discover better routes to more just forms of social coexistence. Paraphrasing Sartre, we are what we are capable of doing over what others expected to make of us.

As we all know, public schools have not been leaders in the movement for social transformation (Enguita, 2007). However, they do serve as a "knowledge distribution agency...Though not totally equitable, it is the least uneven of those we know" (Sacristán, 2000, p. 95; cf. also Paraskeva, 2011b). A reconceptualization of the relation between the TPE and public schooling is therefore of paramount importance, so as to cancel or disrupt technological determinism as a "discourse of salvation" for all problems involving public school, despite the fundamental issues that remain unresolved.

Note

1. The Socialist Party had an absolute majority.

References

ANACOM/ KPMG. (2010). Estudo sobre a adesão e o impacto das e.iniciativas. Relatório Final. Retrieved from http://www.anacom.pt/render.jsp?contentId=1000836

Apple, M. (1986). *Teachers and tests: A political economy of class and gender relations in education.* New York: Routledge.

Apple, M. (1993). *Official knowledge: Democratic education in a conservative age.* New York: Routledge.

Apple, M. (2003). A extinção dos professores: A política cultural do ensino em casa. In J. T. Santomé, J. Paraskeva, & M. Apple (Eds.), *Ventos de desescolarização: A nova ameaça à escolarização pública* (pp. 116–141). Lisbon: Plátano Editora.

Bauman, Z. (2001). *Modernidade líquida.* Rio de Janeiro: Jorge Zahar Editor.

Beck, U. (2002). *Qué es la globalización: Falacias del globalismo, respuestas a la globalización.* Barcelona: Paidós.

Castells, M. (2004). *A galáxia Internet: Reflexões sobre a Internet, negócios e sociedade.* Lisbon: Gulbenkian.

Connell, R. (1993). *Escuelas y justicia social.* Madrid: Morata.

Enguita, M. (2007). *Educação e transformação social.* Mangualde, Portugal: Pedago.

Fraser, N. (2001). Social justice in the knowledge society: Redistribution, recognition, and participation. Heinrich Böll Stiftung. Retrieved from http://www.wissensgesellschaft.org/themen/orientierung/socialjustice.pdf

Freire, P. (1973). *Uma educação para a liberdade*. Porto, Portugal: José Ribeiro.

Jessop, B. (2003). The spatiotemporal dynamics of capital and its globalization—and how they challenge state power and democracy. Department of Sociology, Lancaster University.

Mendanha, V. (1994). *Conversas com Agostinho da Silva*. Lisbon: Pergaminho.

Paraskeva, J. (2003). Desescolarização: Genotexto e fenotexto da políticas curriculares neo-liberais. In J. T. Santomé, J. Paraskeva. & M. Apple (Eds.), *Ventos de desescolarização: A nova ameaça à escolarização pública* (pp. 57–115). Lisbon: Plátano Editora.

Paraskeva, J. (2005). Circunlóquios de silêncios sobre os conteúdos curriculares. In J. Paraskeva, C. Rossatto, & R. Allen (Eds.), *Reinventar a pedagogia crítica* (pp. 89–106). Mangualde, Portugal: Edições Pedago.

Paraskeva, J. (2006). Se a tecnologia é a resposta qual é a pergunta? In J. Paraskeva & L. Oliveira (Eds.), *Currículo e tecnologia educativa*, vol. 1 (pp. 67–95). Mangualde, Portugal: Pedago.

Paraskeva, J. (2008). *O presente como museu: A(s) tecnologia(s) educativa(s) como réu avant la lettre*. In J. Paraskeva & L. Oliveira (Eds.), *Currículo e tecnologia educativa*, vol. 2 (pp. 19–45). Mangualde, Portugal: Pedago.

Paraskeva, J. (2011a). *Nova teoria curricular*. Mangualde, Portugal: Pedago.

Paraskeva, J. (2011b). *Conflicts in curriculum theory: Challenging hegemonic epistemologies*. New York: Palgrave.

Sacristán, J. G. (1982). *La pedagogia por objetivos. Obsesión por la eficiencia*. Madrid: Morata.

Saramago, J. (1986). *Jangada de pedra*. 6th ed. Lisbon: Caminho.

Sousa Santos, B. (2008). A universidade no século XXI. Para uma reforma democrática e emancipatória da universidade. In B. S. Santos & N. A. Filho (Eds.), *A universidade no século XXI. Para uma universidade nova* (pp. 15–77). Coimbra, Portugal: Almedina.

Steiner, G. (2005). *As lições dos mestres*. Lisbon: Gradiva.

Steiner, G. (2008). *Os livros que não escrevi*. Lisbon: Gradiva.

Torres Santomé, J. T. (2003). Escola e família: Duas instituições em confronto? In J. T. Santomé, J. Paraskeva, & M. Apple (Eds.), *Ventos de desescolarização: A nova ameaça à escolarização pública* (pp. 15–56). Lisbon: Plátano.

Torres Santomé, J. T. (2006). *A desmotivação dos professores*. Mangualde, Portugal: Pedago.

TPE. (2007). Resolução do conselho de ministros nº 137/2007. *Diário da Republica, 1ª série— Nº 180—18 de Setembro de 2007*. Lisbon: Conselho de Ministros. Retrieved from http://diario.vlex.pt/vid/conselho-ministros-setembro-33512976 Id.vLex: VLEX-33512976

World Trade Organization (WTO). (1998). Education services. Background note by the Secretariat, S/C/W/49, 98–3691. Geneva; Author.

Žižek, S. (2006). *Bem-vindo ao deserto do real*. Lisbon: Relógio d'Água.

· 1 0 ·

Official Discourses in the Educational Systems

Competencies—The New Curriculum Password?

José Bravo Nico & Lurdes Pratas Nico

The utility of knowledge has always been assumed to be one of the essential and structural questions in any educational and curriculum narrative. In fact, the utility of knowledge frames different designs for educational systems.

Knowledge, as presented in public education systems, originates in the mainstream culture as an "accumulated capital for a future time or cultural ornament" (Beane, 2002, p. 19). It is shaped and sequentially arranged in a compartmentalized way that often is far removed from everyday context of students. Moreover, knowledge is frequently framed as being needed for a certain or eventual future requirement.

Historically there has always been a hierarchical relation within the formal structure of learning, involving contents (what), time (when), and utility (what for). The traditional difference in social status of the different kinds of knowledge and their utilities is connected with the way education emerges institutionally. as well as the demands of the economy. The concept of competence was born at the center of this tension and has been developing there, and there it must be rebuilt.

From Qualification to the Lonely Responsibility of Individual Education

Nowadays, across all geographic, political, and social latitudes, school attendance in formal learning contexts is associated with motivations directly related to employment and productivity (Sarmento & Ferreira, 2006, p. 331).

In fact, the growing pressure to survive in the labor market for a growing group of individuals with an increasing level of qualifications, combined with the ongoing need among businesses and institutions for qualified employees, has been determining the erosion of the cultural purposes of education. This reality has contributed to an interesting debate about the so-called crisis in education. Some authors defend the idea that this crisis does not refer to the school model but to a legitimate crisis of the school institution, believing there is a certain decline of that very institution that is leading to "the deinstitutionalization of the socializing processes and to growing individualization movement" (Dubet & Martucelli, 1996; Dubet, 2002, quoted by Sarmento & Ferreira, 2006, p. 333).

The school model associated with the Taylor-Ford model was followed for decades—until the 1960s and 1970s in some countries, and it still used in Portugal. The educational system in Portugal (and in too many other nations in the European Union) values the passive transmission of knowledge and overvalues the acquisition of diplomas from formal educational institutions, to the detriment of knowledge built through individual experience in multiple personal and professional life contexts. Such a model "is the one of the diplomas and not the one of knowing how to mobilize the knowledge, the skills and competences in new situations" (Warschauer, 2006, p. 806).

This perspective is contradictory in itself, once the bureaucratic content with which learning concretizes itself has created a growing distance between school learning and the knowledge and skills individuals need to be productive in labor contexts. This is identified as one of the main reasons for the weak social and economic performance of the country. It was also clear in the Portuguese students' recurring weak performance on international assessments.

We are, therefore, already too far away from Freinet, who defended the existence of a school system that allows individuals to build a personal identity even as they take part in the construction of a collective identity. From Freinet's perspective, a school should perceive itself as existing to guide "the formation of the citizen" (Souza & Dantas, 2006, p. 993). This idea is reinforced in the most critical perspectives, particularly that of Freire, where it points out the need for each citizen to define himself in relation to his rights and duties and to develop himself as an autonomous and responsible human being, through a process of *conscientization* (p. 987).

The school model has been widely debated in the field of education since the 1990s. Social, economic, and technological developments require workers to develop new capacities, knowledge, and skills, and develop a diverse set of essential competencies. The concept of qualification is associated with the current political circumstances of the concept of citizenship and is an increasing reality in educational systems, as that conceptual relation provides "a citizenship structured on an order, where the educational and qualification systems legitimate the existing differences" (Alcoforado, 2000, p. 114).

Some scholars including Reinbold and Breillot (1993) defend the idea that the qualification of citizens classifies individuals within the existing hierarchy, revealing differences that "serve socially as...[a] basis for employment, salary questions and attribution of responsibilities" (Pires, 2005, p. 280). Access to employment and a salary is based on this model—whether or not a person has a diploma.

A conceptual alteration that suggests an eventual change of paradigm seems to have occurred in the last three decades of the twentieth century with the slow devaluation of the school model based on qualification—all due to the shift in the job field, the growing valuation of knowledge, and the real-world capacities of individuals as opposed to the simple linear and repeated execution of certain tasks in specific contexts. A contrasting new concept occurs concomitantly—the competencies.

Inside the Conceptual Perimeter

As we reflected on these concepts, we could not help but consider what we deem the perspective of a prison of educational thought. The Portuguese educational system is substantively paced by the instrumentality of what the students learn.

The competencies are defined as the "capacity to mobilize the necessary knowledge to solve a problem which appears in the performed activity" (Gonçalves & Fernandes, 2007, p. 14), never appearing in isolation, but only in connection with other competences. If, as we referred to previously, the concept of competence frequently appears connected to the notion of qualification, then there are competencies that may not qualify. In reality, an individual's qualification may not be synonymous with his competence, although the opposite is also true (Alcoforado, 2001, pp. 78–79; Gonçalves & Fernandes, 2007, p. 14; Imaginário, 2007, p. 9).

There is a new approach to what individuals should learn, since they must always be able to respond adequately to permanent social change. There is a constant need for the qualification, development, and updating of competencies. This continuous quest to gain the qualifications to respond to the job market appears in the literature as a "process of merchandising of education" (Fidalgo & Fidalgo, 2007, pp. 53–59). Ávila (2008) refers to the Zarifian competence model as "a performing way in relation to the strong competitiveness and consequently to the permanent need for innovation" (p. 97).

The competence model associated with a capitalist economic paradigm is based on the importance of the knowledge, capacities, and skills transfer that although acquired in specific contexts can be used in other similar situations (Santos & Fidalgo, 2007, p. 83). When what we know is applied to a certain situation, it means that "the passage to the competence realized in the action, took place" as Le Boterf notes (1994, p. 16; cited by Alves et al., 2006, pp. 255–275). On the other hand, this new approach also leads to the development of new capacities and competences (the new worker profile), to new institutional organizational forms, and to personal, educational, labor and social relations (Alves, et al. 2006; Canário, 1996).

The new worker profile associated with the permanent need to update knowledge has some less positive aspects, such as greater individualization and competitiveness, especially in the so-called qualification centers and workplaces. There is a personal dimension that includes adaptability, employability, and informed citizenship (Alcoforado, 2001, p. 76) that is extremely important because, in our view, it is where an individualized perspective of education stands out. In reality, the building, maintenance, and reinforcement of an individual's productive capacity, employability, and adaptability seems more than ever to be a personal problem and circumstance that must be resolved by the individual himself. At present, individual autonomy and issues of freedom are paradoxically among the greatest dangers to exercising the right to education, because the fundamental collective responsibility and unavoidable social interest in the education of each citizen is being diminished by growing individual responsibility.

In this context, and taking these complex considerations into account, any attempt to define the competence concept is a biased process, in our opinion, because it expresses the axiological and political filters in which the different points of view on these definitions stand. In this context, Perrenoud (2005) has identified what he calls the three controversial but classical views:

1. the view that the competencies depend fundamentally on contextual factors—i.e., they are acquired and thus they depend directly on factors such as access to education and experience;
2. the view of the relationship between knowledge and competencies—some affirm that the overvaluation of the competence model affects the transmission and acquisition of knowledge; others, including Perrenoud (who emphasizes the need to apply multiple cognitive resources to discussion of the concept of competence), contend that the competencies are based on knowledge;
3. the existing notion of competence in the business world, which demands a new worker profile and new organizational forms, as we have discussed.

One of the previous views emphasizes not only the value of experience but also access to formal education systems as factors that contribute to the building of competencies. In reality, the equality of opportunity defended in contemporary societies is a value concretized in, among other things, access to formal education and qualification systems, which in turn must provide access to knowledge for all. The ancestral (yet not so old in the collective Portuguese memory) knowledge of how to read, write, and count is manifestly insufficient nowadays. In the complex information ocean we have plunged into, each individual is required to go beyond the reductive ways of producing knowledge, but he must be able to "transfer, use, reinvest and consequently, integrate that knowledge into competences" (Perrenoud, 2005, p. 69). Roldão (2003) affirms that we are being "bombarded" with different origins and references to the concept. Being more competent is, in his opinion, "being more able to use knowledge adequately" (pp. 15–16) in the different areas of knowledge and life spheres.

According to Auber et al. (1993, pp. 19–20, cited by Pires, 2005, p. 263), the different approaches to the competence concept have derived from three levels of analysis: (1) the individual level (psychology and education sciences); (2) the group/society level (sociology, social psychology); and (3) the business level (law, economy, and management). This multi-subject approach was developed by Pires (2005).

We first refer to the works of Noam Chomsky, who in the 1960s centered analysis within the linguistic point of view. He understood it as "a generic faculty, as a potentiality with a distinct significance of performance…a generative, transverse power, with a capacity which allows the adaptation to new situations" (Pires, 2005, pp. 264–266). Chomsky argued that the notion of competence sends us to an internal dimension as well as the external, which is more visible but often less structured. With that, Chomsky (1969, cited by Ávila, 2008) established a distinction between competence and performance: "The first corresponds to a group of nonobservable rules...in which a possibility of language development lies; the second remits explicitly for the behaviors, that is, for the language expression and use" (pp. 93–94).

In the area of labor psychology, we define competence by distinguishing it from other related concepts such as aptitude: "The competences cannot be developed without the support of the aptitudes; however it is not just related with aptitudes"(Pires, 2005, p. 267). In this epistemological context, the local dimension of competence is important, because a direct relation is established between what the competence is, the contexts and organizations in which it is built, and the circumstances in which it operates. The competence is then considered within the scope of a construction in which it is necessary to mobilize instruments and strategies in the cognitive field, and not only from what is observable through the individual performance (a manifestly behaviorist position). The social/collective dimension is emphasized above all in the Vygotsky theory, because individual learning concretizes itself in the social context, along with the others in the collective.

In the areas of education and qualification we find several definitions of competence. It has been particularly visible in these fields since the 1960s (in the English word *skill*), through the implementation of what was called pedagogy by objectives (Rey, 1998, cited by Pires, 2005, p. 276). Focusing this attention on the notion of an objective reveals the relation between three aspects: "the individual possibilities (postulated competences), his results (observable and measured competences) and the pedagogic action" (Arénilla et al., 2001, p. 106).

The transferability and mobility of knowledge also characterize the concept of competence, because it always builds itself within a certain context and they may be transferred to other circumstances. As Le Boterf (1994, p. 16) explains, the use of what we know indicates that the passage to competence has occurred, having been realized through action.

The competitive performance of an individual is nourished by the capacity to act in certain situations by mobilizing a group of resources (capacities, knowledge, learning, attitudes, and values) acquired in a specific context, but placed subsequently in the service of different tasks, requests, and contexts (Le Boterf, 1994; Perrenoud, 1997 in Rodrigues & Peralta, 2006, p. 233; Gomes et al., 2006, p. 33; Rens, 2001, p. 55; Ávila, 2008, p. 95).

If, as Perrenoud (Genile & Bencini, 2000) assumes, competence is the capacity to mobilize a group of cognitive resources to solve a series of situations with pertinence and efficiency, then competence is primarily "learning in use" (Perrenoud, 1995, cited by Roldão, 2003, p. 20)—that is, an individual's capacity to use that learning in different situations. This learning is not about theoretical content with little practical value but learning applied in concrete actions.

Let us now consider the different categories of competencies. Of the four that seem most significant, the first is presented by the European Industrialists Roundtable, which distinguishes five types of competencies: (1) technical and technological; (2) methodological and creative; (3) social, communitarian and relational; (4) participative and ethical; and (4) self-learning (European Commission, 1995, cited in Alcoforado, 2000, p. 137).

The second involves just two competence categories: technical, or connected to professional performance; and social, or occurring in everyday life and in interpersonal relations. They are called the key or transverse competences, which are useful in several contexts and frequently developed by Non Formal Education (Gonçalves & Fernandes, 2007, p. 15).

The third competence category is defended by Trigo (2002, p. 25), who gives us the competence group developed in the course of his work in adult education, including creation of the Adult Education and Qualification National Agency in Portugal (see Figure 1): (1) symbolic analysis; (2) social and behavioural; (3) directed to action; (4) scientific; and (5) technical and technological.

The fourth (Costa, 2002, p. 189) assumes three competence groups, based on what was proposed by the DeSeCo project: (1) operative, use of text and technologies; (2) self-oriented, acting autonomously; and (3) relational.

The Instrumental Line and the Old Reproduction

The prevalence of lines of learning in the school systems, which are anchored to competence-building based on the presumption that that action alone will lead individuals to a greater ability to create, keep, and develop their productive capacities, has crashed the cultural and humanist dimension of individual and institutional learning history and has diminished the traditional role of the school.

There is a tendency to align curriculum and educational objectives with the needs of the market. Increasingly, the citizens aware that the education system has social validity only if it is geared to the interests of the market. Naturally, the education systems in general and the curriculum in particular exhibit a functionalist structure that almost completely neglects the human and social dimension of education. When they realize the magnitude of this tectonic reorientation of their political priorities and consequent pedagogic approaches, the education systems resituate themselves in terms of their societal missions.

Paradoxically, what seemed to be a decisive step toward greater efficiency in public education may in fact become a setback for civilization. In reality, the educational system will "produce" different and segregated functional content. Such segregation will correspond to diverse and unequal salaries and distinct levels of public recognition. In fact, what we see is the reproduction of (pre)existing cultural patterns.

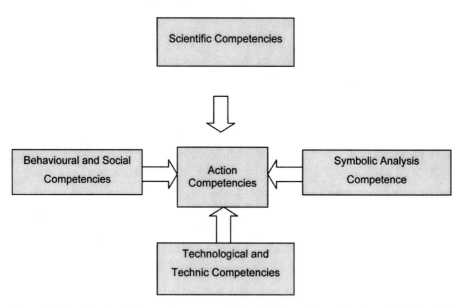

Figure 1. Classification of the action competencies. Reprinted from "Tendencies in People's Education and Qualification," by Maria Trigo, in *Adult Education and Qualification: Development Factor, Innovation and Competitivity*, edited by Isabel Silva et al., 2002, Lisbon: ANEFA. Reprinted with permission.

References

Alcoforado, L. (2000). *Adult education and work*. (Masters dissertation, Coimbra University).

Alcoforado, L. (2001). The competence model and the nonqualified adult Portuguese. *Portuguese Magazine of Pedagogy,*35(1), 67–83.

Alves M., Estevao, C., et al. (2006). Competence developing and assessing at school: Metanarratives of legitimation in confrontation. In G. Figari et al. (Eds.), *Competence assessment and experiential learning: Learning, models and methods* (pp. 255–275). Lisbon: Educa.

Amorim, J. (2006). *The impact of adult education and qualification in the vocational and citizenship development: The butterfly metamorphosis.* Lisbon: Ministry of Labour and Social Security.

Arenilla, L., Gossot, B., et al. (2001). *Pedagogy dictionary.* Lisbon: Piaget Institut.

Ávila, P. (2008). *The adult literacy: Key competences in the knowledge society.* Lisbon: Celta Edition.

Beane. J. (2002). *Curricular integration: The conception of the democratic education nucleos.* Lisbon: Plátano Editition.

Canário, R. (1996). Education and territory. *Noesis, 38,* 55.

Costa, A. (2002). Competences for the educational society: Theoretical issues and investigation results." In Calouste Gulbenkian Foundation (Ed.), *Crossing of learning: Sustainable learning* (pp. 179–194). Lisbon:

Fidalgo, N., & Fidalgo, F. (2007). Social reflections of the competence logic: The individualization process in focus. In Fernando Fidalgo et al. (Eds.), *Professional education and the competence logic* (pp. 17–70). Petrópolis, Brazil: Vozes Edition.

Genile, P. & Bencini, R. (2000). Construire des compétences: Entretien avec Philippe Perrenoud, Université de Genèv. *Nova Escola* (Brasil), 1, September. 19–31.

Gomes, M. et al. (2006). *Key competences reference for the adult education and qualification: Secondary level.* Lisbon: ME/DGFV.

Gonçalves, M., & Fernandes, M. (Eds.). (2007). *MAFL: Motivating adults for learning: The project histories.* Lisbon: National Agency for Qualification.

Imaginário, L. (2007). (Re)valuing learning: European practices and aswers to formal and non-formal learning validation. In *Valuing learning conference: European practices of informal and non formal validation practices* (pp. 1–17). Lisbon. (photocopied text).

Lages, M. (2006). From control evaluation control to process evaluation: The life stories and/or the narrative reason. In Albano Estrela et al. (Eds.), *XVII Conference ADMEE—Europe Minutes* Lisbon: FPCE-UL. (pp. 468–479).

Le Boterf, G. (1994). *De la competénce: Essai sur un attracteur étrange.* Paris: Les Éditions d'Organisation.

Perrenoud, P. (1999). Gestion de l imprevu, analyse de l action et constrution de competentes. *Education Permanente n° 140,* 123–144.

Perrenoud, P. (2005). *School and citizenship: The role of school in the formation for democracy.* Porto Alegre, Brazil: Artmed Edition.

Pires, A. (2005). *Life-long education and learning: Critical analysis of the competence and learning recognition and validation systems and processes.* Lisbon: Calouste Gulbenkian Foundation.

Rens, J. (2001). [Untitled text]. In *European conference on adult education and qualification: The key competencies for citizenship and employability* (pp. 51–53). Lisbon: ANEFA.

Rodrigues, P. & Peralta, H. (2006). Community programs of university exchange: Competence learning and development: Exploratory study in the Lisbon University. In Gérard Figari et al. (Eds.), *Competence assessment and experiential learning: Learning, models and methods* (pp. 229–254). Lisbon: Educa.

Roldão, M. (2003). *Curriculum management and competence evaluation: The teacher issues.* Lisbon: Presença Editor.

Santos, N., & Fidalgo, F. (2007). The (astray)way of competence certification in Brazil. In Fernando Fidalgo et al. (Eds.), *Professional education and the competence logic* (pp. 71–110). Petrópolis, Brazil: Editora Vozes Editor.

Sarmento, T, & Ferreira, F. (2006). Histories of life in adult education and qualification. In Albano Estrela et al. (Eds.), *ADMEE-Europe XVII conference minutes*. Lisbon: FPCE-UL (pp. 329–436).

Souza, D., & Dantas, J. (2006). Uma prática pedagógica interactiva na construção do saber. In Albano Estrela et al. (Eds.), *ADMEE-Europe XVII conference minutes*. Lisbon: FPCE-UL (pp. 986–999).

Trigo, M. (2002). Tendencies in people's education and qualification. In Isabel Silva et al. (Eds.), *Adult education and qualification: Development factor, innovation and competitivity* (pp. 23–30). Lisbon: ANEFA.

Warschauer, C. (2006). Portfolio: An instrument for experience acquired learning recognition. In Albano Estrela *et al.* (Eds.), *ADMEE-Europe XVII conference minutes*. Lisbon: FPCE-UL (pp. 803–810).

· 1 1 ·

Competencies

The Key to the New Curriculum

Juan Bautista Martínez Rodríguez

With the passing of time, the discourse of competence takes on a variety of meanings, until it eventually loses certain aspects of its history and begins to adopt new implications. It is important to recognize that there has been a certain loss of memory throughout the history of education, and that ideas used in the past such as "project methods," "integrated curriculum," "problem-based curricula," "situational learning," and "active schooling" do bear some relation to the different meanings of competency. Discourses, however, are forgotten; they mix and compete with others as they forge a path in pedagogical rhetoric or become part of daily practice. Yet, the problem still exists as to whether competence as a global discourse reaffirms professional autonomy, whether it takes into consideration our differences, thus allowing individual and creative development, whether it destroys them, or if there is a new epistemological colonization.

It is important to decide what social competences or skills students are to gain at school, and what other competences every professional should have after graduation, with special emphasis on the case of teachers. This concern for the skills students need now and later has long existed, and it has been expressed using different discourses and practices without specifically employing the term *competency*. In this chapter we do not attempt to unravel the confusion that exists around the definition of the word, nor do we attempt to give a precise definition of the approaches the word may represent as used in explicative or comprehensive theoretical and practical models (Jones & Moore, 2008). We are more interested in discovering why this approach based on competencies has been adopted in Spain; who has promoted it; the personal, political, or industrial interests of the groups that endorse it; and the social-science values and theories to which it may be related. In short, in this chapter we examine the benefits that the adoption of competences may provide to students in terms of knowledge and training, as well as the effects these political and professional decisions might have on the type of learning generated and the social control this competence-based approach might exert on students.

The Influence of International Agents, Curricular Policy, and Competence Discourse

The processes of globalization are marked by the local contexts of each country, but if we focus on the impact of external assessment models that operate therein, we can see how economic international bodies directly or indirectly affect educational policies and practices by means of highly complex processes (Teodoro & Montané, 2003).

The International Monetary Fund and the World Bank, created in 1944, took on board the theories of human capital. This led to the creation in 1948 of the Organisation for European Economic Co-operation (OEEC), within the framework of the Marshall Plan, which was designed to aid Europe's recovery after World War II. In 1961 this body became the Organisation for Economic Co-operation and Development (OECD). The OEEC/OECD has taken responsibility for collecting and publishing statistics on educational systems since 1959 and has been involved in major international statistical projects, including the Indicators of Educational Systems[1] project, conducted in conjuction with the OECD Centre for Educational Research and Innovation (Teodoro & Montané, 2008).

The impact of this research can be found in our educational policies, which have considered the curriculum an area of conflict, thus highlighting the political nature of such policies. Among other things, this implies that the curriculum selection of contents and training in competences are to be understood as a sociopolitical issue with clear economic influence. What began as an informative instrument is today interpreted as regulation of what to teach at schools. In this way, politics, curriculum, and assessment form part of a trilogy that legitimizes national educational policies through a kind of low-intensity globalization, which is based on the subtle and indirect influence of statistical indicators and competences in education. The curriculum has been invaded by a psychologistic vocabulary based on the terminology of competences, which, in this context, represents the introduction of curricular policy based on the accountability and transferability of competences and skills of students to the world of work (Teodoro & Montané, 2008).

The OECD is essentially an economically oriented body that, through the development of statistical projects such as Education at a Glance, is strongly influencing the transnational regulation of education. According to Bottani (2006), the OECD appeared once the International Association for the Evaluation of Education Achievement (IEA), which was created in 1961, had established a monopoly on research of the assessment of teaching systems.[2] This institution replaced the International Assessment of Educational Progress:

> The strategy of the United States has managed to weaken IEA, resulting in this institution losing its academic autonomy and, above all, bringing it into the sphere of influence of the U.S. In fact, the door was open for a third actor, the OECD, which came into play in 1993, when the latter realized that it could not assemble the information about students' learning which it needed to complete its indicators. The former IEA did not get it, and the new IEA was too much under the control of the U.S. to gain the confidence of every country. In 1997 the OECD Ministries of Education decided to launch a new type of survey about students' knowledge. In spring 2000, around thirty countries took part in the first Programme for International Student Achievement (PISA) (Bottani, 2006).

Today, useful and valued knowledge is considered that which is determined by the market through its regulating, prescriptive, and accepted narratives, in which adaptability, flexibility, effectiveness, and quality of knowledge is the most vivid exponent of a new protagonist: the OECD. Specifically, in 1988 the OECD began the Indicators of Educational Systems project, thus creating an international system of indicators for educational systems. The first version appeared in 1992, and the initiative was later expanded and improved until it gave rise to the Programme for International Student Assessment (PISA). The PISA was designed to provide recommendations to participating countries based on test results for 15-year-old students.

Although the PISA moved away somewhat from the work conducted by the IEA, it kept some major features of the original assessment: International support is strengthened—albeit the area of application is wider in PISA; tests are applied every three years to 15-year-old students; the focus is on three learning domains (reading, mathematics, and science); and competencies are adopted as an object of assessment. However, decisions about the PISA assessment produced some conflicts. The International Assessment of Educational Progress (IAEP) for mathematics and science adopted guidelines from the U.S. National Assessment of Educational Progress, and this caused problems with assessing local educational programs outside the United States because it ignored the influence of different settings on the teaching-learning process. At this point, the PISA and IAEP decided to become free from all national educational programs and measure only students' competences, thus becoming "neutral" with regard to the contexts of teaching and learning. This acquired "neutrality" allows for comparisons, but at the same time it destroys the contextualization of curriculum objectives, which are only superficially and fictitiously linked to competences.

As Bottani (2006) explains, the need for transition from IEA to PISA is clear, because the responsibility and resources for leading and regulating the evaluation process falls on the OECD-PISA rather than on each national government. Consequently, the academic community is, to an extent, relieved of its duties of evaluation for the benefit of this transnational agency. So there is a process of politicization that we must examine critically.

The information PISA provided should have enabled stakeholders to observe the factors associated with educational success, rather than just make comparisons of students' learning among countries in an isolated fashion. The respective national governments structured the results they wanted from PISA from a political perspective, grouping them into four thematic areas: "the quality of results in learning; equality in learning results and equal educational opportunities; effectiveness and efficiency of educational processes; and the impact of learning results on social and economic well-being" (Schieicher, 2006, p. 23). The tests were based on competences and given at three-year intervals, and countries were expected to participate for at least twelve years. The focus was on reading comprehension, mathematics, and scientific culture, and the population studied was 15-year-old students. The social, educational, and political impact of these tests has been significant. Results have been discussed in the media, and a parallel discussion on the state of education has been initiated in society and by scholars. On the one hand, PISA determines the structure of competencies; on the other hand, it defines social and educational success, which to a large extent determines educational reforms and curricular adjustments. Paradoxically, in the PISA findings, the only cause influencing the students' outcomes is the social makeup of population (Carabaña, 2008).

The current education indicators are not intrinsically "good" or "bad." Theoretically they are neutral and, indeed, may be useful for certain types of studies. As Díez (2007) notes, the term *indicator* has diverse meanings that depend on the context in which it is used. The PISA reports are what Díez calls the "externalization of failure, blaming the victim" (p. 10), which means that if school success depends on students' individual performance on the competencies, this implies that the responsibility for training is transferred from educational institutions to individual students. Montané (2008) argues that PISA represents a move away from previous large-scale studies in the sense that learning is no longer measured in terms of the acquisition of knowledge, but by assessments based on the development of human capital.

PISA is contained within another OECD program, the objectives of which are framed within the financial domain, which also influences decisions made about educational policy in different countries. This initiative, Education at a Glance, applies a generalized system of educational indicators, and it has direct repercussions on national policy in that it provides a statistical comparison of educational systems and gives the OECD a critical role as a globalizing agency. It is necessary to point out that its economic discourse does have an effect on the political discourse and that this in turn affects pedagogical discourse. However, this transfer from the economic discourse to pedagogical is not total, because the concept of competitiveness supported by the economic sphere differs from the idea teachers defend, at least in the case of Spain.

Historically, the OECD has provided a forum for the free exchange of ideas in matters relating to education. It also offered a space in which legislators and politicians could speak about their curriculum problems and governments could compare their views on educational policy. Today, however, the organization has become a political actor that attempts to influence, persuade, and direct member states toward a neoliberal ideology in the field of education (Rizvi, 2008). Thus, the OECD has gone from being a place of deliberation to being a channel for neoliberal proposals. Certain regions such as the Scandinavian countries have not engaged in this type of game.

The simple comparison of performance among countries is probably the least interesting form of analysis, even if this data is given the most attention in the media of many countries and is mostly likely to stir a desire to act when results are disappointing. With evidence of better performance in other countries in hand, a country with lagging results can raise national expectations or, alternatively, sell an apocalyptic vision of that national curriculum, depending on the electoral interests of each party.

Media interest in the PISA results has been widespread in most of the countries that take part in this project. In the case of Spain, there was less interest in the 2003 results of the comparison among countries than there had been for PISA 2000. Few articles provided complex analysis or examined areas such as the relationship between quality and equity. But these issues have been addressed by some educational administrations and are being discussed nationally and internationally.

A large-scale study carried out in Spain (Gil & Vilches, 2006) has shown that teachers have little or no knowledge of the contents and guidelines of the tests used in the PISA project. This is expected because, as the teachers interviewed indicated, they have received no official information at the school level, nor have they been encouraged to use the web pages that provide examples of the tests and the reasoning behind them.

Competencies at a National Level: The Case of Spain

In Spain, educational legislation passed in 1990 (LOGSE, 1990) introduced the concept of competencies into the field of vocational training and established the skills required for compulsory secondary education. A year later, the National Institute of Statistics established its own social indicators. Yet, the most important influence in terms of educational indicators came from elsewhere in Europe and from the OECD, which had published the first Education at a Glance report in which an entire group of indicators was specified. Spain's involvement in this new area of rhetoric became evident with the enactment of another educational law aimed at regulating the participation, assessment, and governing of schools (LOPEG, 1995), which attempted to support a new concept of "quality" and to introduce the "external assessment" of schools. Although the concept of a quality public education for all had been established by the LOGSE in 1990, the idea took on new meaning a few years later.

This change took root when the conservative Partido Popular assumed power in 1996, the year the Spanish National Institute for Quality and Evaluation presented its Assessment of Primary Education. One year later, in the northwestern region of Catalonia, proposals were made in regard to the definition of basic competencies. This was the same year the European Union backed the Definition and Selection of Key Competencies (DeSeCo) and the OECD began the PISA project, which established competence-based assessment.[3] Meanwhile, at the European political level, at the Lisbon Summit the establishment and recognition of professional competencies for member states was proposed. This suggests that the EU had a "regulatory ideal" in establishing educational policies aimed at the subordination of education to economics.

There is no doubt that the PISA reports raised expectations. The first report, PISA-2000, reached Spain when the Partido Popular had just won a second term by an absolute majority and was working on a global education proposal through their own legislation, Ley Orgánica de Calidad de la Educación (LOCE). This law was accompanied by a conservative counter-reform movement that favored the suppression of several Socialist Party initiatives included in the 1990 law. The PISA report's impact on the counter-reform was guided by conservative ideology that defended a "culture of effort" and greater elitist demands on the educational system, such as a greater concentration on conceptual-based and rote knowledge to the detriment of skills-based knowledge, for instance. These demands were maintained during debates on discipline, the repetition of academic grades based on the number of subjects failed, and streaming students according to their ability. This conservative attitude coincided with a certain distancing from European policies. In fact, no major study of the PISA results was undertaken in Spain, nor did the government disseminate the results. It was not until five years later, with the Socialist government again in power, that the National Institute for Evaluation and Quality of the Education System published the results from PISA-2000. Carabaña (2008) described the general results of the PISA studies as rigorous in describing student learning but weak in explanations of those differences that, in general, render them irrelevant as guides for educational action.

Reaction to the supposedly negative results of the PISA brought about modifications in educational legislation (Real Decreto 3473/2000, December 29), with an increase in the number of teaching hours per week assigned to reading and mathematics. There was no debate of the results of the national and international surveys, nor any serious reflection, apart from demands for greater effort on the part of students, more control and assessment of student performance, and differentiation of curriculum for secondary education students through a premature process of curricular pathways. The Education at a Glance reports continued to appear regularly, and in 2001 an important document was published by the Council of Europe, *Education and Training 2010*, which addressed the skills and competencies that formed the educational policy to be established by 2010.

The competencies introduced in Spain with the 2002 law that regulated qualifications and vocational training (Ley Orgánica 5/2002 de Cualificaciones y de la Formación Profesional) essentially applied the proposals made at the Lisbon Summit two years earlier. At the same time, the government published the major reform legislation LOCE, in which the concept of quality was seen in an intensified neoliberal light. During the years of right-wing rule there was an increase in the use of indicators and competencies, particularly at the university level, in response to proposals made at the Bologna Summit and demands from ANECA, the National Agency for Evaluation of Quality and Accreditation. What happens in higher education is in many respects a referent for the compulsory educational system, so this promotion of competencies and indicators at tertiary level created new arguments and increased pressure to adopt teaching through competencies in primary and secondary education.

The second PISA report, PISA-2003, was published in Spain in 2004, the year the right-wing Partido Popular lost the elections to the Socialist Party. The new government decided to suspend the introduction and development of the proposals made in LOCE, and via a high court ruling it withdrew the most important proposals. The Socialist government then passed its own new education law (LOE, 2006) that used results from other parts of Europe as a goal and moved closer to EU policies, despite the fact that these policies were mostly conservative. The main changes to the curriculum provided in LOE followed the same lines as those proposed by PISA, including organizing the curriculum around competencies. Time assigned to reading and mathematics was increased, and the controversial subject of "education for citizenship" was introduced.

To date, work on competencies has not begun in kindergarten, whereas primary and secondary education are regulated by the 2006 law. The preamble of the law alludes to the students' acquisition of "basic competencies" needed to function in society and "professional" competencies necessary for the labor market. These basic competencies are a core curricular element and are very much related to the historical process of assessing competencies. Specific aspects of assessment and promotion of basic competences are also treated in this bill, which specifies, for instance, the evaluation process and the promotion of these basic competencies, and alludes to the macro political context of the country within the diagnostic evaluation of competencies. However, Spanish tradition and the earlier influences on the adoption of competencies prompted the greater attention to professional rather than basic competencies in this law and in later legal and curricular developments. The 2006 bill also presents a more open and flexible set of competencies, undoubtedly taking into account possible future changes in circumstances. At the same time, the introduction of competencies as part of the basic curriculum had to fit with other curricular elements such as objectives, contents, and the three levels of specification of the curriculum—national and regional, school, and classroom—that are usual in Spain. Clearly, the history of the country initially conditioned a weak introduction of competencies as a curricular component because the classical curriculum design through objectives coexists with this concept of competencies.

Since the promulgation of this law in 2006, the competencies have been developed more fully in the annexes of legislation specifically aimed at primary and secondary education (Real Decreto 1513; Real Decreto 1631). This national legislation coincides with the recommendation of the European Parliament and of the European Council for the introduction of eight Key Competencies for Permanent Education (Official Journal of the European Parliament, 2006). Some questions arise about the way competencies were developed in Spain: Do the competencies appear as annexes in those decrees as a result of a possible contradiction between a national curriculum still based on objectives and the European recommendations developing a competency-based curriculum? That is, why is the traditional format of subjects and objectives placed alongside that of basic competencies? Are they compatible with the objectives, content, and assessment criteria of the objective-based curriculum, or do competencies make way for another type of organizational structure? For us, the answer is that political and administrative rationales force a decision that weakens the potential of competencies. The professional structure is not reformed, nor is professional development; subjects and subject areas are not changed, nor are curricular formats renewed. In order to facilitate the introduction of competencies, moves are made to rely on the much desired autonomy of schools and the framing of competencies in the second level of curriculum specification. Once again, an opportunity for a profound and progressive debate on the school curriculum has been lost.

As professional competencies as part of the curriculum historically have been one step ahead of other educational competencies in Spain, legislation passed in 2008 (Real Decreto 34/2008) regulates professional qualifications. A year later, additional legislation (Real Decreto 1224/2009) recognized that professional competency is to be gained through work experience. Moreover, proposals for professional background have sparked the introduction of competencies not only in vocational training, but also in the European Space for Higher Education. This implies the reinforcement of a technical rather than humanistic or practical approach that deals with the application of social skills, integral knowledge, and academic values in a different way. Curiously, we observe how few advances have been made with regard to the competency approach in comparison to older taxonomies based on skills, knowledge, and attitudes.

How the European Convergence in Higher Education Was Developed in Spain

Along with legislative developments in Spain, we have examined scientific and professional publications from Spain's ISOC database that deal with the subject of competencies during the last twenty years, and we have observed certain paradoxes that are illustrated in Figures 1 and 2. Here we highlight publications on competencies at the university level alongside those on secondary education and kindergarten, and we point to the large number of publications dedicated to linguistic communication.

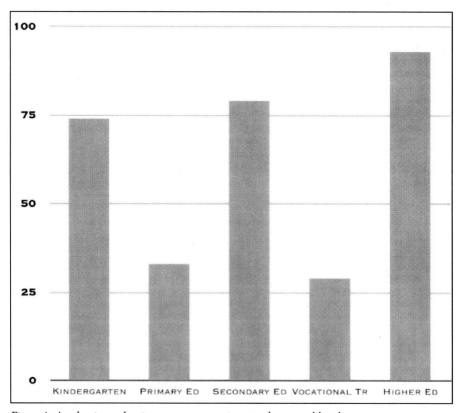

Figure 1. Academic production on competencies per educational level.

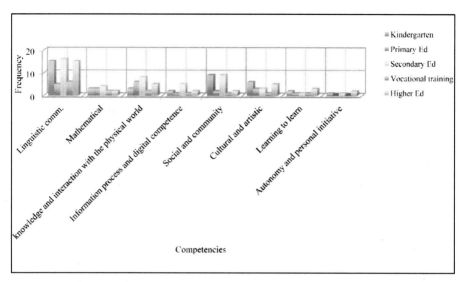

Figure 2. Academic production on competencies per competency and educational level.

The process of reform that accompanied the European convergence process in higher education basically consisted of the application the European Credit Track System (ECTS) as a way to unify the teaching and learning process in higher education in Europe; the implementation of competencies in programs; and adoption of the lifelong-learning model based on the student's learning.

The model of lifelong learning that is focused on the student again shifts responsibility for learning onto students themselves, overlooking the necessary and complex requirement of creating the right conditions for learning. Placing the burden of the teaching and learning organization on its learners requires an acute awareness of the conditions under which students should accept involvement in their own training. At the same time, the permanent nature of lifelong learning (Popkewitz, 2009) acquires a certain defective dimension—a pathological characterization that identifies the permanent deficits of citizens before examining their opportunities and needs in order to enable students to adapt themselves to these new conditions. Essentially, we are talking about the difference between a deterministic and uncritical vision of life and one that reinforces students' autonomy and their ability to intervene and, indeed, to participate.

In university circles, the evolution of the implementation of competencies has certain characteristics that are based on the political agents' ability and the convergence process in higher education with the EU. The Sorbonne Joint Declaration of 1998 gave the EU countries a statement on harmonization of the architecture of the European higher education system. This essentially began the process—strengthened by the Bologna Declaration a few years later—that created an easily comparable system of grades and cooperation in quality control that was adopted by EU countries, and promoted a European dimension in higher education through curricular development. But for universities, it was the Berlin Communiqué of 2003 that first used the word *competencies* and then created a general framework of qualifications for European higher education. During that same year, the Tuning Report provided a rich description of what competencies should be in higher education, based on empirical work (González & Wagenaar, 2003). ANECA almost simultaneously called for proposals (known as *Libros blancos*, or White Books) for different university degrees and applied the Tuning model of competencies. These White Books provided dissemination and application of this new model of teaching and learning in higher education to be implemented with the European convergence in both general and practical terms.

The work of Rychen and Salganit (2006), which was published about the same time, was by and large ignored, in spite of the fact that they have a much better defined theory on competencies based on a wider background, including social and cultural issues. Unfortunately, given the earlier mentioned DeSeCo project on competencies for Europe and the ANECA's stance, the impact of Rychen and Salganit was reduced.

The Socialist Party won the 2004 elections, and Executive Director of Education Alejandro Tiana collaborated with the DeSeCo authors on questions relating to competencies. The higher profile given to the White Books, which were ordered by ANECA and distributed the same year, meant that the Tuning model was strengthened. In 2005 the Bergen Communiqué adopted the proposal for quality standards from the European Association for Quality Assurance in Higher Education, as well as its competencies for European convergence and the new structure of higher education.

The history of the introduction of competencies in Spain's universities culminated with legislation in 2007 (Real Decreto 1393/2007 de Ordenación de las Enseñanzas Universitarias) that regulates general and specific competencies for undergraduate programs and master degrees. In 2010 the changing of ministers of education, the involvement of autonomous communities in university development, and the elitist decision taken at university level by bureaucrats and technicians all make up a picture of precipitate decisions, inbred powers, and political regulation that has led to an accommodation of what already existed rather than a projection into the future.

We agree with Lessard (2008) that there is something that does not quite work with the introduction of competencies. A lot of care has been taken with the introduction of new degree programs, as if they alone could constitute an effective curriculum. In reality, it is possible that we would have been better served with simpler programs that allowed the collective autonomous development of contents by those directly responsible for teaching in European universities.

Notes

1. See http://www.oecd.org/edu/eag2010 for 2010 indicators.
2. Association dedicated to the construction of large-scale student performance which compared results in different learning contexts.
3. PISA defines a competency as a combination of knowledge and skills "which is concerned with the capacity of students to apply knowledge and skills in key subject areas and to analyse, reason and communicate effectively as they pose, solve and interpret problems in a variety of situations" (OECD, 2007, p. 16).

References

Acevedo, J. A. (2005). TIMSS y PISA: Dos proyectos internacionales de evaluación del aprendizaje escolar en ciencias. *Revista eureka sobre enseñanza y divulgación de las ciencias, 2*(3), 282–301.

Bottani, N. (2006). La más bella del reino: El mundo de la educación en alerta con la llegada de un príncipe encantador. *Revista de Educación*, extraordinario, 75–90.

Carabaña, J. (2008). Las diferencias entre países y regiones en las pruebas PISA. Retrieved from http://www.colegiodeemeritos.es/DocumentosDelColegio_Document02_InformePisa/seccion=32&idioma=es_ES&id=2008052910570001&activo=1.do

Comisión Europea. (2005). *Progress towards the Lisbon objectives in education and training*. Brussels: European Community Commission.

Comisión Europea Dirección de Educación y Cultura. (2004). Competencias clave para un aprendizaje a lo largo de la vida: Un marco de referencia europeo. Programa de trabajo Educación y Formación 2010 Grupo de trabajo B Competencias Clave.

Diez, E. (2007). *La globalización neoliberal y sus repercusiones en la educación*. Barcelona: Roure.

Eurydice. (2002). Las competencias clave: Un concepto en expansión dentro de la educación general obligatoria. Madrid: Unidad Europea de Eurydice.

Gil, D., & Vilches, A. (2006). ¿Cómo puede contribuir el proyecto pisa a la mejora de la enseñanza de las ciencias (y de otras áreas de conocimiento)? *Revista de Educación*, extraordinario, 293–311.

Gimeno Sacristán, J. (2008). *Enseñar por competencias: ¿Qué hay de nuevo?* Madrid: Morata.

González, J., & Wagenaar, R. (Eds.). (2003). *Tuning educational structures in Europe. Final report. Phase 1*. Bilbao: University of Deusto.

Instituto de Evaluación (IE). (2007a). PISA 2006.I Informe Español. Madrid: MEC.

Instituto de Evaluación (IE), (2007b). PIRLS 2006. Informe Español. Madrid: MEC.

Instituto Nacional de Calidad de la Educación (INCE). (2000). *Sistema estatal de indicadores de la educación 2000*. Madrid: MECD.

Instituto Nacional de Evaluación y Calidad del Sistema Educativo (INECSE). (2003). Evaluación PISA 2003. Resumen de los primeros resultados en España. Madrid: MECD.

Instituto Nacional de Evaluación y Calidad del Sistema Educativo (INECSE). (2004). Sistema estatal de indicadores de la educación 2004. Proyecto. Madrid: MECD.

Instituto Nacional de Evaluación y Calidad del Sistema Educativo (INECSE). (2005). *Resultados PISA 2000*. Madrid: MEC.

Jones, L., & Moore, R. (2008). La apropiación del significado de competencia: El movimiento de la competencia, la Nueva Derecha y el proyecto de cambio cultural. *Revista de Curriculum y Formación del Profesorado, 12*(3). Retrieved from http://www.ugr.es/~recfpro/rev123ART7.pdf

Las competencias básicas y el currículo: Orientaciones generales. (2007). Cuadernos de educación 2. Santander, Spain: Consejería de Educación de Cantabria.

Lessard, G. (2008). Entrevista a Lessard. *Revista de curriculum y formación del profesorado, 12*(3).

Martínez Rodríguez, J. B. (2008). La ciudadanía se convierte en competencia: Avances y retrocesos. In J. Gimeno Sacristán (Ed.), *Enseñar por competencias: ¿Qué hay de nuevo?* (pp.103–142). Madrid: Morata.

Martínez Rodríguez, J. B., & Rivera. G. E. (2002). *La evaluación de la elaboración de los Proyectos Curriculares en los centros educativos*. Madrid: CIDE.

Organisation for Economic Co-operation and Development (OECD). (2002). *DeSeCo. Symposium: Discussion papers*. Paris: Author.

Organisation for Economic Co-operation and Development (OECD). (2005a). *Informe PISA 2003: Aprender para el mundo del mañana*. Madrid: Editorial Santillana.

Organisation for Economic Co-operation and Development (OECD). (2005b). *Mirada sobre la educación: Indicadores de la OECD 2004*. Paris: Author.

Organisation for Economic Co-operation and Development (OECD). (2005c). *The definition and selection of key competences. Executive summary*. Paris: Author.

Organisation for Economic Co-operation and Development (OECD). (2007). *PISA 2006: Science competencies for tomorrow's world*. Vol. 1: *Analysis*. Paris: Author.

Pérez Gómez, A. (2007). La naturaleza de las competencias básicas y sus aplicaciones pedagógicas. *Cuadernos de educación, 1*. Santander: Consejería de Educación de Cantabria.

Pérez Gómez, A. (2008). ¿Competencias o pensamiento práctico?: La construcción de los significados de representación y de acción. In J. Gimeno Sacristán (Ed.), *Enseñar por competencias: ¿Qué hay de nuevo?* (pp. 59–102). Madrid: Morata.

Perrenoud, C. (2004). *Diez nuevas competencias para enseñar*. Madrid: Graó.

Popkewitz, T. S. (2009). *El cosmopolitismo y la era de la reforma escolar*. Madrid: Morata.

Recommendation 2006/962/EC of the European Parliament and of the Council of 18 December 2006 on key competences for lifelong learning. (2006, December 30). Official Journal L 394 of the European Parliament.

Rizvi, F. (2008). La globalización y las políticas en materia de reforma educative. In J. L. Aróstegui & J. B. Martínez Rodríguez (Eds.), *Globalización, posmodernidad y educación: La calidad como coartada neoliberal*. Madrid: Akal-UNIA.

Rizvi, F., & Lingard, B. (2009). *Globalizing education policy.* New York: Routledge.

Rychen, D. D., & Salganik, L. H. (2006). *Las competencias clave para el bienestar personal, social y económico.* Archidona, Spain: Ediciones Aljibe.

Schleicher, A. (2006). Fundamentos y cuestiones políticas subyacentes al desarrollo de PISA. *Revista de Educación,* número extraordinario, 21–43.

Simone, D., & Hersh, L. (2004). *Definir y seleccionar las competencias fundamentales para la vida.* Mexico City: Fondo de Cultura Económica.

Teodoro, A., & Montané, A. (Eds.). (2008). *Espejo y reflejo: Políticas curriculares y evaluaciones internaciones.* Alcira: Germanía.

Torres Santomé, J. (2006). Los indicadores de rendimiento como estrategia y medida contrarreformista en las reformas educativas. In J. Gimeno Sacristán (Ed.), *La reforma necesaria. Entre la política educativa y la práctica escolar* (pp. 155–180). Madrid: Morata.

· 1 2 ·

Disability and Education

Transforming Difficulties into Possibilities

Miguel Lopez Melero

We are aware that when we take the first step we will not avoid making many and serious mistakes. Nevertheless, the entire problem is that the first step has to be taken in the right direction. The rest will happen at its own time. What is wrong will be eliminated, what is missing will be added (Vygotsky, 1979, p. 32).

To talk about disability and about education means talking about educational solutions to diversity-related problems, and the way these solutions have been implemented in schools. What disabled students must learn and how such learning process is carried out ought to be considered as fundamental aspects for the school curriculum.

During the second half of the twentieth century, educational responses to diversity were of two types, both influenced by medicine and psychology: Students were either "normal" or "disabled," and the two types required different teaching and learning processes. This dichotomy was justified by a diagnostic evaluation to determine who should receive "normal" or "special" education. Educational responses advanced from total exclusion of disabled people, who were overlooked and hidden in their homes, to their present recognition and participation in school life. This path began with disabled students being educated in separate schools, followed by educational reforms that recommended educating disabled students along with the rest of the student body. However, these latest changes were implemented without appropriate measures to guide the significant institutional transformation or to prepare teachers to deal with this new student population.

Human Diversity and Educational Responses

Many educational models aim for an educational response that takes into consideration the diversity of human beings. Historically, efforts to achieve social and cultural changes have been preceded by a general vision of the nature of humanity and society; that is, by reconceptualizing society and human existence, and offering a new concept of social and educational change.

When we realize the difficult situations and manipulations exceptional individuals experience—including educational inequalities that result from applying different pseudo-educational models—a two-pronged approach has to be taken in order to re-establish the right of education. First, we must assess educational practices that do not respect human diversity and that discriminate. Secondly, a more theoretical perspective makes it clear that inclusion does not mean that minority cultures and exceptional individuals[1] have to bend to conditions imposed by the hegemonic culture—in fact, precisely the opposite. A culture of diversity requires that society change its behaviour and attitude toward exceptional individuals so they are not forced to live under the tyranny of normality (Barton, 1998, 2008).

This new vision of exceptional individuals requires terms such as *deficient*, *retarded*, *subnormal*, and *sick* to be replaced by others that recognize these people's individuality and dignify them as human beings. This is the ethical value of the necessary paradigm shift, which aims to create a consciousness that stops us thinking about exceptional individuals as lesser beings and enables us to consider them human beings who are at school to be educated, not to undergo therapy.

It is easy to define these individuals but difficult to understand and to educate them. Thus, there are large differences between the various educational responses, which range from total exclusion to full inclusion. Although the inclusive process stems from integration programs, it should not be confused with them; indeed, inclusion arises because integration promises have not been kept and because of certain human rights violations. In this sense, several education strategies are offered:

Neglect or Abandonment Perspective (Exclusion)

It is important to remember that for much of history, individuals with a handicap did not count at all. They were excluded from any relationships or human interaction, were considered "nonhuman beings," and were treated with curiosity or disgust. Being different meant being subnormal, or invisible to the rest of the society. Moreover, although these individuals were not able to participate in building society, they were expected to follow the rules it imposed (Nussbaum, 2006). From this perspective, two kinds of exclusions were taking place: an *active* one, that is, a direct process of excluding or marginalizing individuals who were different; and a *silent* one, in which their rights and duties were taken away.

Perspective of Assimilation (Segregation)

At the beginning of the second half of the twentieth century, special education had no public profile; it was left up to charities or philanthropists. In 1968 a group of experts at UNESCO studied the conditions under which special education was taking place and then outlined principles of action for the necessary and adequate educational intervention. This group agreed that special education should be an enriched form of general education, but despite UNESCO's significant efforts to integrate special education into general education, all countries continued to offer special schooling in response to diversity, mainly because of strong medical and psychological influences. From a medical perspective, exceptional individuals are inferior biologically or physiologically. Psychology defines handicaps using instruments to categorize the abnormal and pathological behaviors of exceptional individuals. Psychology's attempt to classify these individuals does not seek to eliminate or heal deficits, as the medical model does, but instead tries to identify, classify, and adapt interventions to the handicap. Under this model, special education was understood as a technical educational response based on a student's handicap, a natural deficit that was part of the individual and independent of the context under which he or she developed. From this perspective, the classification itself seems to be more important than the transformational educational models which turn the difficulties or handicaps into opportunities for learning.

In Europe, political changes during the 1960s and 1970s also led to changes in how these inequalities were viewed, and a movement began to integrate and include minority cultures and exceptional individuals into normalized conditions (Nirje, 1979; Wolfensberger, 1972; Bank-Mikkelsen, 1973). Taking steps toward the educational and social integration of handicapped individuals was considered progressive.

In my view, a "before and after" in special education began in 1978 with the publication of the Warnock Report, which led to two important outcomes. First, exceptional individuals were addressed in less disparaging (if somewhat euphemistic) terms as those with "special educational needs," which provided a more optimistic vision of their cognitive and cultural possibilities. The emphasis is on competencies. Human development relates strongly to the context and should not be seen as a natural maturing process.

Second, it brought about changes in the teaching and learning process by proposing more open and integrative educational models. Yet, although thirty-three years have passed since the report was published, it has not achieved its two major goals: avoiding labeling and its negative effects, and changing teacher's minds about the cognitive and cultural competencies of exceptional individuals. In fact, in 1982 Mary Warnock criticized her own concept:

> Maybe the main reason for evident poverty in special needs lies in its definition...or better, in its lack of definition....The concept of "special need" encloses a false objectiveness. Because one of the main difficulties, certainly an overwhelming one, is to know who has special needs, or what special means. (cited in Slee, 1998, p. 137; translation my own)

Despite the shortcomings of the Warnock Report, an "integrative" path that led to the 1994 Salamanca Declaration[2] was undertaken after the speech on "Education for All" in Jomtien, Thailand in 1990.[3]

Integrative Perspective (Integration)

After the Warnock Report and continuing into the 1980s we witnessed a pedagogical movement that planned to change the goals and general benchmarks of schools—not only special education, but education in a broader sense. Three types of integration were possible: (1) physical integration, which satisfied vital and primary needs; (2) functional integration, such as the use of public transport, restaurants, sports facilities, and so on; and (3) personal integration, which addressed secondary needs and personal self-fulfilment.

This process of integration started in the 1960s and gradually paved the way to a movement that respects diversity and heterogeneity. Traditionally, schools had been homogeneous and uniform; this initiative opened up schools to become more heterogeneous and diverse.

One of the most forceful arguments segregationists used against these reforms was that "deficient" individuals did not develop cognitive or culturally because they had permanent defects. Yet, research in the field of integration has demonstrated the intellectual potential of exceptional individuals. Using adequate educational models, arguments that exceptional individuals' capabilities would not improve were dismantled. Results frequently showed these students adapting successfully to the school culture.

Integration was considered one of the greatest educational innovations, one that would allow all children the right to an education and would improve the quality of teaching and professional teacher training. Later, in 1990, the UNESCO conference in Jomtien reaffirmed the right of all children to education, regardless of their individual differences. At the Salamanca Conference in 1994, the idea that all countries should guarantee this right to education for all in their respective constitutions was solidified, and the international community recognized education as a fundamental human right. The Action Framework of the Salamanca Statement commits to this ideal:

> The Action Framework principle is that schools must welcome all children independently from their physical, intellectual, emotional, linguistical and other conditions. They must welcome handicapped and gifted children, children working or living on streets, children from distant or nomad populations, children of linguistic, ethnic or cultural minorities and children of other groups or underprivileged or marginalized areas. They all are challenges for school systems. In the context of this Action Framework, the term "special education needs" refers to children and young people whose needs stem from their capacity or their learning difficulties. Many children have learning difficulties at some time in their school life. Schools must find the way to successfully educate all children, including those with severe handicaps. (UNESCO, 1994, pp. 59–60; translation my own)

In summary, the Action Framework held that inclusion is a matter of human rights and not of charitable attitudes; inclusion exists when all children are educated in an ordinary education system; and when building an inclusive school, we help to achieve a more inclusive society.

Inclusive education humanizes us; exclusive education makes us less human. Thus, the right to an education becomes a right of all children—not only those who have special educational needs, but all those not currently receiving an education:

> [Education is the right of all children, even] those children deprived of the opportunity to learn and to obtain knowledge and capabilities to which they are entitled. It

is evident that the sources of difficulties are found not within themselves, but in the environments where they live. One of the greatest tasks for the future is to determine how this school, part of the social environment, can offer greater learning opportunities to all children, and try to unmask the idea according to which the greatest source of learning difficulties is the education system. (UNESCO, 1994, p. 15; translation my own)

Inclusive Perspective (Inclusion)

Inclusion in education means talking about social justice. If we call for a more just society, we need educational models that are more equal and fair, models where nobody is discriminated against because of handicap, religion, gender, ethnicity, country of origin, and so on. This is the position held by numerous authors (Barnes, 1992; Booth, Ainscow, & Dyson, 1998; Oliver, 1990; Shakespeare, 1993) who emphasize that inclusion is a social and political movement for change. Booth, Ainscow, and Dyson (1998) link their definitions of inclusion to two other concepts to help explain what inclusion means: the community concept and the participation one. They also add two more dimensions to further clarify and enhance the extraordinary force of this concept of inclusion. For the authors, inclusion is seen: 1) as a process always under construction, and 2) it is always connected to exclusion. Their stance is highly relevant because they highlight the interrelatedness of two key features: Inclusion means increasing exceptional students' participation in curriculum activities of ordinary school communities, while reducing their exclusion from communities and culture. In short, this process reduces exclusion and expands inclusion. If we make a statement about a certain school, saying that it is not inclusive, we must know why exclusion happens. Booth, Ainscow, and Dyson (1998) try to develop the general guidelines and proposals needed to produce changes in schools and classrooms.

To emphasize the importance of this understanding of inclusion, I present my own model of inclusive schools in which I explain the implementation of Project Roma in schools.[4] Our yet incomplete but heuristic approach to inclusiveness addresses the need for a school without exclusions, a school where the main aim is to avoid discrimination of all kinds. From my point of view, it is those individuals who are exceptional in some way that are the main reason for cultural change in public schools. Because of them, schools recover one of their reasons for exiting and functioning: to recognize and legitimize diversity as a human right and a value.

Talking about inclusion brings us to an examination of democratic practices, both educational and social. A democratic education relates to values of respect, solidarity, tolerance, cooperation, and participation. We understand that school democracy is about learning a lifestyle. Discussion of inclusive education relates to the search for equity, for social justice, for democracy and the fulfilment of human rights. It means talking about a humanization process that legitimates diversity and allows people to live their differences.

Inclusive Education as a Humanization Process

Europe's classrooms today are a cultural mosaic that presents a unique opportunity, a challenge to provide an education that aims at values such as mutual respect, participation, and coexistence. As Bengt Linqvist rightly recalled:

> Now, the challenge is to draw the requirements of a school for all. All children and young people of the world, with their strengths and weaknesses, their desires and expectations, have a right to education. It is not that our educational systems have a right to certain types of children. The country's school system must adapt to respond to the children's needs. (Lindqvist, 1994, p. 28; translation my own)

Inclusiveness has been and continues to be one of the central concerns of education policy in liberal democracies. It requires having schools and teachers who are adequately trained to welcome all children regardless of their physical, intellectual, emotional, and linguistic abilities. Some education professionals' understanding is that inclusive education is postmodern special education, and they assume that having handicapped children in their classrooms is what makes their schools inclusive, but this is not the case. Inclusive education is not related specifically to special education, but to education in general. However, as long as teachers keep talking about "special education" and integration of "special educational needs" and of "adapting curriculum," segregation will continue to be an accepted practice in our schools (Tilstone, Florian, & Rose, 2003).

Inclusive education is not the same as integration. Inclusive education is about breaking down barriers that prevent some children from learning in school. We should not blame learning difficulties on individuals, but on the curriculum. From this perspective, inclusive education is a process by which we learn from students' differing needs and abilities—in other words, it is a humanization process. Integration, in contrast, implies that individuals and minority groups who differ from the norm must adapt to the hegemonic culture. From a didactic standpoint, inclusive education means breaking down barriers that interfere with any child's participation in the knowledge-building process in the classroom. What are the barriers that make it hard for children to live and to learn together with their classmates? To identify the problems and learn how to overcome them is the ethical commitment of inclusive education.

Below, I provide a brief description of these barriers. The first is political in nature and relates to contradictory laws, rules, and norms regarding education for all individuals of all cultures. For example, while laws reference UNESCO's *One Education for All* (1990), at the same time they stipulate the existence of special schools; one curriculum for all children coexists with adapted curriculum, in common practice. There are laws that deal with cooperation among teachers, and there are laws that allow teachers to separate children with handicaps from regular classrooms. These contradictions blur the road toward building inclusive schools.

In addition, a widespread cultural barrier significantly hinders inclusion in education: teachers' obsession with diagnoses and assessments that look for reasons (and maybe excuses) why some children are unable to learn. In fact, the problem might be their own inability to teach these students. Intelligence tests and other evaluations have proven to be as discriminatory and segregationist as other barriers, which prompts the questions, what is intelligence, and what exactly do we mean by these diagnoses and by curriculum adaptations?

Is it appropriate to ask about the nature of intelligence? Historically, we have concluded that each human being is born biologically predetermined to be less gifted, gifted, or more gifted, following a Gauss curve. Therefore, intelligence has been considered an attribute of the individual regardless of the context. However, human beings come into this world, first and foremost, as raw material; culture completes us. Intelligence, like "handicap," is built by culture or its lack.

Diagnosis is a concept closely linked to the issue of intelligence. Conventionally, diagnosis has been a tool for labeling individuals as sick, retarded, subnormal, deficient—all of which fall into the human subcategory of disability. This concept of diagnosis is fragmented, static, and deterministic, and allows no possibility for change or growth. In my understanding, it is less a diagnosis and more a sentence that tells a child they will be as they are for the rest of their days. Diagnosis has to be understood not as a perverse control measure but rather a thereshold of knowledge—an open door to discovery and to inquiry: a permanent search. Individual development depends on education and culture—it is about what we can become with the help of others. A quality education will lead to quality development. These are the educational and ethical aspects of diagnosis.

Classroom Competitiveness Versus Cooperative Communities of Coexistence and Learning

Classrooms will have to be reorganized so that all children have the same opportunities in the knowledge-building process based on cooperative and dialogical learning (Freire, 1990). Thanks to handicapped individuals, those who are not handicapped in some way will benefit from interactions with others. Their dialogue, their sharing of different opinions and points of view and activities, the fact that they will establish common rules of coexistence, will improve and enlarge their world of knowledge and will transform the classroom into a truly coexisting and learning community. If all children are to have the same opportunities to participate in knowledge-building, the classroom will have to be reorganized.

Discipline and Textbook-structured Curriculum Versus Problem-solving Curriculum

In modern systems, the role of learning material has changed. It does not simply pass on information, but invites reflection and action. Moreover, gaining knowledge is not to be confused with accumulating information. Learning today must be based on real-life problem-solving. It should not be about imparting certain information, but about knowing what the learning potential is of each individual. We have to teach students how to think, how to communicate and how to act correctly.

Is it possible to generate teaching and learning processes in the classrooms that allow all children to learn together, regardless of their cognitive, cultural, ethnical, or religious peculiarities? This question has engendered two opposing educational practices. The first belongs to those who defend the idea that schools have to offer a common curriculum, the second to those who believe that a dual curriculum is necessary.

From a didactic point of view, curriculum adaptation means deciding a priori to offer a lesser quality education based on lower education expectations to the handicapped/diverse student body. Certainly, those who receive an education of poorer quality would not achieve the same results as their peers who receive a higher quality education, nor would they develop their full potentials.

In agreement with Vygotsky (1995) that cognition depends on culture, and without falling into a blind pedagogical optimism, I assert that there are reasonable expectations about all students' cognitive potential, as all individuals have the ability to learn. They only need the right kind of education, which can be achieved only by turning classrooms into democratic learning communities in which difficulties become possibilities. The project method (Dewey, 1916/1971; Kilpatrick, 1918) offers a good model, particularly the research projects developed by Project Roma, which have shown good results since 1990. This methodology favors autonomous learning for all students by using real-life decisions and developing strategies to "learn how to learn." This involves developing a logical thinking process and knowing how to create mental routes for children, which I consider to be more important than focusing primarily on results (López Melero, 2004).

The Traditional Classroom Organization in Time and Space Versus an Ad-hoc Classroom Organization

Working according to the project model requires heterogeneous grouping of children and change in the classroom in terms of time and space. Interactive teaching and working in heterogeneous groups should be guiding the new classroom structure. Students will learn to help each other, and those without disabilities will provide important support to those who do have difficulties, essentially creating a student support unit. Accomplishing this will require schools to be organized in a cooperative way. Students will no longer passively receive information and follow rules, but instead will learn by actively selecting, exploring, and transforming their learning material together with their peers. Ideally, students will learn to love a learning culture they share with their teachers and peers in which they build knowledge through cooperative learning with the teacher as the cornerstone.

Teacher as Rational Technician Versus Teacher as Researcher

In an inclusive school, the role of the teacher is not to transmit past knowledge to students, but to communicate to students how knowledge not yet existing is built. The corpus of knowledge will be constructed through a process of inquiry carried out by children, together with the teacher. The teacher traditionally has had three roles: to transmit learning material, to evaluate student progress and achievement, and to provide a model of an educated person. In inclusive schools, the role of the teacher is different. He or she first must know how to work in classrooms that are heterogeneous in terms of ethnicity, gender, handicap, religion, origin, language, and so on. Therefore, he or she will not think in terms of an "average" student, but will consider each child's individual needs and potential.

This will require teachers to learn other teaching models. They should participate in projects, seminars, teamwork, and other situations in which knowledge is built cooperatively. This will make the teacher's work more original and more creative, but also more demanding. Socioconstructivism offers many possibilities by underpinning the theory that development of individuals depends on culturally rich contexts. Human cognition is due to culture (Vygotsky, 1975).

A new type of professional is necessary to bring about the transformation that the diversity culture requires. From being a teacher who implements techniques and procedures, he or she will become a researcher who knows how to open spaces so that the classroom can become a place of shared and autonomous learning rather than an instrument of the system. By promoting autonomy and freedom, the teacher will express his or her commitment to change and social transformation. This emancipated individual will improve practices by sharing reflections on their classroom practices (Kemmis & McTaggart, 1998). From my own experience as director of a research group and working directly with school teachers, participative action-research has allowed us to change our thinking and our speech by sharing our thoughts on problem situations in classrooms (self-reflection). This has lead to better teaching practices. Thinking about practices is a good example of how we can break classroom routines. The dialectic action-reflection-action conditions the thinking as well as the action by mutual enrichment. We agree with Freire, who reminds us that conscience is not transformed by attending seminars and speeches or by eloquent sermons, but by the action of human beings It implies a union of theory and practice that will constitute and become a steady movement from practice towards theory and from here to new practices (Freire, 1990).

From Antidemocratic Schools to Democratic Schools

Values education is essential in public schools to help students become responsible citizens. However, this is not only the teacher's duty; it is a responsibility that must be shared among families, teachers, and other educational stakeholders (NGOs, the media, and so on). This educational co-responsibility brings together children, their families, and their teachers in a way that enables them all to learn from one another and together. Families and teachers will learn to understand and value the role each has in educating our children and in changing today's social values of competition, divisiveness, and lack of respect for diversity. We will alter the antidemocratic educational model only by creating a living democracy in our schools, one that values liberty, generates respect and tolerance, and promotes equality.

Education for democratic and participative coexistence will allow us to build a society and a new humanization process in which pluralism, cooperation, tolerance, and liberty will be the values defining relationships between families and teachers, teachers and students, and teachers and the teaching community—where human diversity is recognized as an element of value and not as a human disgrace.

Finally, building schools that have inclusive cultures, inclusive policies, and inclusive pedagogical practices will not be accomplished by simple pedagogical practices. A more complex pedagogy is needed to help individuals of all abilities and cultures to "learn how to learn." In addition to the aforementioned Project Roma, other examples of cooperative pedagogical practices include the School Development Program of Professor James Comer at Yale University (1968, 1998, 2001); the Accelerated Schools Program created in 1968 by Professor Henry Levin at Stanford University; and the group of projects called Education for All, created by professors Robert Slavin and Wade Boykin (1996, 2001) of the Research Center at Johns Hopkins University. These programs demonstrate that a school without exclusions is possible, and that it only takes a change in attitude to start the transformation processes.

Through our own educational practice and our research, we have contributed to the construction of an inclusive quality education. By respecting the individual needs of each child, Project Roma, as an ethical model, upholds public schools as one of the cultural spaces responsible for ensuring a democratic coexistence and quality education. By accepting diverse cultures, public schools today are demonstrating respect for human rights. This entails avoiding injustice by not allowing two types of curriculum in the classroom, thereby contributing to a type of education that helps build a new civilization. What is needed are teachers who commit to democratic principles and who believe that the most important matter is not instruction or the delivery of previously constructed knowledge, but knowing how to create democratic environments in which students are socialized and receive values education. In school, students must learn how to live, or better, how to live together. It is not about teaching diversity as a value, but about living democratically in classrooms with respect, participation, and coexistence. This is what inclusive education is about.

Notes

1. I define exceptional person as a person who is having learning difficulties because of a peculiarity/handicap of some kind.
2. The Salamanca Statement on Principles, Policy and Practice on Special Needs Education and Framework of Action held in Salamanca, Spain on June 7–10, 1994 (UNESCO).
3. The World Conference on Education for All held in Jomtien, Thailand, on March 5–9, 1990 (UNESCO).
4. Project Roma has established inclusive schools in Mexico (Guadalajara), Brazil (Belo Horizonte), Chile (Santiago), Argentina (Mendoza), Peru (Lima), and Spain (Málaga, Murcia, Alicante). As a research project, it examines ideas on building a new theory of intelligence through development of cognitive, metacognitive, linguistic, emotional, and autonomous processes of the human being. As an educational project, its final and fundamental purpose focuses on improving family, school, and social contexts based on democratic coexistence and mutual respect, as well as personal, social, and moral autonomy.

References

Ainscow, M., Hopkins, D., Southworth, G. Y., & West, M. (2001). *Hacia escuelas eficaces para todos, Manual para la formación de equipos docentes*. Madrid: Narcea.

Bank, Mikkelsen, N. E. (1973). *The principle of normalization*. Copenhagen: Danish National Board of Social Welfare.

Barnes, C. (1992). Qualitative research: Valuable or irrelevant? *Disability, Handicap and Society, 7*(2), 115–124.

Barton, L. (1998). *Discapacidad y sociedad*. Madrid: Morata.

Barton, L. (2008). *Superar las barreras de la discapacidad*. Madrid: Morata.

Booth, T., Ainscow, M., & Dyson, A. (1998). England: Inclusion and exclusion in a competitive system. In T. Booth & M. Ainscow (Eds.), *From them to us* (pp. 193–225). London: Routledge.

Comer, J. (1968). *Comer school development program*. New Haven, CT: Yale University.

Dewey, J. (1971). *Democracia y educación*. Buenos Aires: Losada. (Original work published 1916).

Freire, P. (1990). *La naturaleza política de la educación. Cultura, poder y liberación*. Madrid: Ed. Paidós.

Kemmis, S., & McTaggart, R. (1988). *Cómo planificar la investigación-acción*. Barcelona: Alertes.

Kilpatrick, W. (1918). The project method. *Teachers College Record, 19*, 319–335.

Levin, H. (1994). *Accelerated schools after eight years*. Palo Alto, CA: Stanford University.

Lindqvist, B. (1994). Necesidades educativas especiales: Marco conceptual, planificación y factores políticos. En UNESCO. *Informe final: Conferencia mundial sobre necesidades educativas especiales: acceso y calidad. 27*. Madrid: UNESCO/Ministerio de Educación y Ciencia.

López Melero, M. (2003). *El proyecto Roma. Una experiencia de educación en valores*. Málaga, Spain: Aljibe.

López Melero, M. (2004). *Construyendo una escuela sin exclusiones. Una forma de trabajar con proyectos en el aula*. Málaga, Spain: Aljibe.

Nirje, B. (1969). The normalization principle and its human management. In R. Kugel & W. Wolfensberger (Eds.), *Changing patterns in residential services for the mentally retarded* (pp.179–195). Washington, DC: President's Commission on Mental Retardation.

Nussbaum, M. (2006). *Las fronteras de la justicia. Consideraciones sobre la exclusión*. Barcelona: Paidós.

Oliver, M. (1990). *The politics of disablement*. Basingtoke, UK: Macmillan.

Shakespeare, T. (1993). Disabled people's self-organization: A new social movement? *Disability, Handicap and Society*, 8(3), 249–264.

Slavin, R. (1996). *Education for all*. Lisse, Netherlands: Swets & Zeitlinger.

Slee, R. (1998). The politics of theorising special education. In C. Clark, A. Y. Dyson, & A. Millward (Eds.), *Theorising special education* (pp. 126–137). London: Routledge.

Tilstone, C., Florian, L., & Rose, R. (2003). *Promoción y desarrollo de prácticas educativas inclusivas*. Madrid: Editorial EOS.

UNESCO. (1981). *Declaración sobre la raza y los prejuicios sociales*. Paris: Organización de las Naciones Unidas para la Educación, la Ciencia y la Cultura.

UNESCO. (1990). *The Dakar framework for action*. Dakar: Author.

UNESCO. (1994). *Salamanca statement and framework for action on special needs*. Salamanca, Spain: Author.

Vygotsky, L. S. (1979). *El desarrollo de los procesos psicológicos superiores*. Barcelona: Crítica.

Vygotsky, L. (1995). *Fundamentos de defectología: Obras completas*. 5 vols. Havana: Editorial, Pueblo y Educación.

Warnock, M. (1978). *Special educational needs: Report of the committee of enquiry into the education of handicapped children and young people*. London: HMSO.

Wolfensberger, W. (1972). *The principle of normalization in human service*. Toronto: National Institute on Mental Retardation.

· 1 3 ·

Curricular Tensions and the Struggle for Justice in Neoliberal Times[1]

Jurjo Torres Santomé

Despite its disastrous consequences, the current worldwide economic crisis provides an excellent opportunity to rethink our position regarding the types of societies we should aim for, given the enormous authoritarian power now exercised by large economic corporations whose operations are fed by insufficient regulation from the political establishment. This situation arises as a result of policies that have progressively weakened citizenship, thus creating ever more obstacles that keep citizens from analyzing and evaluating local and global events. In the last few decades, progressive social and community organizations have been subject to attacks that have left them completely debilitated; at the same time, individuals concerned with the public sphere have become suspect. Community ties have been severed, and it is now becoming clear that only by recovering these community institutions and reinforcing the values of a democratic and responsible citizenship, including solidarity—in other words, by regaining the true value and significance of politics—will we be able to find our way out of the crisis. The direction taken should be guided by a key objective: to transform the world, its institutions, and the obscurantism that underlies their functions in order to build societies that are more open-minded and just, and that include strong democratic frameworks whereby citizens may regain their true role: that of exercising control over, and making decisions about, the present and future of humanity.

Drifting Concepts and Demobilizing Resignifications

A first step toward citizen[2] empowerment at the current historic juncture involves awareness about the main obstacles to active civic engagement. One difficulty relates to language: specifically, to the extent to which many political concepts are adrift in a sea of words. These words have been stripped of their original meaning and are all too often distorted, misinterpreted, and taken to mean the opposite of their widely accepted signification. Thus, it is becoming increasingly difficult to discern exactly what speakers are referring to when they resort to such discourse.

Since the mid-twentieth century, the political Right has developed a series of manipulation strategies including this kind of resignification of progressive concepts embraced by the Left, concepts that have been arduously defended in order to create a better world, such as democracy, social justice, equality, fraternity, solidarity, redistribution, recognition, and so on. Right-wing appropriation of such value-laden terms sets out to "change the frame associated with a word so that it fits the conservative worldview" (Lakoff, 2006, p. 43). Thus, when the right wing speaks of "a return to values," it is in fact an attempt to promote greater submission, obedience, and discipline through education. When it alludes to the importance of the family, the call is for a return to patriarchal values. When it proclaims the "right to life," the sole concern is prohibiting abortion. In contrast, advocating for accurate and informative sex education, or even for something as basic as combating hunger and poverty—which are the chief causes of infant mortality today—is not on the agenda.

The same holds true for "quality" and "excellence" in education, in which case the aim is to ensure that only children from the most economically and culturally powerful groups have the right to higher education, and to the benefits it entails. On the road toward this right-wing resignification of language there is a moment just before the process is set in motion when concepts holding the greatest potential for social mobilization are stripped of their true meaning. This is accomplished when such terms are actively and almost exclusively employed in and associated with routine bureaucratic contexts—a process which obfuscates their original meaning, true scope, and potential mobilizing force for change. Making the commitment to organize a school democratically is easier said than done, as is putting into practice an open curriculum that is both relevant and significant to students. These are goals that have generated reams worth of writings but unfortunately they rarely have been achieved.

As these concepts, which usually arise within the framework of progressive philosophies, are legislated and implemented, they eventually lose their power to transform, and thus become depoliticized. From then on they are used quite flippantly and, more critically, without any concern for changing the practices and routines of those who now ascribe to them.

This appropriation of progressive language also accomplishes another important objective right-wing supporters have long striven for: persuading people to believe there are no longer any conflicting ideologies or political alternatives. A glance at statements that abound in the media quickly confirms how these same concepts, which once appeared on banners protesting injustice, have been reduced to mere slogans and pet phrases that anyone can use, as they no longer have critical meaning.

It is precisely this depoliticization of thought adopted by most public and private institutions that is behind the growing pressure to privatize education in Spain. This type of reorientation is all too frequently found in alarmist discourse around educational institutions today, whereby information about poor school performance or problems and conflicts in the classroom is exaggerated. This arouses the interest of authoritarian personalities whose worldview is rooted in the educational, social, cultural, and military policies enforced during the forty-year dictatorship to perpetuate its own power. These personalities, who have remained dormant or lethargic over the last three decades of democracy, have now been awakened by a much younger group of right-wing supporters whose leaders have easy access to influential media to serve their interests. These leaders have received a classist, sexist, racist, and conservative education based on silence in some cases and on the manipulation of human history in others. The groups at the bottom rung of the social ladder, for whom gaining access to culture and relevant information is particularly difficult, are most easily persuaded by the strategies employed by the most populist and demagogic sector of the political right.

The advance of this neoliberal and neoconservative agenda paves the way for the acceptance of policies that reflect a strong mercantilist orientation, which implies strict authoritarian control of the educational system (Santomé, 2007). These policies are supported by the manipulation of words with positive connotations, such as *efficiency*, *excellence*, *quality*, and *competition*, now used as slogans to disguise measures designed to reorient curricular content, methodologies, and assessment methods. The criteria upon which the external evaluation of schools is based are never subject to public debate, because such evaluation relies on supposedly fair tests or ostensibly objective data. As currently conducted within the Spanish context, this type of evaluation helps reinforce the imposition of a curriculum that is becoming increasingly standardized. This trend is supported by large textbook publishers, some of which are multinational corporations feared by the government due to their control of the major information networks: newspapers, television networks, magazines, Internet portals, and so on. These types of tests further accentuate the privatization policies being applied in schools, and legitimize pressure from the entrepreneurial sector to render the educational system subservient to its needs by promoting the kind of knowledge and lines of research that maximize financial, strategic, and corporate benefits.

The Curriculum at the Neoliberal and Neoconservative Juncture in Global Societies

It is essential that a detailed analysis be conducted of the principal measures undertaken in the last few decades by institutions focused on globalizing policies, for they are presented to the public as if they hailed directly from the Oracle of Delphi. Institutions such as the Organisation for Economic Co-operation and Development (OECD), the World Bank, the International Monetary Fund (IMF), the G8, and the World Trade Organization (WTO) cooperate with and advise the majority of the world's countries based on their diagnoses. An analysis of their track records demonstrates that their efforts and reports are designed to redirect educational systems toward models that are in line with neoliberal philosophies. Their objective is to persuade not only the ruling classes but also a significant part of the citizenry that the main objective of schools—in fact, their sole objective—should be to train and prepare students to compete in the workplace in the current capitalist market. Meeting this objective entails redirecting school content and tasks, primarily by reducing the time devoted to the social sciences, the humanities, and the arts, while reinforcing the knowledge and skills required for the workplace.

The analysis and advice offered by these institutions serve their objective: to contribute to the production of "human capital" rather than fostering concerned citizens interested in public affairs. Thus, little by little, classic educational goals are taking on a secondary role, including helping to increase the levels of justice and equity in society; eliminating discrimination and marginalization; reinforcing models and structures that promote participation in democracy; and educating citizens for the kind of democratic participation that includes identifying the repercussions of specific models of globalization and condemning global warming, petroleum wars, the oppression of certain ethnic groups, cultural and political and economic neocolonialism, and hunger and disease in particular areas of the world.

It is striking that with every change of government in Spain over the last few decades, new educational reforms have been developed and implemented. This is particularly evident in market-driven policies that call for redirecting "the information society" toward a "knowledge-based" economy. This latter term refers to the focus on knowledge as raw material in order to maximize profits in a market economy.

Documents that urge countries to adopt a knowledge-based economy, such as those drawn up by the OECD (1996b), highlight the new ways market economies function. At the same time, they set the guidelines in terms of priorities and the direction educational systems and research policies should take. Measures designed to force educational systems and research networks to take on this challenge—for example, the Programme for International Student Assessment (PISA), and the Trends in International Mathematics and Science Study (TIMSS), which saturate the mass media and policy makers with exclusively scientific data and subject matters and thus relegate into a very secondary place the value of the social sciences, humanities, arts education and sex education—have multiplied in the last few decades, due to the intimidating pressure these economically oriented organizations impose on our social reality. Their influence is also seen in governments' redirection of investment toward this end.

As a result of these new economic models, evaluations and comparative studies play important roles in telling both governments and citizens when we are or are not headed in the right direction. Comparative diagnostic studies highlight theoretically relevant results that indicate how far we have come and how much further we must go before goals are met.

It is no coincidence that in assessing social progress, only variables that help calibrate the power of the market economy are taken into account, such as the number of personal computers per capita; the percentage of people with Internet access and the type of access they have; the number of mobile phones; the number of households with a satellite dish or cable television; the amount of economic transactions carried out via the Internet; and so on. These surveys focus on the volume of business generated by the industries that manufacture and commercialize these technologies, rather than determining how they are used by citizens able to purchase them.

The demand is for knowledge that will help increase business opportunities and thus allow companies to continue to innovate, thereby generating new consumer needs so that people will be willing to do whatever it takes to acquire the new products.

At present, given the enormous impact of the Programme for International Student Assessment (PISA) and the apparent neutrality of its sponsoring organization, the OECD, this institution claims sufficient power and authority to impose a model of quality in education that has real potential to generate progress, wealth, welfare, and the justice this implies. Michael N. Barnett and Martha Finnemore (1999, p. 713) refer to these types of economic, transnational, and extra-governmental organizations as the missionaries of our time who are intent on spreading good news about the true keys to economic, cultural, and social progress. However, these organizations do not feel obliged to explain such models or to identify the criteria upon which their guarantees of success are based.

These redirecting strategies are based on empirical data claimed to be objective and neutral and are therefore more easily accepted by a public accustomed to perceiving statistics as irrefutable evidence. We should not forget that schools have taught citizens to highly value numerical data, and that in a number of cases it was in the aforementioned "hard science" subjects that many students struggled through purely rote learning pedagogies. We live in a time dominated by statistics, which are professed to offer an x-ray of contemporary life. However, the variables are chosen, organized, and interpreted according to the interests of the organizations that publish them.

True to its etymology, statistics—from the Latin *statisticum*, as well as a political arithmetic originating in seventeenth-century England that gave rise to "the science of the state"—are associated with the construction of the state inasmuch as only those data and variables that governments selectively publicize have been used to administer state territories and resources, and to unify cultures and the various mindsets that make up nations (Desrosières, 2004, p. 8). It is claimed that such studies of the state offer an objective description of its peoples and possessions, the actions it undertakes, and the events occurring within its boundaries. The kind of data collected therefore facilitates state control and administration. At the same time, publishing such statistics convinces the population that the measures adopted by the government are, in fact, the most pertinent in terms of resolving the inadequacies brought to light.

We cannot overlook the fact that the present PISA results have the power to persuade the public about what constitutes a good educational system and, by extension, sound educational policy. The results are presented as objective and neutral, and are therefore not open to debate.

Moreover, to avoid accusations that the OECD may be attempting to introduce specific cultural content into the curriculum or to favor certain cultural groups, the organization resorts to using the terminology of "competencies." This involves analyzing cognitive competencies that can be developed within any of the content areas under evaluation. The results of comparative studies have been presented as evidence of the success of an open curriculum that may be applied to any subject area, thus ensuring administrative approval because such diagnoses protect administrators from accusations of bias in terms of the educational choices adopted for the so-called basic curricular design. The result is a model of education where content takes second place to a focus on developing "competencies." This is the underlying philosophy that allows PISA tests to be administered without taking into account the fact that certain subjects are compulsory in every country that uses the test.

We cannot ignore the fact that PISA assesses only three areas: reading comprehension, mathematical ability, and scientific literacy. Once the test results are made public, these areas of knowledge immediately become the focal point for state and regional administrations, which subsequently direct their efforts at reinforcing these three content areas by allowing schools to dedicate more time and greater resources to them. The results also become a focal point for families and students, who soon become aware of the hierarchy of subjects in the school curriculum and accept that what really matters are scores in mathematics and science, while the remaining subjects are considered easier and/or less important.

It is important to point out that these tests do not assess the content of either the compulsory curriculum imposed by the national and regional education ministries or any other subject areas. In other words, they do not evaluate fundamental knowledge, procedures, and values, including artistic knowledge and skills; the capacity to interpret historic, political, and social processes; communicative competence; literary knowledge and critical thinking skills; ideas about affection and sexuality; and psychomotor skills and sports education. Nor do they address concepts of responsible citizenship within a democratic framework, such as human rights education; conflict resolution; student participation in school life; debating skills; cooperation and the value of helping others; civic responsibility and commitment to democracy; and education in human values, among others. Interestingly, educational policies give these areas of knowledge low priority, and they are consequently generally neglected in schools.

The emphasis on reorienting knowledge along neoliberal lines affects research policies, teaching practices, and learning, and it is also evident at elitist forums such as the meetings of G8 and G20 education ministers. For example, at the 2009 G8 summit, where representatives from twenty nonmember countries and ten international organizations were also invited to participate, the report "Sharing Responsibilities to Advance Education for All"[3] was approved. In addition to making some rather altruistic declarations of intent that in no way imply any obligation or decisive action, the report states that after primary school, the main objective of the educational system is to enhance "skills development for employability" (p. 6).

It is also striking that the few curriculum revisions proposed by educational authorities in terms of compulsory content incorporate these economy-oriented dimensions. This is certainly true of the new subject matter proposed for economics taught at the secondary level in Spain, which includes "financial education" (Ministerio de Educación, 2009). According to Education Minister Angel Gabilondo, this type of education "allows our youth to learn about and understand things like mortgages, bank accounts or shares. This will prepare them to face the necessary and complicated world of economics and finance" (Ministerio de Educación, 2009). The Ministry of Education claims that this educational program is being developed in collaboration with the Bank of Spain and the Spanish National Securities Market Commission, and is expected to be launched in the 2011–2012 academic year. Spain's BBVA Bank is designing a similar curriculum project for children at the primary school level. In addition, from 2012 the PISA assessment of many countries, including Spain, will include the evaluation of financial education.

These subjects are a necessary part of a well-designed curriculum in a market-oriented society, but the minister of education affirms that their introduction is the result of "principles and recommendations from the OECD and the European Commission regarding the promotion of financial education" (Ministerio de Educación, 2009). A financial education program based on directives from these institutions implies that the same institutions develop, or at least provide advice on, the choice of textbooks covering these subjects, and determine who is responsible for preparing teachers. The Ministry of Education explicitly acknowledges its participation in these tasks:

> The three institutions will develop the appropriate action plan to implement the program through teacher training and the creation of materials and supporting resources, including the use of a wide range of media (video games, simulation programs, etc.).
>
> This collaboration between the Ministry of Education, the Bank of Spain and the CNMV [Comisión Nacional del Mercado de Valores, or Spanish National Securities Market Commission] is fundamental for teaching financial education as a curricular

subject in secondary education, and for achieving one of the basic objectives of the Financial Education program. (Ministerio de Educación, 2009)

This advice and support should trigger an alarm regarding the content. Does such support aim to turn students into the kind of financiers who are responsible for the grave economic crisis currently affecting our global society?

Incorporating this subject, financial education, into the compulsory curriculum raises several issues; how they are resolved will provide insight into how far this technocratic and mercantilist approach to curriculum planning will go. How many hours per week are to be dedicated to this new subject? How many courses will be offered? Since the Ministry of Education has not proposed extending the school day, which of the current subject areas will have their instructional hours reduced?

The decision to include these market-related content areas is consistent with recommendations from both the OECD and international organizations directed by multinational corporations that are less mercantilist oriented. From the beginning, it was market priorities that spearheaded the creation of the European Union. Entrepreneurial organizations have always maintained important ties with the EU working committees, and their recommendations, and of course their lobbies, have left their mark on European legislation from the start.

One example is that as early as 1998, the European Round Table of Industrialists (ERT),[4] which brings together the most important multinationals operating in Europe and was highly influential in the creation of the EU, published its report "Job Creation and Competitiveness through Innovation." The report addresses the need for greater deregulation and flexibility in employment contracts for educational systems. Even in the face of criticism of this mercantilist view of the educational system, the ERT continues to insist on the importance of the connection between the two: "Greater emphasis must be placed on entrepreneurship at all levels of education. Despite the pressing need to manage better the transition from school to work, school-industry cooperation is still underdeveloped in Europe" (ERT, 1998, p. 18).

If previous reports underscored the need for educational systems to maintain close ties with big business, the emphasis in this case is on *lifelong learning* to ensure that individuals are able to adapt to ongoing industrial innovation, and thus remain employable in an ever more competitive and unpredictable job market.

This notion of lifelong learning has been adopted by UNESCO and is claimed to have been the point of reference for educational philosophy since the 1960s, when the concept of permanent education was first introduced. This was taken up again in the 1970s in documents such as "The Planner and Lifelong Education" (1977), and in the early 1990s the idea became one objective UNESCO sought to have countries incorporate into their educational policies. The concept was instrumental in furthering exclusively economic and market interests, as demonstrated in the document "Lifelong Learning for All" (OECD, 1996a). The concept of a humanistic and integral education has gradually lost ground, although it is still instrumentalized as cultural capital.

The OECD's interests are clearly in line with those supported by the ERT. The current minister of education explicitly refers to OECD recommendations to justify the implementation of financial education, but the ERT also calls for this curricular focus. In the document previously cited, the ERT considers "building basic business education into school curricula" a priority for the different governments, along with greater emphasis on providing "state of the art education in science and technology" (ERT, 1998, p. 19).

At the same time, pressure from the World Trade Organization[5] cannot be overlooked. This organization is also pursuing pro-globalization objectives and is certain to exert tremendous pressure to mercantilize educational programs and liberalize the education market. This will merely accelerate the privatization process already under way.

Generally, in a society where conservative governments and institutions attempt to persuade the public that capitalism is the best economic and social model, the fact that those who derive the most benefit from such a system—the banks and the stock markets—are also responsible for designing the content, the syllabus, and the materials, is unsettling at best, and dangerous at worst. It is time to clarify the fact that large corporations that control the market increasingly promote economy-oriented educational policies that do not value the kind of education hitherto received by the general population, for fear that such an education could lead to a rebellion against exploitive corporate policies.

There is no legislation that includes persuading and indoctrinating students with a particular worldview and a system of values and attitudes that serve to reproduce the current version of capitalism, thereby obtaining acquiescence to the idea that there are no other economic or political alternatives—a conviction once expressed by the former conservative Prime Minister Margaret Thatcher with her famous TINA acronym ("There Is No Alternative") (Berlinski, 2008). Teaching students how to play the stock market, for example, implies showing new generations that welfare, happiness, and personal success are contingent on extrinsic incentives of a monetary nature. Within this context, the development of critical thinking skills will be relegated to other subjects and material that large sectors of the population consider "easy" or less important.

At a time when the world is struggling to stay afloat amidst a grave financial crisis, this could be a good opportunity to highlight the fact that it is the practice of usury on the part of large banks and the behavior of stock market experts (who hold academic degrees from large universities) that are responsible for this situation.[6] Neither the middle classes nor the socially disadvantaged are responsible, although it is they who suffer the consequences. The crisis is not the result of First World social justice policies in the poor countries, former colonies, or countries whose material and human resources have been historically exploited by more powerful nations. Nor can it be blamed on teachers, students, and educational systems that have been most affected by the crisis.

On the contrary, never before have education or literacy levels among the general population been so high. It is time to clarify that large corporations controlling the market increasingly promote economy-oriented policies that disqualify or do not value the education achieved by the general population, as this may lead the latter to rebel against the former's policies of exploitation. The number of people who now qualify as the "1,000-euro earners" attests to the fact that there is an excess of qualified candidates for a very limited number of jobs. Moreover, the problem posed by dislocation in the case of large multinational monopolies reveals exactly how important it is for workers to submit to the rules of the game: more flexible dismissals; longer working hours; lower salaries; and relaxed safety conditions that allow for higher pollution levels and wider margins of environmental destruction.

Functions of the Educational System and Implications for the Curriculum

One main objective of every educational system is to contribute to the construction of individual identity, which is understood as the knowledge, procedures, skills, and values each individual learns, develops, and implements in order to understand, evaluate, interact, and represent the self and others in the world. If the elements that are used in the context of daily life—language, aptitudes, beliefs, rites, procedures, attitudes, values, representations—discriminate against any individual, then the system can be said to be unjust, classist, sexist, racist, homophobic, and so on. Analyzing the various dimensions of bias allows us to determine the levels of injustice present in an educational institution.

Jacques Hallak and Muriel Poisson (2002) argue that corruption in educational systems can be understood as "the systematic use of public office for private benefit whose impact is significant on access, quality or equity in education" (p. 29). A corrupt system of education can be defined as one in which disadvantaged social groups have few educational resources at their disposal, and those they have are of poor quality. Commitment to social and curricular justice implies identifying and monitoring the ways this unfair distribution of resources becomes institutionalized. For instance, public schools located in disadvantaged neighborhoods or in isolated rural areas where access is difficult suffer this injustice. It is also not unusual to find a concentration of inexperienced teachers working in these areas; their more experienced colleagues generally work in less problematic schools that have better resources and facilities and are located in better neighborhoods.

Another sign of corruption in the education system is that families find access to education difficult. This occurs, for example, when children are denied a place in their school of choice because the school administration has established discriminatory criteria related to gender, social class, ability, previous knowledge, ethnic background, religion, and so on. This represents a clear violation of the rights granted in the UN Convention on the Rights of the Child, which was adopted on November 20, 1989. Article 19.1 specifically asserts that "States' Parties shall take all appropriate legislative, administrative, social and educational measures to protect the child from all forms of physical or mental violence, injury or abuse, neglect or negligent treatment, maltreatment or exploitation, including sexual abuse, while in the care of parent(s), legal guardian(s) or any other person who has the care of the child [sic]."

A truly democratic education provides cultural content that facilitates a rational understanding of the world in which we live; employs pedagogical methodologies that promote the development of critical and creative thinking; and helps students develop the ability to understand, communicate, and live with people who come from other cultures and/or have different ideas and ideals. This educational praxis should go hand in hand with organizational and participatory models that promote greater interaction and collaboration with people from different social groups and cultural communities within the same country.

In current capitalist societies, it is possible for the state to develop its economic markets and increase its gross domestic product without necessarily increasing its citizens' level of education. A small elite well educated in scientific and technical areas, coupled with able economists, requires a minimally educated workforce to generate wealth and profit that directly benefit these more privileged sectors. One example is the so-called economic miracle of the construction industry, which is guided in Spain by a banking system managed by economists solely interested in short-term profits. We need to keep in mind that it was during this economic boom that the decline in humanistic education and interest in the arts took place, followed by criticism of transversal and interdisciplinary education and education for citizenship and human rights.

It is obvious that the new economy is closely linked to the capacity to produce and process information in order to construct the knowledge needed to generate the markets and services consumers demanded. This knowledge requires constant updating and training so that new products can be offered to satisfy the ever-increasing demands of a society trained to consume more and more. Unfortunately, this type of economy has already demonstrated its capacity to generate discrimination and increase the distance between the haves and have-nots. Technical knowledge alone does not generate injustice; however, within the context of the new information society, "inequality, polarization, poverty, and misery all pertain to domains of relationships of distribution/consumption or differential appropriation of the wealth generated by collective effort" (Castells, 1998, p. 69). Inequalities in the relationships of production and consumption lead to the exploitation of workers, as well as most processes of discrimination and social exclusion. Thus, scientific and technical knowledge may not appear to promote such injustice until the consequences of the information society are examined from an interdisciplinary perspective.

One consequence of neoliberal economic policies and conservative ideology is that economics seems to have become the science that sets the rules for what should or should not be done. Contributing to this dominant tendency is, on the one hand, the secondary role allotted to philosophical, ethical, and sociological discourse, and on the other hand, school policies that fragment knowledge. Moreover, the way departments and subject areas are organized makes them wary of each other, for fear that subjects that are perceived as exclusive territory will be interfered with. This is manifested in educational policy that presents the different subject areas as independent of each other, which results in a lack of interdisciplinary discourse and debate. This compartmentalization of knowledge makes it even more difficult to perceive the ideological and political functions behind the knowledge we do come into contact with.

Creating obstacles to acquiring knowledge about the realities of schooling gives rise to a perverse social phenomenon known as the *infantilization of youth*. This occurs through the use of programs and materials that discourage young people from taking an interest in how society functions, or from reflecting on how their activities and behaviors facilitate and reproduce oppressive power structures, including those they complained about throughout childhood and adolescence. Confronted with a curriculum based on such traditional content and methodologies, it is unlikely that students will opt for alternative forms of knowledge or exercise their civil right to act in ways that contribute to a world characterized by greater democracy, justice, and solidarity.

Never before have educational systems been subject to such an onslaught of mercantilist and utilitarian scrutiny. Although schools previously may have been used and manipulated to construct chauvinistic national identities, their present mission seems to be to train a workforce capable of increasing economic profits in capitalist societies. The current labor market is taken as a point of reference in planning the curriculum, and it becomes the basis for the decisions educational authorities make regarding students and their families (Torres Santomé, 2011).

This mercantilist perspective explains why the curriculum is weaker in the social sciences, humanities, and the arts than in science, engineering, and mathematics, which are not only the focus of diagnostic tests, alternative approaches, and new educational programs, but also the areas in which most resources are invested.

Mathematics, science, and foreign languages are the star players of economy-oriented education policies. They are presented as the cultural content that has the power to resolve every social problem and guarantee jobs. These clearly are essential subjects, but a more interdisciplinary approach is needed if the goal is to educate people to make democratic and informed decisions.

Instructional resources and the teaching and learning strategies used in classrooms also need attention. Students often are not given content that helps them develop critical thinking skills or democratic attitudes and values; instead, content is conditioned by its links to the dominant productive and entrepreneurial models. This lack of an interdisciplinary perspective makes it difficult to identify the political, social, developmental, and economic dimensions underlying current research. The same holds true of the production of, use of, and access to knowledge in these scientific fields.

The sciences and mathematics are generally associated with concepts such as progress, development, and wealth, and seem less related to such issues as democracy, ethics, solidarity, and justice. The former concepts are presented to teachers as well as students as being more authoritative and less open to debate. Furthermore, because knowledge in these areas stems from research carried out in laboratories, it is possible to control most of the variables that may condition the results of experiments conducted in these somewhat artificial contexts. This characteristic of positivist research allows science and math to be considered politically neutral subjects. However, this is not the case with the humanities and the arts.

Experimental science explains how today's world functions, whereas the arts and humanities deal with today's problematic issues. The latter are essential to educating citizens rather than mere consumers. They give insight into the origins of the current state of the world, and help us develop strategies for changing what we do not like. Subjects under the umbrella of the arts and humanities allow us to imagine and construct other worlds and realities; therefore, it is critical that they be considered just, and that they spur active mobilization to turn them into reality.

Academic subjects that encompass sociohistorical, artistic, or humanistic knowledge offer students the opportunity to perceive and critically analyze traditional models of exploitation based on social class, gender, race, sexual orientation, religion, territorial boundaries, and so on. Working within these areas of knowledge allows for the development of individual social dimensions, including aspects such as affection, compassion, empathy, and solidarity. These dimensions are particularly important because youth are harshly criticized for lacking in values; for the inability to relate to others; and especially for a lack of respect for parents, teachers, or anyone in a position of authority. It is no coincidence that we are seeing the emergence of Spanish television programs such as *Aula del 63* (Class of 63)—an adaptation of the television show *That'll Teach 'Em*, produced for the Channel 4 network in the United Kingdom, in which twenty young people must live in a boarding school set in 1963— which highlight the "benefits" of an authoritarian educational system. Here, a group of students are chosen to undergo an experience where they are deprived of any democratic right to participation in decision-making, yet they are expected to make the effort to work hard and blindly obey without complaint, as was the case in schools under the iron dictatorship of General Francisco Franco.

A democratic society requires an educational system that produces citizens who can apply reason to their decision-making; who have the ability to engage in democratic debate; and who are held responsible if they neglect their commitments.

Attempts to disguise the motives behind neoliberal and technocratic educational policies make it difficult to identify the objectives behind such policies. This explains the limitations of reports on the failure of public schools. The conditions under which these schools operate—such as amount and quality of material resources; the number of skilled teachers and other professionals working in the system; and the characteristics and social class(es) of the school population—are rarely considered. This lack of in-depth analysis is behind the reductionist philosophy informing corrective measures called for by the educational administration. In most cases, these measures focus exclusively on technocratic and disciplinary practices justified by a discourse that puts the blame for the schools' social and educational failure solely on students and parents.

Over the last few decades, right-wing politics in Spain—which often go hand-in-hand with the Episcopal Conference (representing the Roman Catholic Church hierarchy in Spain)—have drawn attention to legislation on education and curriculum content at the national level, and in the autonomous communities. The primary concern has been that the main points of reference for students continue to be neoconservative ideology and values: the traditional family model; the orthodoxy dictated by the Catholic Church; heteronormativity; entrepreneurial and capitalist free-market models; classist and traditional cultural frameworks; and the cultural hegemony of groups that support, produce, and consume the most centrist state models. These sectors are also the least respectful of the diversity that characterizes the autonomous community model of regional administration currently in effect in Spain. The conservative discourse insists again and again that young people today are amoral, disrespectful, and incapable of following rules; yet, conservative groups also mobilize the media and families to declare the subject of *Education for Citizenship and Human Rights* as illegitimate, as a precursor to challenging its illegal base, because, they claim, this subject belongs exclusively to the private sphere and the family.

It is important to note that in Western societies, values education is increasingly mistaken for religious or moral education. With each passing day, there is growing support for the notion that this kind of learning should remain the responsibility of the family, not the schools.

The priority for neoconservative groups (including the Episcopal Conference of Bishops in Spain) is cultural reproduction. Therein lies their concern with the "rectitude" of curricular content, to elude any "dangerous" humanistic or critical educational stances. From their standpoint, these elements run the risk of encouraging students to start asking questions that would threaten the status quo and, consequently, the Right's privileged position within the current productive, social, and political model.

The economically powerful elite and ideologically conservative sectors consider the social sciences, the humanities, and the arts potentially dangerous. Thus they take great pains to reduce the role these subject areas play in the educational system. Questioning what is considered to be true, good, and fair and what solidarity actually consists of is not something that either the authorities or many teachers would like to see become the key component of the core curriculum, or of the standards that guide the choice of instructional materials, classwork, or the evaluation of learning in educational institutions.

There are performance indicators for mathematics, reading, and science, but they only provide information on a small part of the school system. Relying solely on PISA data may therefore mask other more relevant failures in the education system and delay appropriate solutions.

It is important to point out that we lack "civic standards"—a central concern at a time when there is such a clear bias toward directing citizens into accepting that their primary role in modern societies is that of spectators and consumers. The political and social functions inherent in the notion of a truly educated, informed, and civically committed citizenship are increasingly relegated to second place.

What type of citizenship should we foster, then, in order to maintain and improve modern democratic societies? The answer to this question should guide how we plan and evaluate our educational systems. However, those who are responsible for this important concern tend to shy away from dealing with it directly.

An Educational Project
for a Democratic Society

The new technocratic discourse in education is used to distract attention from the relevant cultural content citizens require in order to understand and participate fully in modern society. Currently, dominant cultural policy is so obsessed with comparative international test results that determining which curricular content is truly constructive and desirable and which is secondary, inappropriate, or discriminatory is continually overlooked or postponed.

It appears that there is now general agreement among educational authorities and the majority of the population as to what constitutes a relevant curricular content for new generations. Since there is no ongoing debate on this issue, the impression is that there is consensus about what should be taught and why. Consequently, evidence of the political and conflicting nature of knowledge and of the educational process itself is not taken into account. This legitimizes both the lack of concern for fostering critical thinking in students and the lack of dialogue, reflection, and critical analysis of the methodology and instructional approaches employed in most educational institutions. Ignoring these dimensions of knowledge puts others at the forefront, in particular those legitimized and endorsed by the more powerful social groups.

Developing a critical stance, which the pertinent legislation highlights as a primary objective of education, cannot be taught through authoritarian approaches that discourage participation or in one isolated lesson. It requires a commitment by the entire institution to set in motion a working philosophy that informs planning, developing, and evaluating curricular projects. This approach is incompatible with a passive student body willing to blindly follow orders from those in charge.

Educating autonomous, responsible individuals involves a pedagogical praxis that holds each student responsible for and able to justify his or her actions. Modern global and multicultural democratic societies require citizens to be educated in three important values: (1) the capacity for Socratic self-criticism and critical thought about one's own traditions; (2) the ability to see oneself as a member of a state and a heterogeneous world while understanding fundamental aspects of the diverse groups that inhabit it; and (3) the capacity to understand what it is like to be in someone else's shoes (Nussbaum, 2009, pp. 10–12). Merely having information and knowledge about realities different from our own does not automatically guarantee that citizens will treat others with respect and a sense of social solidarity. However, ignorance and prejudice are widely recognized as the source of most inappropriate, aggressive, and offensive behavior.

In terms of content, curricular justice requires taking into account the inclusion, representation, contributions, and values of all individuals and social and cultural groups who share our classrooms and the wider social context of our educational institutions. Creating this kind of content calls for methodological strategies and resources that shed light on the hidden curriculum behind the more traditional pedagogical models generated by classifying areas of knowledge into distinct subject categories (Torres Santomé, 2005).

Working within an interdisciplinary approach allows the student to learn to ask complex questions and not to fear experimentation. An interdisciplinary approach also encourages students to explore the new paths they discover as a result of their exposure to alternative dimensions. This is how we can best ensure a genuinely democratic education that fosters reflection and critical awareness.

By now we should all be well aware of the drawbacks of specialized, expert disciplinary knowledge. The twentieth century was witness to its devastating effects. For example, nuclear weapons are the result of a narcissistic fascination with discoveries in the field of physics with a disregard for the consequences of their application, until it was too late.

One factor that has contributed to social fracture is the division of labor and specialization, whereby specific tasks are assigned exclusively to specific professional groups. A consequence of this practice is the reduction of the functions of citizenship. More and more matters are considered the sole concern of specialized individuals or experts who are not required to justify their actions or decisions. As John Dewey accurately pointed out as far back as 1927, "a class of experts is inevitably so removed from common interests as to become a class with private interests and private knowledge which in social matters is not knowledge at all. The ballot is, as often said, a substitute for bullets" (1927/1988, p. 207).

We live in a time when public concerns, including educational issues, are presented as technicalities to be dealt with by experts and specialists. This is one of the most dangerous ideas put forward by right-wing groups in an attempt to isolate the debate about possible alternatives to this specialized knowledge, and the social, economic, cultural, political, and environmental consequences.

Dewey (1916/2008) also argued that schools are not independent entities separate from society, but quite the contrary. They are responsible for encouraging students to engage in constant inquiry and investigation into the realities of everyday life, and into the human affairs that directly concern them. Education is a process that involves a reconstruction or reorganization of both social and personal experience, "which adds to the meaning of experience, and which increases the ability to direct the course of subsequent experience" (1916/2008, p. 63).

We should not ignore the fact that educational systems have long been the network that serves to "domesticate" people to varying degrees, depending on the extent to which the various social groups within that society manage to organize the struggle against such forces. Nonetheless, classrooms remain the most appropriate space for new generations to find the support and incentives they may need to construct other possible realities. A truly critical education is the best antidote for the "poisonous" discourse with which right-wing sectors attempt to persuade us to accept their guise of an immoral, authoritarian, and unfair world. This is clearly a dominant practice against which we should rebel. Investing in education that serves the needs of an active citizenry as an empowering force requires revealing the resignification of language conducted under the auspices of new conservative frameworks. This is paramount if we are to recover the original capacity of education for mobilization. Concepts such as democracy, justice, inclusion, solidarity, and dignity should continue to help cement the conviction that alternatives do indeed exist, and that they can help us forge a better world.

Notes

1. This paper was funded by Research and Development Project EDU2008–04858, corresponding to the Sixth National Plan for Scientific Research, Technological Development and Innovation 2008–2011, sponsored by the Ministry of Science and Innovation of Spain.
2. In this work, the notion of citizenship is used in its most inclusive sense: Everyone who lives in the same state territory, regardless of any legal stipulations in effect, is considered to be a citizen of that country. For example, this would include everyone living in the Spanish state, regardless of legal status.
3. See http://www.g8italia2009.it/static/G8_Allegato/G8_Preliminary_Accountability_Report_8.7.09,0.pdf.
4. Currently, ERT has forty-eight members, each of which represents a major multinational corporation headquartered in Europe. Jorma Ollila, who represents Nokia, is the current chairman. Representing Spain are César Alierta Izue for Telefónica, Antonio Brufau for Repsol YPF, and Pablo Isla for Inditex.
5. See http://www.wto.org/spanish/thewto_s/thewto_s.htm.
6. Corporations and economic analysis tend to blame educational systems for the mistakes and dysfunctions of the labor and financial markets. In contrast, the contributions of educational institutions and teachers are rarely ever acknowledged.

References

Barnett, M. N., & Finnemore, M. (1999). The politics, power, and pathologies of international organizations. *International Organization, 53*(4), 699–732.

Berlinski, C. (2008). *There is no alternative: Why Margaret Thatcher matters.* New York: Basic Books.

Castells, M. (2000). *The information age: Economy, society and culture.* Vol. 3: *End of millennium* (2nd ed.). Oxford, UK: Blackwell.

Desrosières, A. (1998). *The politics of large numbers: A history of statistical reasoning.* (C. Naish, Trans.). Cambridge, MA: Harvard University Press.

Dewey, J. (1988). *The public and its problems.* Athens, OH: Swallow Press Books. (Original work published 1927).

Dewey, J. (2008). *Democracy and education.* Whitefish, MT: Kessinger. (Original work published 1916).

European Round Table of Industrialists (ERT). (1998). *Job creation and competitiveness through innovation.* Retrieved from: http://www.ert.eu/ERT/Docs/0093.pdf

Hallak, J., & Poisson, M. (2002). Ethics and corruption in education. Policy forum no. 15. Results from the expert workshop held at the IIEP, November 28–29, 2001, Paris. Paris: IIEP–UNESCO.

Lakoff, G. (2006). *Thinking points: Communicating our American values and vision*. New York: Farrar, Straus & Giroux.

Ministerio de Educación. (2009, September 14). Los estudiantes de secundaria recibirán educación financiera en sus clases. Retrieved from http://www.educacion.es/horizontales/prensa/notas/2009/09/educacion-financiera.html

Nussbaum, M. C. (2009, Summer). Education for profit, education for freedom. *Liberal Education*. 95, 6–13.

Organisation for Economic Co-operation and Development (OECD). (1996a). Lifelong learning for all. Paris: Author.

Organisation for Economic Co-operation and Development (OECD). (1996b). The knowledge-based economy. Paris: Author.

Torres Santomé, J. (2005). *El curriculum oculto* (8th ed.). Madrid: Morata.

Torres Santomé, J. (2007). *Educación en tiempos de neoliberalismo* (2nd ed.). Madrid: Morata.

Torres Santomé, J. (2011). *La justicia curricular. El caballo de Troya de la cultura escolar*. Madrid: Morata.

UNESCO. (1977). The planner and lifelong education. Paris: Author.

· 1 4 ·

Deconstructing Discourses on Racism in Educational Contexts in Spain

Along a Continuum of Racialization, New and Old[1]

Cathryn Teasley

The mass media, the political elite, and dominant academic and educational circles in Spain have contributed variously to a hegemonic discourse on statewide cultural diversity and racism, which is heavily centered on the challenges posed by the country's rapid transition over the last two decades to a destination for migrants from poorer countries. Indeed, a remarkably sharp increase in the overall immigrant population between 1998 and 2010 caused this group to rise from 1.5% of Spain's population to just over 12% (INE, 1999, 2010). That trend has been paralleled by a steady rise in reports of racist and xenophobic incidents in recent years,[2] and by findings such as those presented in a 2003 report on racism and xenophobia conducted by the European Monitoring Centre on Racism and Xenophobia (2003). Focused specifically on Spain, the report concludes that "racial or xenophobic violence continues to increase almost in tandem with the increase in immigration" (p. 3).

In these ways, mainstream discourse on racism in Spain has centered on its newness as a reaction to novel stimuli. However, while these reports reflect necessary and laudable efforts to expose and denounce such disturbing developments, I find that most of the reportedly new or exceptional racist and xenophobic reactions to human difference and cross-cultural contact are hardly unprecedented in Spain. Many do, however, represent the most recent manifestations along a continuum of racism that extends far back into the multicultural contours of Iberian history—a kind of volcanic racism, if you will, whose activity may periodically slow down or remain dormant, but may also build and eventually erupt.

Although the current wave of globalization has given rise within the Spanish state to sustained contact among formerly distant and predominantly racialized subjectivities and collective identities, historian José María del Olmo (2009) has revealed how various manifestations of racist response to these recent interactions are far from new to the ethnic minority groups native to the Iberian Peninsula. The Roma/Gypsies,[3] for example, who began to settle on the peninsula more than 500 years ago, are arguably the most affected by racist prejudice and violence (see Leblon, 1993; San Román, 1997; Calvo Buezas, 2003). But while it is most pronounced in the case of the Roma, experience with racism is certainly not limited to them. Other larger historic cultural groups such as the Moors and the Jews of late- and postmedieval Iberia also experienced such oppression, the most severe of which was unleashed against the Jews during the Spanish Inquisition.[4] Nor are racist reactions new to the indigenous inhabitants of Latin America, once colonized and aggressively exploited by the Spanish monarchs. These populations now constitute significant sources of immigration to Spain and Europe. In all these ways, then, racism has been an essential part of the Hispanic cultural tradition.

Establishing this continuity in the historic ebb and flow of racism in Spain helps situate today's racist outbreaks within the broader perspective of an enduring undercurrent of racism. To prevent the periodic eruptions, then, this undercurrent must be disrupted. The analytical tool of deconstruction, as advanced by Jacques Derrida (1974), is powerfully positioned to serve this purpose. Deconstruction exposes the artificial constraints in mainstream discourse, canonical texts, and epistemologies that not only tend to naturalize what is not natural in ontological concerns, but also are necessarily filtered, interpreted, and (re)presented through subjective human perception. Furthermore, where grand narratives about historical realities are concerned—such as those represented in textbooks—the written word, as opposed to speech, tends to limit the degree to which directly interactive interpretation of the various meanings involved can take place. This limitation makes comprehending the historical complexities surrounding the writers' original intentions more difficult, while simultaneously reifying textual representations. Yet, deconstruction is not meant to silence or replace such discourse; its purpose is to reveal omissions, contradictions, and distortions, much as Edward Said's (1993) contrapuntal analysis offers alternative understandings of historically significant events, but without aiming to replace one hegemonic discourse with another, or to mimic the canonical appropriation of discursive legitimacy.

Beyond drawing from these analytical tools, Michel Foucault's (1970) archeological mode of inquiry into the origins of current social science principles and practices offers another powerful means of historicizing, and thus relativizing, destabilizing, and deconstructing, the epistemological foundations upon which certain positivistic assertions around racism rest. These foundations of the human sciences have come to be accepted as unquestionable, solid, stable truths because they were laid through modes of inquiry modeled after the natural sciences, and have therefore been considered throughout the modern era to be the most rational, objective, and legitimate forms of inquiry. The postmodern perspective has now thrown such legitimacy into question. By embarking on a kind of postmodern analysis that aligns with Derrida's deconstruction, Said's contrapuntal analysis, and Foucault's archeological perspective, but that—in keeping with Boaventura de Sousa Santos's (2005) approach to postmodern critique[5]—remains critical, my aim here is to historicize the manifestations of racism in Spain in ways that seek to unsettle dominant representations and justifications of racism now in circulation, particularly as they apply to educational settings.

As occurs with archeological excavation, this inquiry will start with the present and gradually work its way back in time in ways intended to challenge the "truths" frequently reproduced in school textbooks and mainstream discourse on social groups in Spain—narratives that education sociologists Julia Varela and Fernando Álvarez-Uría forcefully critique in their book *Arqueología de la escuela* (*Archeology of the School*, 1991). These authors observe, for example, that it is through the very codes that determine "justice for all" that certain injustices materialize among school youth: "[Codes] through which 'the political management of illegalities,' to use Michel Foucault's notion, operate for the underclasses [through] the penal code, prisons, and reformatories; [and] for the middle and upper classes [through] the civil code, fines, bail, and impunity" (p. 260).[6]

Whereas this observation is directed at social *classes* of youth, it retains a latent correlation with the discursive treatment of racialized youth as well. Cameron McCarthy (1990) has highlighted this connection in his analysis of the nonsynchronous nature of mutually yet unevenly influential and interactive forms of discrimination related to race, ethnicity, class, gender, and other determinants of human diversity. Another scholar of racism, bell hooks, reminds us in her book *Where We Stand, Class Matters* (2000) that while wealth can indeed shelter those who might otherwise be targeted by harsh racism, it still "does not mean that racism does not daily assault [those] with class privilege" (p. 94).

Precisely because much of the racism expressed today is channeled beyond the reified cultural constructs or imaginaries consolidated in textbooks—consider the immediacy of racist encounters among children in the schoolyard or among neighbors in the local community, as well as the filtering and magnifying effects of the mass media, the Internet, video games, and so on—such active discourse must therefore be met and confronted with the same immediacy at school. This can be accomplished through a dynamic critical pedagogy and a curricular approach that prioritize ongoing democratic deliberation on the ethical significance and ramifications of racist discourse, ideologies, and practices. For this reason and more, I argue that public schooling specifically—as one of the "final frontiers" of cosmopolitan encounter—must be protected from neoliberal incursions (privatization policies) and promoted as a privileged site, along with cyberspace, for the collective deconstruction of racism in all of its manifestations, and for the creative construction of cross-cultural justice in today's ever more interconnected world.

Eruptions

Annual reports from various sources such as SOS Racismo (2006a, 2006b, 2007, 2009, 2010), one of Spain's largest antiracism advocacy organizations, the European Monitoring Centre on Racism and Xenophobia (2003, 2006, 2009), and the Ministry of Labor and Immigration's Spanish Observatory of Racism and Xenophobia (see, e.g., D'Ancona & Valles Martínez, 2008) all point to a notable rise in negative attitudes among native Spaniards toward immigrants from poorer countries, and to increasing violence, conflict, and discrimination directed at or involving non-native inhabitants of Spain. For example, the racism and xenophobia detected in the answers to an attitude survey conducted by the Observatory of Racism and Xenophobia, which was repeated over time, were found to increase in the following terms: "The growth is gradual and advances the momentum of Spain's establishment as a destination country for immigration. The greater visibility of immigrants…seems to be acting against the [autochthonous population's] receptiveness toward immigrants" (D'Ancona & Martínez, 2008, p. 301). Here, the immigration process under way is directly linked to increasing expressions of racism found in the "autochthonous population" construed as a whole. I find, however, that the roots of such racism are not necessarily *growing*, precisely because they have always been present, albeit latent, in an ethnically diverse Iberian population that in fact has never been a monolithic cultural whole. But before exploring this aspect, some additional information on the racism directed at Spain's immigrant populations will provide a context for the ways such oppression is now represented.[7]

The series of high-profile, openly racist hate crimes and other incidents reported in the Spanish media at the outset of the sharp period of growth in the immigrant population in 1999 attest to this reality. The primary victims of these attacks were immigrants from the North African Maghreb, particularly Morocco—a former protectorate (colony) of Spain. They constituted the largest non-European immigrant group at the time. In Catalonia, for example, neo-Nazi groups took their violence to the streets, mugging individuals, vandalizing homes, and burning down a mosque in one town; in other locations, the construction of mosques was (and still is) widely protested. Following the murder of a Spanish woman by a Moroccan man in El Ejido, Andalusia, hundreds of native Spanish residents began to riot and randomly attack people of Maghreb origin who resided in the area. And following the Madrid train bombings orchestrated by Islamic extremists on March 11, 2004, in which nearly 200 people were killed, some Islamophobic activities have since been linked to that event.[8] In fact, the most recent report from the European Monitoring Centre on Racism and Xenophobia (2009) reflects the sustained nature of a growing trend in openly xenophobic and neofascist activity in Spain, and it is once again immigrants who have become the new scapegoat of this racist discourse and activity.

By contrast, low-profile discrimination against immigrants in education, housing, employment, healthcare services, and law enforcement has only recently captured more media attention. The now familiar controversy over the use at school of the hijab (the headscarf worn by many women of Maghreb origin) resurfaced in the media yet again in April 2010, in the case of a secondary school outside Madrid. Another example occurred in the municipality of Vic, just outside Barcelona, where the city has developed a selective school busing policy designed to evenly distribute newly arrived children of foreign origin among the schools. The reasoning behind this is to avoid the formation of "ghetto" schools in the lower-income neighborhoods where many such families tend to reside. Nevertheless, this policy is itself racially and ethnically segregational because no native residents must submit to the same busing requirement (Sevillano, 2007).

In the meantime, Fortress Europe—to use the powerful metaphor advanced by David Morley and Kevin Robin (1995)—is increasingly fortified in Spain through more restrictive immigration policies such as stricter border controls (SOS Racismo, 2006b), the racial profiling and persecution of undocumented immigrant youth in schools (Wagman, 2005),[9] deplorable conditions in detention centers for undocumented migrants (SOS Racismo, 2010; European Monitoring Centre on Racism and Xenophobia, 2006; Migreurop, 2009; Wagman, 2005), and the ongoing tragedies suffered by those whose only means of migrating is by crossing the sea in makeshift vessels.[10] What is more, the media help to fortify the borders by emphasizing the "onslaught," "threat," or "avalanche" of growth in the population of immigrants from poorer countries. Daniel Wagman (2003) argues that this kind of *social racism* in the media—a term that encompasses Teun Van Dijk's (2008) *elite racism*[11]—must not be obscured by the dominant reporting of high-profile cases of racist violence, as the former is fed by deeply rooted prejudice and stereotypes evident in the metaphors employed above, which associate immigration with security issues. Echoing this critique, the aforementioned 2003 European Monitoring Centre on Racism and Xenophobia report claims that the influence this news trend has on public opinion in Spain is causing "a media-driven perception that immigration is causing an increase in violence" (p. 3).

New Racism in Spain?

Scholars of the kind of racism now emerging in Spain point to its novel qualities. For instance, in her recent study on Islamophobia in Spanish press discourse, Ángela Ramírez (2010) finds that women and girls wearing the hijab are manipulatively construed as the quintessential exponents of the so-called clash of civilizations, which was famously and dualistically hypothesized by conservative ideologue Samuel Huntington (1996). Ramírez further explains that this elite form of racism diverges from Spain's historic Maurophobia (rejection of the Moors; see Corrales, 2004) in that it centers on religious practices over racial/ethnic origin per se.

Michel Wieviorka (2009), a theorist of racism, synthesizes the distinctions between newer and earlier forms of racism postulated by Martin Barker (1981), Taguieff (1988), and Étienne Balibar and Immanuel Wallerstein (1991). He asserts that this neoracism emerged with the advent of decolonization and tended

> to dismiss the principle of biological hierarchy, while favoring that of cultural diversity.
> This new racist discourse is less legitimated by the invocation of the inequality of "races,"

as it is by the idea of the irreducibility and the incompatibility of certain cultural, national, religious, ethnic, and other specificities. (Wieviorka, 2009, pp. 44–45)

But while Wieviorka recognizes the differences here, he questions whether the deeper logics of racism—hierarchism and differentiation—have indeed been overcome. He argues that pure differentiation as "a logic that is present throughout modern history" (p. 49) is now merely emphasized over hierarchism.

Sociologists Michael Omi and Howard Winant (2005) offer the view that "the meaning and salience of race is forever being reconstituted in the present. In the last half century new racial politics emerged in a process, usually decades long, that constituted a hegemonic shift or postcolonial transition" (p. 7). They claim that "very old patterns" (p. 8) of Islamophobia are resurfacing in the North, with the United States assuming a civilizing mission in the Muslim world "much as the British and the French (not to mention the Crusaders) did in the past" (p. 8). They add that this and related processes signal a regression in the West to a kind of twenty-first-century Orientalism, in the sense denounced by Edward Said (1993).

Other such "classic" expressions of racism are directed at the Roma/Gypsy people as well. Currently representing just over 2% (approximately one million) of Spain's population,[12] the Roma are arguably the most disenfranchised of the historic ethnic groups of the Spanish state. Since their establishment on the Iberian Peninsula in the 1400s, the Roma have endured everything from enslavement to ethnic cleansing through expulsions and genocide missions such as historic "hunt-to-kill" campaigns and Nazi concentration camps. While related practices continue to this day in some parts of Europe (a tragic reality that cannot be adequately addressed here), I examine just a few cases of racism recently directed at the Spanish Roma.[13]

Spanish anthropologist Teresa San Román (1997) has found that current-day racism toward Gypsies can be grouped into at least two major expressions: a popular version of street militancy, and a refined, semi-institutionalized, indifferent version of omission. Examples of the former unfortunately abound in recent years. For instance, just before I conducted an ethnography at a public elementary school in 2001–2002 in a costal city of Galiza, a nearby provisional school located on a Romani settlement had been shut down. This prompted the transfer of some twelve Gypsy children to the mainstream school. The scene at opening day, I was informed, took the school staff by surprise. Angry protests were mounted by the majority-culture parents due to the first-time enrollment of these Romani children. My informant was a teacher who had taught there for many years. She asked me to remain as discreet as possible about the incident because she did not want her school to attract the same bad press another school had the year before in the Basque town of Barakaldo. In that case, a Catholic elementary school had been required to accept three Romani siblings tuition free because the school was receiving state funding for applying the same admission standards required by any public school. The frightened children had to be escorted in by local police—and by students and parents from a nearby secondary school, who also came to their defense—through a crowd of angry parents, some of whom were aggressive toward school personnel.

What did not come to the fore in the extensive reporting of this latter case, however, was the fact that such open manifestations of racism in Spain are far from new and are much more prevalent than is generally reported, as Tomás Calvo Buezas (2003), researcher of educational racism in Spain, has long argued. And while the roots of this racism run deep, I have noticed in interviews with both parents and teachers that "new" justifications are nonetheless offered, such as, "It's not that we're racist; it's that *those* kids are a bad influence on *the rest*. They demand more attention in class, which keeps *the majority* from learning to their fullest potential" (emphases added). With adult attitudes like these, it is perhaps no wonder that researchers Gonzalo Jover and David Reyero (2000) have found that children of Spain's majority culture tend to judge Gypsies more negatively than they do immigrants.

The second form of racism identified by San Román, institutional indifference, is particularly evident in a news item I came across in 2002 that involved the Roma in the curriculum. Its headline read, "Five hundred secondary students to receive lessons on Gypsy culture."[14] While a first reading of this news captures the progressive promise of the cross-cultural learning scheduled to take place, a second reading, this time from the perspective of deconstruction, reveals the tragedy behind the fact that this kind of learning is even considered news. In other words, is such cultural knowledge really so novel in a country that has been home to a significant share of Europe's Roma for over half a millennium? Unfortunately, it is. The racism in this information occurs, then, by omission. Galizan pedagogue Jurjo Torres Santomé (1991) has referred to the silenced cultures produced through this process, and Portuguese sociologist Boaventura de Sousa Santos (2005) has developed what he calls a sociology of absences to detect such instances of discursive void, marginalization, or censorship—an important aspect of elite racism. In one way or another, this kind of silencing, intentional or not, is present in all four interactions involving the Roma depicted here, but perhaps most clearly and directly in the first two cases at the schools in Galiza and the Basque Country. There, not only did the parents' blatant rejection of Roma children echo "old" forms of racism—their *justifications* tended to gather, however, on the "new" end of the racism continuum—but also the fact that a teacher informant requested discretion about the existence of such rejection belied her particular contribution to racist omission and silenced cultures.

Since the founding of the current Spanish state in 1978, official steps have been taken to reduce both popular and elite racism through various compensatory measures designed to make compulsory and postcompulsory education equally accessible to formerly excluded Romani youth. José Eugenio Abajo and Silvia Carrasco (2004) have found that, since the 1980s, Gypsy youth have indeed tended to be fully schooled at the elementary level. However, while those under age 30 are now generally literate, secondary school absenteeism and dropout rates among the Roma continue to be the highest of all ethnic groups, which is due to a considerable extent to their own patterns of cultural resistance (Fernández Enguita, 1999).

Furthermore, misguided educational policies have been found to exacerbate the de facto segregation of Romani children. One such policy was in fact involved in one of the racist confrontations described above: The Gypsy children who were relocated to another public school in Galiza had until then been attending a so-called bridge school. Bridge schools were built in Romani communities as a result of an official policy implemented in the 1980s to bring formal schooling to the Roma. But after a decade of experience, this policy resulted in segregated "infra-schooling" (see Fernández Enguita, 1999). At a broader level of recent policy-making, Jurjo Torres Santomé (2001) has revealed how neoliberal school-choice policies have led to a segregated schooling situation in Spain that is comparable to the white-flight occurring elsewhere (see McCarthy, 1990), as the state funds private schools that (officially) apply the same tuition-free, nondiscriminatory admission standards as public schools. But in reality, these schools often maintain covert selection practices. For example, at the school in Barakaldo, the bigoted parents' violent outbreak demonstrated just how much they had come to rely on the social distance such schools usually provide from community members tragically perceived as "undesirable."

A Continuum of Racisms in Spain

To claim that most of the racism now occurring in Spain is hardly new is not to say that the social circumstances of the Spanish state—with its relatively recent transition from dictatorship to democracy in the 1970s and 1980s—have been immune since that time to the broader cultural impact of the globalization of communications and transportation technologies, or of global capitalism. Quite the contrary: Sociologist Manuel Castells (2000) has revealed that the accelerated and fluid circulation of ideas, products, capital, and (albeit much less fluidly) people across borders, coupled with the corresponding rise in cultural hybridity or "porosity" (to borrow a vivid term from McCarthy, 2008)— especially since the establishment of grand neoliberal projects such as the European Union, NAFTA, and other international free-trade regions—all have greatly influenced not only the economy, the collective identities, and the very organization of the Spanish state, but also those of practically all sovereign states across the globe today. Nevertheless, globalization is understood here as an ongoing historical process that periodically coalesces into key moments of transformation. As Zygmunt Bauman (2010) asserts, ours is one of those moments of interregnum, in the Gramscian sense of the word, characterized by social rupture and transition. In other words, just as historic instances of interregnum have allowed all-too-familiar racist attitudes to surface, so too has the current transitional period of neoliberal globalization.

Intertwined in this process is the fact that Spain, like Portugal, is a relatively young democracy. This is significant, considering the fact that the greater contexts of coexistence may serve to lay—or, in contrast, to dismantle—the kinds of social foundations that support racism. In Spain, some of these foundations can be found in the fascist culture of authoritarianism, which was officially eschewed during the transition to democracy but far from fully eradicated. Remnants of Franco's doctrine of National Catholicism, for instance, can be found in the crucifixes still hanging on many *public* school walls today, or in some sectors' strong opposition to recently instated citizenship education, or in the privileged role Catholicism occupies even in teacher education programs. As the president of the Federation of Jewish Communities of Spain recently claimed, "Some still see us as foreigners" (Bedoya, 2009, p. 9). Thus, on this and other levels, Spaniards are still struggling with long-held and unresolved claims to cultural recognition (a term borrowed from Nancy Fraser, 2008) dating back to well before the contemporary accelerated arrival of immigrants.

This is why we must dig deeper into Iberian multicultural history, right down to the roots, for example, of anti-Semitism or the aforementioned Maurophobia. Central to Iberian cultural heritage, following the Roman Empire's period of influence, is that of the al-Ándalus, the Iberian territory of the Islamic empire, which lasted from 711 to 1492. Spain owes much of its art, music, science, and literary legacy to that period. But the al-Ándalus eventually succumbed to the *Reconquista*, or reconquering, led by Christians from the north and completed by the Catholic monarchs in Granada, who then proceeded to "conquer" the Americas via the *Conquista*. In the meantime, the newly founded Kingdom of Spain (previously Castile) exiled, tortured, and executed all non-Christians, particularly Jews, through that brutal mockery of justice known as the Spanish Inquisition. As for the *Conquista*, still represented in some Spanish textbooks as the "Discovery" (García Sebastián et al., 2004), while Spanish domination and occupation of the Americas dates farther back than most other colonial processes there, it nonetheless set the stage for a continuing legacy of economic and cultural exploitation and dependency between the imperial North and the subjugated South—an indirect consequence of which is today's migration patterns. For instance, today we certainly are *not* witnessing a continuous flow of poor emigrants abandoning the North for the South.

Implications for an Anti-Racist Pedagogy

Awareness of this continuum of racism in Spain, then, as well as the interruption of its reproduction, can be promoted through a dynamic critical pedagogy that involves interdisciplinary deconstruction, contrapuntal analysis, archeological inquiry, and a sociology of absences through ongoing democratic deliberation at school on the ethical implications of dogmatic discourses, unsolidary values, and historically constructed ideologies that serve to justify racism, xenophobia, and other forms of oppression. A major goal here is to uncover the ways racism is undergirded by neoliberalism, ethnocentrism, classism, and other expressions of discrimination. Schooling that is truly public provides one of the last social spaces for direct, cosmopolitan, cross-cultural encounters, and the collective negotiation of meanings that can destabilize the foundations of racism. Cyberspace also offers such contact, albeit indirectly and on a much broader scale. In these ways, then, let us create common ground at school on which to combat all of these impediments to the pursuit of intercultural justice—justice that relates past to present (historical/temporal), Third World to First (geographical/spatial), and "us" to "them" (cultural/symbolic).

Notes

1. This paper was funded by Research and Development Project EDU2008–04858, corresponding to the Sixth National Plan for Scientific Research, Technological Development and Innovation 2008–2011, sponsored by the Ministry of Science and Innovation of Spain.

2. See, e.g., the Permanent Observatory on Immigration (1999–2000).

3. These groups generally refer to themselves in Spanish as *gitanos*—meaning Gypsies—as opposed to *Rromà*, or Roma. In Spain, the latter term has been embraced primarily by Romani activists and scholars as a means of promoting a historically informed, transnational ethnic identity. Out of respect for both postures, the terms *Gypsy* and *Roma* will be used interchangeably in this chapter.

4. Del Olmo (2009) and others also argue that native Iberian linguistic groups with nationalist aspirations and identities have themselves experienced certain rooted forms of racism, a contention that cannot be adequately addressed here.

5. What Sousa Santos (2005) has termed "critical postmodern theory" or "oppositional postmodernism" resists nihilistic strands of postmodern thinking that downplay, even negate, the role of agency in social transformation, especially where historic oppression is concerned.

6. This and all subsequent translations of Spanish-language sources are translated by the author (C. Teasley).

7. Fortunately, representations that condemn this kind of racism are also on the rise in Spain through reports such as those cited above.

8. Researcher Ángeles Ramírez (2010) argues a strong case for their existence, as do the authors of one of the reports from the European Monitoring Centre on Racism and Xenophobia (2006, p. 73). Nonetheless, broadly supported resistance to the outbreak of Islamophobia after the attacks was also reflected in the media.

9. Additionally, a collective press statement was issued in 2009 by the immigrant rights organizations SOS Racismo Madrid, APDHE, CEAR Madrid, ENAR España, and FERINE, condemning racially motivated identification checks by police in public transportation stations, at schools, or near immigrant advocacy offices. See: http://www.sosracismo-madrid.es/index2.php?option=com_docman&gid=26&task=doc_view&Itemid=41.

10. 1,271 immigrants were reported to have died between 1988 and 2006 while attempting to cross the sea from the Maghreb to Spain (see SOS Racismo, 2006b).

11. Van Dijk describes elite racism as subtle, indirect and primarily discursive, and as channeled via laws, reports, the mass media, and textbooks, among other sources.

12. State census information on the Roma is not available. This figure is based on the combined estimates of Roma advocacy organizations such as the Unión Romani or the Fundación Secretariado Gitano.

13. A growing proportion of this population is composed of immigrant Roma from Romania and other eastern European countries. Researcher Juan Gamella (2007) presents a critical analysis of their particular situation.

14. From the article "Quinientos alumnos de Secundaria recibiran clases de cultura gitana" (no authorship specified), appearing in *La Opinion de A Coruna*, June 16, 2002, p. 8.

References

Abajo, J. E., & Carrasco, S. (Eds.). (2004). *Experiencias y trayectorias de éxito escolar de gitanas y gitanos en España*. Madrid: Instituto de la Mujer.

Balibar, E., & Wallerstein, I. (1991). *Race, class, nation: Ambiguous identities.* New York: Verso.

Barker, J. F. (1981). *The new racism.* London: Junction Books.

Bauman, Z. (2010). *44 letters from the liquid modern world.* New York: Polity Press.

Bedoya, J. G. (2009, March 1). Jacobo Israel: Algunos nos ven aún como extranjeros. *El País, Domingo,* p. 9.

Calvo Buezas, T. (2003). *La escuela ante la inmigración y el racismo.* Madrid: Popular.

Castells, M. (2000). *The information age: Economy, society and culture.* Vol. 1: *The rise of the network society* (rev. ed.). Cambridge, MA: Blackwell.

Cea D'Ancona, M. A., & Valles Martínez, M. S. (2008). *Evolución del racismo y la xenofobia en España. Informe 2008.* Madrid: Ministerio de Trabajo e Inmigración, Observatorio Español del Racismo y la Xenofobia.

Corrales, M. (2004). Maurofobia/islamofobia y maurofilia/islamofilia en la España del siglo XX. *Revista CIDOB d'Afers Internacionals, 66–67,* 39–51.

Del Olmo, J. M. (2009). *Historia del racismo en España.* Córdoba, Spain: Almuzara.

Derrida, J. (1974). *Of grammatology.* Baltimore: Johns Hopkins University Press.

European Monitoring Centre on Racism and Xenophobia. (2003). *National analytical study on racist violence and crime: RAXEN focal point for Spain.* Brussels: Author.

European Monitoring Centre on Racism and Xenophobia. (2006). *Muslims in the European Union: Discrimination and islamophobia.* Brussels: Author.

Fernández Enguita, M. (1999). *Alumnos gitanos en la escuela paya.* Barcelona: Ariel.

Foucault, M. (1970). *The order of things.* New York: Pantheon.

Fraser, N. (2008). *Scales of justice.* New Jersey: Polity.

Gamella, J. F. (2007). La inmigración ignorada: Romá/gitanos de Europa oriental en España, 1991–2006. *Gazeta de Antropología, 23*(8). Retrieved from http://www.ugr.es/~pwlac/G23_08JuanF_Gamella.html

García Sebastián, M., Gatell Arimont, C., et al. (2004). *Ecumene 4. Ciencias sociais, historia de Galicia moderna e contemporánea.* A Coruña, Spain: Vicens Vives.

hooks, b. (2000). *Where we stand: Class matters.* New York: Routledge.

Huntington, S. (1996). *The clash of civilizations and the remaking of the world order.* New York: Simon & Schuster.

Instituto Nacional de Estadística (Ed.). (1999). *España en cifras, 1999.* Madrid: Author.

Instituto Nacional de Estadística (Ed.). (2010). *Avance del padron municipal a 1 de enero de 2010: Datos provisionales.* Madrid: Author. Retrieved from http://www.ine.es/prensa/np595.pdf

Jover, G., & Reyero, D. (2000, Fall). Images of the other in childhood. *Encounters on Education/Encuentros sobre Educación/Rencontres sur l'Éducation, 1.* Retrieved from http://library.queensu.ca/ojs/index.php/encounters/article/view/1765

Leblon, B. (1993). *Los gitanos de España.* Barcelona: Gedisa.

McCarthy, C. (1990). *Race and curriculum.* London: Falmer Press.

McCarthy, C. (2008). Understanding the neoliberal context of race and schooling in the age of globalization. In C. McCarthy & C. Teasley (Eds.), *Transnational perspectives on culture, policy, and education* (pp. 319–340). New York: Peter Lang.

Migreurop (Ed.). (2009). *Fronteras asesinas de Europa.* Paris: Author. Retrieved from http://www.apdha.org/media/FronterasAsesinas09.pdf.

Morley, D., & Robin, K. (1995). *Spaces of identity*. London: Routledge.

Observatorio Permanente de la Inmigración. (1995–2000). *Inmigración y racismo: Análisis de radio, televisión y prensa española*. Madrid: Ministerio de Trabajo y Asuntos Sociales. Retrieved from http://www.eurosur.org/CIPIE/prensa.htm

Omi, M., & Winant, H. (2005). The theoretical status of the concept of race. In C. McCarthy, W. Crichlow, G. Dimitriadis, & N. Dolby (Eds.), *Race, identity and representation in education* (pp. 3–12). New York: Routledge.

Ramírez, Á. (2010). Muslim women in the Spanish press: The persistence of subaltern images. In F. Shirazi (Ed.), *Muslim women in war and crisis: Representation and reality* (pp. 227–244). Austin: University of Texas Press.

Said, E. (1993). *Culture and imperialism*. New York: Alfred Knopf.

San Román, T. (1997). *La diferencia inquietante*. Madrid: Siglo XXI.

Sevillano, E. (2007, December 17). Soluciones contra el gueto. *El País*. Retrieved from http://www.elpais.com/articulo/educacion/Soluciones/gueto/elpepiedu/20071217elpepiedu_1/Tes

SOS Racismo (Eds.). (2006a). *Informe anual 2006 sobre el racismo en el estado español: Dossier de prensa*. Barcelona: Author.

SOS Racismo (Eds.). (2006b). *Informe frontera sur. 1995–2006: 10 años de violación de los derechos humanos*. Barcelona: Author. Retrieved from http://www.mugak.eu/noticias/99

SOS Racismo (Eds.). (2007). *Informe anual 2007 sobre el racismo en el estado español: Dossier de prensa*. Barcelona: Author.

SOS Racismo (Eds.). (2009). *Informe anual 2009 sobre el racismo en el Estado español: Dossier de prensa*. Barcelona: Author.

SOS Racismo (Eds.). (2010). *Informe anual 2010 sobre el racismo en el Estado español*. Barcelona: Author.

Sousa Santos, B. de. (2005). *El milenio huérfano*. Madrid/Bogotá: Trotta/ILSA.

Taguieff, P. A. (1988). *La force du préjugé*. Paris: La Découverte.

Torres Santomé, J. (1991). *El curriculum oculto*. Madrid: Morata.

Torres Santomé, J. (2001). *Educación en tiempos de neoliberalismo*. Madrid: Morata.

Van Dijk, T. (2008). Elite discourse and institutional racism. In C. McCarthy & C. Teasley (Eds.), *Transnational perspectives on culture, policy, and education* (pp. 93–111). New York: Peter Lang.

Varela, J., & Álvarez-Uría, F. (1991). *Arqueología de la escuela*. Madrid: La Piqueta.

Wagman, D. (2003). Violencia racista: La punta del iceberg. *Documentación Social, 131*, 245–259.

Wagman, D. (2005). *Perfil racial en España*. Madrid: Open Society / Justice Iniciative y Grupo de Estudios y Alternativas. Retrieved from http://www.bantaba.ehu.es/obs/ocont/obsinter/doc/racialespa/

Wieviorka, M. (2009). *El racismo: Una introducción*. Barcelona: Gedisa.

· 1 5 ·

Social Class and Education in Spain

Jaime Rivière & Mariano Fernández Enguita

The Spanish Civil War (1936–1939) was, among other things, a class war, as was, in a way, the Second Republic (1931–1936). The conflict was difficult to prevent in Spain, a country that had missed the European train of modernization, particularly in terms of the civil, political, and social rights that were already recognized by the liberal democratic governments on the continent. This development also affected education as a civil right, with restricted freedom of thought and the confessional character of the state; as a public asset, in the absence of a consolidated democracy and under the enormous power of the Catholic Church; and as a social right, with inadequate and traumatic inequalities in access to schooling. This is the context within which the education policy of the Second Republic should be understood, including its proclamation of the Unified School in the constitution of 1934, its massive school-building programs, and its training of thousands of schoolteachers (Molero, 1977), for which it became known as the Pedagogic Republic. This is also the context for the military-fascist dictatorship headed by General Franco, which in its early years embarked on a large-scale deschooling policy by reducing compulsory education from eight to six years, purging the teaching ranks, and closing fifty of the scarce secondary schools and handing them over to the church (Lozano, 1994).[1]

This social and educational disaster was not remedied until the 1950s. The regime signed the Concordat with the Holy See in 1953, was admitted to the United Nations in 1955, began a school-building plan in 1956, and in 1959 launched the Economic Stabilization Plan, which allowed the country to be included in UNESCO's Regional Mediterranean Plan of 1961. In the decades from 1950 to 1970, two long alphabetization campaigns were organized, and the Ministry of Education was entrusted for the first time to politicians who were not partisan fascists but members of the National Catholicism political groups: first the Propagandists—a conservative group under the aegis of the Catholic hierarchy—and then the Opus Deists. In the 1960s the creation of vocational schools and labor colleges (*universidades laborales*) provided a parallel education path that reflected the populist face of the regime and allowed the Falange[2] to gain influence over public education despite having lost control of the education ministry.

The big modernization drive came in 1970 with the General Education Act (Ley General de Educación, or LGE).[3] Although it was written in fascistic and technocratic jargon and it provided for a system that was subordinate to the regime and lacked the financing that would enable it to succeed fully, the LGE reorganized the school system in a way comparable to the prosperous, democratic, and social education systems operating in Europe north of the Pyrenees. The law established Basic General Education (*Educación General Básica*, or EGB) for students aged 6 to 14, which corresponded in other countries to primary and lower secondary education combined. It therefore extended compulsory education down to 6 (from 8) years of age, and doubled the number of common years in order to achieve some uniformity. The preamble to the EGB promised educational opportunities for all: "It is aimed, ultimately, to attain a permanent educational system conceived not as a selective sift of pupils, but able to develop to the maximum the capacities of every Spaniard."[4]

Despite being the work of a regime that denied the existence of social classes and class inequalities, achieving the end of social classes was its central promise: "The educational reform is a pacific and silent revolution, but the most effective and sound to attain an equitable society and an increasingly humane life."[5]

However, the LGE was burdened with the mechanism of double credentialing that allowed EGB graduates to choose between baccalaureat and vocational education, while those who did not graduate were relegated to the latter, which essentially made it the garbage collector of the education system. The system that resulted, which was ostensibly selective and classist and therefore lacked legitimacy, prompted an almost universal clamor for a new reform. This reform extended common compulsory education from age 14 to 15 or 16. This was done through the System General Organization Act (Ley de Ordenación General del Sistema Educativo, LOGSE), which emphasized egalitarian values. It replaced the eight-year cycle of EGB with six years of primary schooling and four years of compulsory secondary schooling. The words *equality* and *inequality* appear as many as thirteen times in the preamble to the law.

Schooling and Participation in the Educational System

During the twentieth century, the expansion of Spanish public education was slow but constant, as seen in Figure 1. For the generations that attended school before the Spanish Civil War and in the years immediately after, only half continued their education at the end of the *bachillerato elemental* (basic secondary cycle). Indeed, for the older living generations, only 70% of children received an education. Between 1939 and 1954, the number of those schooled grew to 80.1%, but without a corresponding improvement in the years they stayed in school. Despite a general halt to development in Spain after the war, there was some improvement of retention in primary schooling. Substantial changes did occur between 1955 and 1981, initially during the second half of the Franco period and continuing after Spain's transformation into a democratic society, which benefited the generations born after the Civil War.

In order to refine this analysis and focus attention on the influence social origins have on educational attainment, we selected cohorts whose schooling occurred under one of the three educational models applied in Spain in the last fifty years. The first one corresponds to the acts of 1945 and 1953 (LIP and LOEM) and includes pupils who joined the education system between 1945 and 1960 (i.e., those born between 1938 and 1953). The second one corresponds to the act of 1970, whose first students graduated in 1975; they began under the previous system but spent their last three years under the new system. These students attended school between 1967 and 1978 (born between 1961 and 1972). The third corresponds to the act of 1990 (LOGSE), which has been in effect since 1993–1994 and began with students who were to be enrolled in third and fourth grades of EGB, which means that students born in the youngest cohort were born in 1984; we include students who entered the system between 1980 and 1990 and were born between 1974 and 1984.

The expansion of the education system did not affect all children equally. Figure 2 shows how the expansion affected first the offspring of certain social classes, based on the number of them schooled. That is, the data shown in the

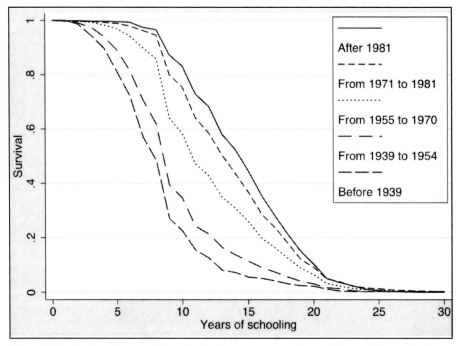

Figure 1. Distribution of years of schooling for five generations. Source: Centro de Investigaciones Sociológicas survey 2634. Analysis by the authors.

figure do not take into account the fact that one important factor in the educational differences by social origins concerns the enrollment in the system, at least at the beginning of the period for which we have statistical information. These figures show historically the perspective of which may have been lost. At the beginning of the period, there was a clear pattern of leaving school early that affected substantial numbers of students of all social origins. Children of humblest origins dropped out early and in great numbers; children of the middle classes also left school early in significant numbers. Compared to other European countries during this period, Spain's educational backwardness was considerable (Ishida, Müller & Ridge, 1995; Immerfall & Therborn, 2007). Among those schooled between 1967 and 1978, there was a change in the schooling pattern of the middle classes; for those of lower social origins, the original pattern remains: early and generalized selection, higher among rural students. Among the middle classes, we saw a reduction in dropouts in response to the dynamics between the aspirations of well-off families and the requirements of the education system. The working classes drop out at an early stage that is linked to specific moments of transition between school stages.

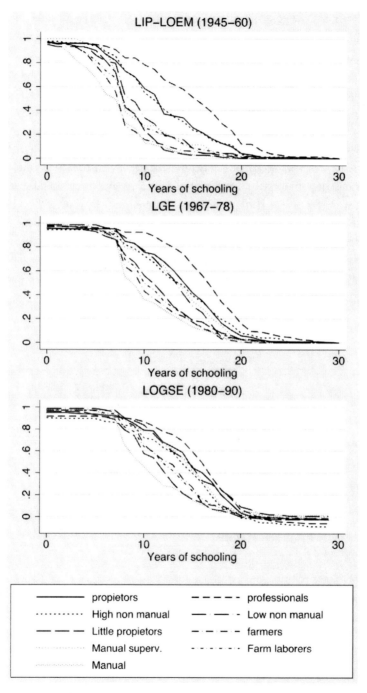

Figure 2. The effects of class on schooling in three generations. Source: Centro de Investigaciones Sociológicas survey 2634. Analysis by the authors.

Students follow one of two general trajectories: completing compulsory schooling and stopping there, or going as far in the education system as family resources and personal ability allow. Children of the working classes can now pursue the latter path more easily due to the expansion of the education system and its relation with industrialization.

In terms of access to the education system, we found differences according to class origins (see Table 1). Among those born before 1939, 25% of the children of manual workers, 32% of the children of farmers, and 52% of the children of farm laborers were not schooled at all. A minority of middle-class children was never schooled, probably because they were educated at home. After the war, the rate of the unschooled dropped to less than 20% overall, and 42.5% among the children of farm laborers. By the 1960s, close to full attendance rates had been achieved, but schooling of the entire population was not achieved until well into the 1970s. Increased participation in the school system resulted in a complete transformation of the educational landscape. However, class differences persist; children of the middle classes are still receiving more and, we suspect, better education.

Table 1. Schooling Rates by Class of Origin and Period of Entry into the Educational System

Class	After 1987	1973–1987	1955–1972	1939–1954	Before 1939
High Business and/or Property Owners	97.6	97.9	96.0	91.1	85
Professionals (Not Prop.)	99.2	99.3	97.3	100	91.3
High Nonmanual	97.4	98.5	97.6	92.9	86.4
Routine Nonmanual	98.3	97.2	98.7	100	100
Small Business and/or Property Owners	96.2	98.5	96.7	84.1	84.0
Farmers	96.2	95.2	95.6	82.8	67.7
Manual Supervisors	100	100	100	89.5	63.6
Manual Workers	97.9	97.3	96.6	86.7	74.2
Farm Workers	94.8	96.5	91.4	58.5	47.2

Source: Centro de Investigaciones Sociológicas survey 2634. Analysis by the authors.

The Determinants of Compulsory and Postcompulsory Schooling

Table 2 shows the results of a logistic regression model of the probability of graduating in compulsory, postcompulsory, and higher education for the three cohorts defined above. The original model included a variable not shown in the table—the seven regions where students had spent their childhoods, to allow for regional differences in the development of the system. The results do not include interaction effects with age. In all the models, the reference group for comparisons is the same: high-level nonmanual, nonprofessional work.

The basic pattern of educational attainment by class is similar at all levels: The children of proprietors (business or property owners) and professional proprietors (professional business or property owners) have no significant advantages or disadvantages vis à vis the reference group. The relative disadvantages of the children of small property owners and manual workers are present in all the cases. We have already seen how the children of *jornaleros* (agricultural laborers)—a specific category associated with the agrarian economies of southern Spain—sustain higher levels of delay in schooling. Children of professionals, on the contrary, have advantages in the education system, some variations notwithstanding. It should be noted that, in contrast to the method for years of schooling, in this case we are using the definition of educational levels reflected in the Spanish educational code to measure attainment.

In Table 2 we can see clearly the stable level of influence social origin has on educational outcomes, as well as a general trend, in the case of compulsory education, toward a loosening of these effects. There are, nevertheless, differences between educational periods, which are due in part to the abrupt extension of compulsory schooling. Moreover, there are relative differences in employment. Opportunities are not strictly coherent between different educational levels, as it is not evolution in time that counts. Children of small business or property owners, for example, have seen their relative disadvantages diminish by the end of the secondary education as defined here, but such disadvantages have increased in postobligatory cycles, and they are erratic with respect to university education—a trend that is on the increase. It is probable that these effects are in part the result of changes in the internal composition of small business ownership, which is sliding from commercial into industrial and building occupations, thus diminishing the cultural and social assets of the class as a whole. Using mandatory schooling or secondary school graduation as a reference, the effects of social origins were stronger in the period immediately after

Table 2. Conditional Probabilities of Achieving a Given Educational Level by Class Origins, Sex, and Private Schooling for Three Generations

Compulsory Education

	LIP-LOEM (1945–1960)	LGE (1967–1978)	LOGSE (1980–1990)
High Proprietors	-0.021	0.026	0.002
Professionals (Not Prop.)	0.179	0.260***	0.146***
Routine Nonmanual	-0.117	0.032	-0.022
Small Proprietors	-0.301***	-0.179***	-0.182***
Farmers	-0.377***	-0.328***	-0.059
Manual Supervisors	-0.229*	0.007	-0.042
Manual Workers	-0.275***	-0.245***	-0.113**
Farm Workers	-0.420***	-0.340***	-0.292***
Women	-0.126***	-0.005	0.053**
Private	0.078***	0.169***	0.089***

Postcompulsory Education

	LIP-LOEM (1945–1960)	LGE (1967–1978)	LOGSE (1980–1990)
High Proprietors	-0.049	0.015	-0.001
Professionals (Not Prop.)	0.207**	0.277***	0.085
Routine Nonmanual	-0.123**	0.022	-0.087
Small Proprietors	-0.203***	-0.246***	-0.251***
Farmers	-0.250***	-0.305***	-0.071
Manual Supervisors	-0.195***	-0.019	-0.090
Manual Workers	-0.212***	-0.256***	-0.198***
Farm Workers	-0.275***	-0.341***	-0.375***
Women	-0.147***	-0.012	0.070***
Private	0.117***	0.172***	0.135***

University

	LIP-LOEM (1945–1960)	LGE (1967–1978)	LOGSE (1980–1990)
High Proprietors	-0.003	0.017	-0.016
Professionals (Not Prop.)	0.051**	0.220***	0.140**
Routine Nonmanual	-0.023*	-0.020	-0.049
Small Proprietors	-0.050***	-0.125***	-0.177***
Farmers	-0.047***	-0.125***	-0.143***
Manual Supervisors	-0.053***	-0.161***	-0.180***
Manual Workers	-0.052***	-0.152***	-0.184***
Farm Workers	-0.048***	0.006	0.083***
Women	0.021**	0.055***	0.076***

Note: *: p < 0,1; **: p < 0,05; ***: p < 0,01. Note: Control by region, coefficients not shown.
Source: Centro de Investigaciones Sociológicas survey 2634. Analysis by the authors.

the war through the reforms of the mid-1950s. The exception to this rule can be found in the learning attainment differences found between learners raised in the professional classes and those raised by nonmanual workers, which are not significant for this period; such differences reach a maximum for cohorts schooled between 1967 and 1978.

In this period, the effect of class on attainment is higher at postcompulsory levels. The frequency with which children of farm workers believe they can reach this level is 23% lower than that of the children of nonmanual workers, and 30% below that of children of farmers. In the higher levels of the occupational structure, children of the middle classes increased to 27%, although the differences between the reference category (i.e., middle class) and the professional and managerial class are clearly stable over time. The reason for these differences rests in the gradual expansion of schooling. As we have seen, the period of maximum expansion of the education system paid off immediately for children in the middle and well-off sectors of Spanish society, but results were much slower to arrive for the working classes. This explains why differences in attainment levels are higher precisely at the moment of greater expansion of the educational system. The result is an effect similar to that foreseen by Kuznets for the evolution of income: The period of highest inequality exists during maximum expansion of the system and is sandwiched between periods of minimum inequality.

Opportunities for advancement for women in the educational system have been steady during the period. The path indicated in our data can be summarized to represent a disadvantage in the first of the three main periods of between 0.12 and 0.15 probability points in compulsory and postcompulsory education, and of 0.05 points at the university level; complete equality in the intermediate period; and a widely acknowledged advantage in the later period, which increases slightly with each additional level. However, gender inequality in the educational system has not reversed, and we have yet to see its eventual evolution. In terms of educational attainment and schooling, and despite the general trend toward a female advantage in attainment levels, there are examples of complete equality, at least in purely statistical terms, between men and women in the education system (Goldin & Katz, 2001, p. 21). In the case of postcompulsory education, the effect is much more extreme, resulting in a net advantage, other factors considered, of 0.09 probability points. At both levels, as at the university, the turning point occurred around 1970.

With respect to schooling in private schools, the effect on attainment is consistently positive (when significant), reaching a maximum of 17.8% for postcompulsory education in the period between 1955 and 1972, and the positive effects reach around 10% for the remaining cohorts and levels. The distinction between public and private schools appears as a factor of attainment *as independent from the effects of class origins.* In other words, having studied for a significant percentage of the schooling period in a private facility improved achievment at all levels. This effect is especially strong in postcompulsory non-higher education and college, especially in the first year and in the LGE period. It is important to keep in mind that the supplementary effects of private education on attainment—marginal to social origins—can be attributed to multiple factors apart from the school itself, including the social and geographic context of the school, the expectations raised by the school's ambience, and multiple other factors associated with the counseling provided by private institutions.

The effects of the region in which learners were raised during childhood are similar at all levels and clearly linked to students' different rate of development. At the university level, those educated in southern regions are significantly less likely to earn a degree than those from the reference region. Differences between regional groups can be significant at other levels, and we can make distinctions among at least four groups: (1) Madrid, Catalonia, and Center-North; (2) Levante (eastern coast) and Balearic islands; (3) Galicia; and (4) Center and South.

Educational Transitions

The international literature on the effects of social class on educational attainment emphasizes the distinction between the stability of the results for overall educational level attained and the decreasing effects of social origin on the transitions between educational levels (Mare, 1980; Rafter & Hout, 1993; Shavit & Blossfeld, 1993; Shavit, Yaish, & Bar-Haim, 2007). This distinction is important because the interpretation of the importance of social origins at various educational levels can be very different in both cases. In terms of the level of higher education achieved, the effects of social origin tend to be stable, or they can be subject to the effects of the fast expansion of the system, which seems to be the case in Spain. If the analysis is restricted to those finishing a given level relative to those who can study it, the results tend to show a decreasing effect of class of origin on achievement through the successive levels of the education system. Therefore, the interpretation can vary significantly.

The usual practice in the analysis of educational transitions is to include all the students who finished the previous level in the denominator of achievement ratios. This means that two different selective effects are used: the effect of the decision to drop out before enrolling in the next level, and the effect of the decision to drop out after enrolling. General results show that the confusion between these two effects has no relevant consequences for the interpretation and does not invalidate the procedure.[6]

Table 3 shows how the expectation is satisfied in the case of Spain that results are linked to social origins in a pattern of decreasing importance with each successive level. However, there are some important qualifications: for example, the effects of social origin on academic postcompulsory education are higher in some cases than for compulsory education, due to the fact that the two different paths at the end of secondary school reflect class; a vocational education is more attractive for the children of manual and farm workers and an academic path is more attractive for the rest. We should interpret this as an artifact of the base—all those finishing compulsory education are factored in the denominator—more than in comparison with other levels. But the final result is a strong bias based on class in the selection of general secondary education, with the children of manual workers 43% less likely to achieve the academic postcompulsory level (*bachillerato superior*) than the children of professionals.

Table 3. Conditional Probabilities of Success in Given Educational Transitions by Class Origins

Class of Origin	Secondary	Academic Postsecondary	Vocational Postsecondary	University
High Proprietors	0.0142	-0.0524	-0.0000	0.0287
Professionals (Not Prop.)	0.0901**	0.1592***	0.0113	0.1156***
Routine Nonmanual	-0.0274	-0.0957**	-0.0108	-0.0709
Small Proprietors	-0.2131***	-0.2081***	-0.1151**	-0.1778***
Farmers	-0.2978***	-0.2287***	-0.1019**	-0.1250**
Manual Supervisors	-0.1033*	-0.2178***	0.1321*	0.1253
Manual Workers	-0.1716***	-0.2726***	-0.0736*	-0.0892**
Farm Workers	-0.2993***	-0.2736***	-0.1285***	-0.0724

Note: *: $p < 0,1$; **: $p < 0,05$; ***: $p < 0,01$. Control by region, sex and private sector. Source: Centro de Investigaciones Sociológicas survey 2634. Analysis by the authors.

Note that even in vocational postsecondary education, the probabilities of achieving a degree among those eligible are lower for the children of manual workers than for the children of nonmanual workers. Nevertheless, in this case, small business or property ownership and farm origins have greater influence on disadvantage, while it remains relatively uniform for the rest. Even without taking into account the role vocational education plays for nonmanual workers, these results show the important effects social selection has on participation in the system.

A Few Lessons

Forty years of reforms and analysis of the reforms, particularly in reference to class inequalities, have shown many things, but two are of particular interest. The first is the persistence of the significance of social class in school results and achievement. Relentless reforms, extensions, and restructuring of cycles and stages, pedagogical changes and related policies, and class origins still strongly affect schooling results in every way it is measured: skills, objective tests, permanence, promotion, expectations, and so on. This does not mean that these effects are invulnerable to policies or that they are irrelevant or useless, but that class effects are more resistant to policy changes than expected, and that policy results do not come with the awaited changes. This probably has more to do with our limited knowledge of the real processes of school selection and with the distance between theory and practice or between micro and macro levels of policy implementation than with any inexorable misfortune. Nevertheless, and with all these caveats, there is a contrast between the persistence of the effects of class and the speed at which, in the limited milieu of the education system, gender effects have disappeared, as indicated by the trends in our statistical data.

The second aspect is that social class counts in a way wich is not exactly the one predicted in the usual critical discourse on the structure and function of the institution on capitalist society. This narrative presents repeatedly the educational system as the school of capital (see Baudelot & Establet, 1971; Bowles & Gintis, 1976). This means that education was supposed to serve the interests of the capitalist class as a whole by means of diverse mechanisms—ideological domination, socialization for labor, social stratification, reduction of variable capital costs, and so on—and the interests of its members in particular by allocating them a position of advantage by arbitrarily choosing and rewarding their culture, allowing them to profit from their economic advantages and, finally, guaranteeing success to them and only to them by the mechanism of choosing those already chosen, in keeping with Bourdieu and Passeron (1977). In contrast, increasingly detailed data on who attains success at school and who fails or drops out have modified this image, showing that the most advantaged are not the children of the rich but of the cultured; that is, those who have *cultural capital* rather than *economic capital*. It is true that having money allows people to send their children to better schools, to buy all kinds of support services (incurring more direct educational costs), and to not rush their children into the workforce, by necessity or choice (this involves more opportunity costs). It is also true that those with more economic capital are likely to have more cultural capital as well. But it is also certain that the single most important factor in academic success is the family: the student speaking the same language at home and school, experiencing the same culture, valuing the same educational degrees.

With the birth of an information and knowledge society—which played an increasing role in the creation and appropriation of value and in social stratification—we can ask how inequalities and class strategies in education will evolve, thus becoming a more valued asset. The data presented here are inconclusive and indicate ambiguous trends. If we had to summarize them, we would say that there is considerably more equality in the compulsory stage of education, ambivalent effects in the upper secondary levels, and significantly more inequality between the middle and working classes in higher education.

Notes

1. The Primary Education Act of 1945 (Ley de Instrucción Primaria, or LIP) reduced compulsory education to six years, and the Middle Education Act of 1953 (Ley de Ordenación de la Enseñanza Media, or LOEM) established the 4+2+1 secondary education system (basic and higher baccalaureats and college preparatory course).
2. In Spain, the Falange was a political organization based on the principles of fascism and founded in 1933 by Madrid lawyer José Antonio Primo de Rivera. Its members believed in state planning and government intervention in the economy and therefore professed to be anticapitalist, but it was also anticommunist. During the bloody Spanish Civil War, General Francisco Franco Bahamonde (otherwise known as El Caudillo, or as Generalísimo Franco) took over the ideological framework of the Falange by arresting and executing Primo de Rivera. When the Civil War ended in 1939, Franco declared himself Head of State, thereby initiating a dictatorship that lasted until his death in 1975.
3. LEY 14/1970, de 4 de agosto, General de Educación y Financiamiento de la Reforma Educativa (LGE), *Boletín Oficial del Estado*, No. 187, August 6, 1970, pp. 12525–12546.
4. See LEY 14/1970, de 4 de agosto, General de Educación y Financiamiento de la Reforma Educativa (LGE), *Boletín Oficial del Estado*, No. 187, 6 de agosto de 1970, p. 12526 ("Se trata, en última instancia, de construir un sistema educativo permanente no concebido como criba selectiva de los alumnos, sino capaz de desarrollar hasta el máximo la capaci-

dad de todos y cada uno de los españoles").

5. See LEY 14/1970, de 4 de agosto, General de Educación y Financiamiento de la Reforma Educativa (LGE), *Boletín Oficial del Estado*, No. 187, August 6,1970, p. 12527 ("La reforma educativa es una revolución pacífica y silenciosa, pero la más eficaz y profunda para conseguir una sociedad más justa y una vida cada vez más humana").

6. Again in this case, we include controls by age, gender, private sector, and region, which are not shown in the results.

References

Baudelot, C., & Establet, R. (1971). *L'école capitaliste en France*. Paris: Maspero.

Bourdieu, P., & Passeron, J. C. (1977). *Reproduction in education, society and culture*. Beverly Hills, CA: Sage.

Bowles, S., & Gintis, H. (1976). *Schooling in capitalist America: Educational reform and the contradictions of economic life*. New York: Basic Books.

Breen, R., Luijkx, R., Muller, W., & Pollak, R. (2010). Long-term trends in educational inequality in Europe: Class inequalities and gender differences. *European Sociological Review, 26*(1), 31–48.

Goldin, C., & Katz, L. F. (2008). *The race between education and technology*. Cambridge, MA: Harvard University Press.

Hauser, R., & Andrew, M. (2006). Another look at the stratification of educational transitions: The logistic response model with partial proportionality constraints. *Sociological Methodology, 36*, 1–26.

Immerfall, S., & Therborn, G. (2009). *Handbook of European societies*. Dordrecht, Netherlands: Springer Verlag.

Ishida, H., Müller, W., & Ridge, J. M. (1995). Class origin, class destination, and education: A cross-national study of ten industrial nations. *American Journal of Sociology, 101*, 145–193.

Kerckhoff, A., Ezell, E., & Brown, J. (2002). Toward an improved measure of educational attainment in social stratification research. *Social Science Research, 31*(1), 99–123.

Lozano Seijas, C. (1994). *La educación en los siglos XIX y XX*. Barcelona: Síntesis.

Lucas, S. R. (2001). Effectively maintained inequality: Educational transitions, track mobility and social background effects. *American Journal of Sociology, 106*, 1642–1690.

Molero Pintado, A. (1977). *La reforma educativa de la Segunda República Española. Primer bienio*. Madrid: Santillana.

Pfeffer, F. T. (2008). Persistent inequality in educational attainment and its institutional context. *European Sociological Review, 24*(5), 543–565.

Raftery, A., & Hout, M. (1993). Maximally maintained inequality: Expansion, reform, and opportunity in Irish education, 1921–75. *Sociology of Education, 66*(1), 41–62.

Scherer, S., Pollack, R., Otte, G., & Gangl, M. (2007). *From origin to destination: Trends and mechanisms in social stratification research*. Bonn: Campus Verlag.

Shavit, Y., Yaish, M., & Bar-Haim, E. (2007). The persistence of persistent inequality. In S. Scherer, R. Pollack, G. Otte, & M. Gangl (Eds.), *From origin to destination: Trends and mechanisms in social stratification research* (pp. 37–57). Bonn: Campus Verlag.

Shavit, Y., Arum, R., & Gamoran, A. (2007). *Stratification in higher education: A comparative study*. Stanford, CA: Stanford University Press.

· 1 6 ·

Gendered Agenda in Education[1]

Ana Sánchez Bello

Pedagogical debates about gender issues in Spain's primary and secondary schools, which are relatively recent, include political, ideological, and educational questions. The first steps toward creating an educational model that provides greater gender equality were taken in Spain following two major events in 1975: the death of Francisco Franco, and the United Nations proclamation of International Women's Year. These events highlighted the importance of developing policies to promote gender equality: The dictator's death signaled the end of the patriarchal model of government his rule represented, while the celebration of International Women's Year revealed the gender inequality inherent in the political agendas of the time.

Although 1975 could be considered a critical starting point for the transformation of Spanish society, it is important to realize that this process was set in motion in the late 1960s.[2] In terms of education, the innovative proposals and work carried out by associations that promoted pedagogical reform, progressive activists, and groups against the Franco regime are well documented. These social movements were united under the banner of educational reform, which they believed was the key to social reform. In terms of gender equality, proposals initially focused on eliminating the segregated model of education and instituting a nonsegregated model in which boys and girls would be able to interact and share the same curriculum. This was legally instituted through the General Law of Education, which was passed in 1970. This was the first step toward more complex and elaborate proposals in favor of coeducation. However, there was little debate and reflection on the role of girls in schools until Spain made the transition to democracy and the influence of women's movements in the scientific, social, and political spheres became stronger and more fully developed.

Pressure exerted by women's groups, civil rights groups, and teachers' unions working directly or indirectly to promote a more equal society converged with the Socialist Party's rise to power. The new government sought to implement progressive policies that would bring Spain closer to the rest of Europe. This led to the creation of the Women's Institute, the first government body to promote policies of gender equality. Created in 1983, this institution aims to develop policies that favor gender equality in political, cultural, economic, and social life.

The first actions the Women's Institute took in the field of education were to examine the situation of female students and teachers in the schools, and to bring their findings to light through fieldwork, research, and the publication of reports. It is important to highlight the significant role teachers played in this investigation. Without the efforts and collaboration of teachers at different levels in the educational system, the examination of inequality in education would not have been possible.

Two forces had a decisive impact on finding a solution to the problem of gender inequality: the research carried out at universities, and movements for pedagogical reform organized by the more politically and socially committed teachers. Theoretical frameworks and educational practice became necessary allies in implementing the required changes in schools.

It is important to note that the research in this field is ongoing and continuously updated to adapt to new social demands. Science presupposes that each historic period has a particular way of interpreting the world, given the technological means at its disposal at that point in time and the ideological load of the specific individual or collective context. Current critical perspectives on the philosophy of science hold this to be a human activity that is conditioned by the economic, social, and cultural circumstances of the society that encompasses it, as well as the personal characteristics and commitments of the individuals who carry out this scientific activity. Gender studies are a clear example of this link between individual lives and scientific practice at the university. The connection between scientific knowledge and collective experience must be emphasized in order to prevent university researchers from distancing themselves from people's real lives, because helping people is their prime objective.

Overcoming Segregation:
Major Changes in a Short Period of Time

Gender issues were introduced in schools in Spain later than in neighboring countries, where the feminist movement in the 1960s and 1970s had a greater impact. This movement sought to transform the educational system based on investigation and revew of the actual situation in schools. Schools were considered a fundamental social pillar and, as such, were believed to reproduce inequalities existing in society. At the same time, however, schools had the potential to become a privileged space in which new values and attitudes regarding sexual equality could be instilled in the school population. Schools therefore were expected to carry out a new function: to break gender stereotypes in order to achieve a society based on genuine equality. To accomplish this, concepts of gender and patriarchy were introduced in the schools to be used as theoretical tools for evaluating how sexist stereotypes are reproduced and, subsequently, to attempt to modify these attitudes.

In the 1970s, while the feminist movement had wide social repercussions in Western Europe and the United States, Spain was taking its first steps toward overcoming segregation in the educational system. The General Law of Education of 1970 allowed for the establishment of mixed schools, and this eventually became the norm, particularly after Spain made the transition to democracy in 1975. This is not to suggest that there was any social or pedagogical debate on the role of education in shaping a culture of inequality, or on the specific issue of the role of girls in schools. However, it is undeniable that by opening the door to mixed education, the new law was a giant step toward developing policies and actions that helped establish schools that were nondiscriminatory, at least in terms of gender.

It was not until twenty years later, however, that the legislation against gender discrimination in schools was passed. The Law on the General Organization of the Educational System, which was passed in 1990, explicitly states that curricular design should include objectives and content on equality between boys and girls. This gave rise to several educational proposals for how to accomplish this goal. The law consolidated the work of teachers at all educational levels who had begun working for gender equality in the late 1970s and continued even more forcefully throughout the 1980s. The theoretical and practical work carried out by these educators was based on the principle that the educational system is one of the main socializing institutions and, therefore, is a potential agent for changing the traditional image of men and women. The educational system was considered a suitable place to start educating girls and boys as free, independent, and confident individuals.

Faced with this opportunity for change, questions arose about the type of knowledge, values, attitudes, and skills formal education should transmit to new generations. The answers to these questions are best understood if we accept the thesis that the function of schools in today's society is to make two fundamental aspects compatible: first, to compensate for inequalities based on national or ethnic origin; and second, to reconstruct knowledge, attitudes, and behavior patterns assimilated by students in their social interactions outside school.

The theoretical and practical proposals developed since the 1980s have continued to grow in number and scope. This is evidence of the increasing interest in eliminating gender inequality in the educational context. This concern has not faded, despite legislation by conservative governments in which specific policies and measures combatting gender inequality disappear from the agenda. The Law on Quality in Education, passed in 2002 by the conservative government of José Maria Aznar, is a prime example. This law omits any references to gender inequality, the disadvantaged position of girls, or the process of curricular selection or choice of curricular options, and it allows single-sex schools. These omissions reflected the government's conviction that inequality is not a problem to be dealt with by schools and that, consequently, neither policies nor action directed at its eradication are necessary.

With their return to power the Socialists stopped the law from going into effect and drew up a new law, the 2006 Law of Education. This legislation's most important contribution has been the introduction of a new required subject in the compulsory secondary education system, Education for Citizenship and Human Rights, which includes gender equality as compulsory content. This was firmly opposed by the fundamentalist sectors that support biologically based theories of gender differences. Article 84 of the law explicitly prohibits any gender-based discrimination in the area of student admissions.

The Road from Formal
Equality to Real Equality

The formal equality granted by educational legislation after Spain became a democracy is a reality because segregation is prohibited and there are no longer any differences in terms of curriculum according to gender. This model has guaranteed the success of mixed schools, but it has not been able to accomplish true coeducation. Schools presently function as mixed institutions in that boys and girls study in the same classrooms, learn the same content, have access to the same degree programs, and achieve similar academic results (in fact, girls usually perform better than boys). In short, the explicit curriculum establishes that gender discrimination in terms of content, objectives, activities, and means of assessment is not allowed.

However, much work needs to be done in terms of the hidden curriculum if true equality is to be realized in our schools. This is the ultimate aim of a coeducational model. The fundamental premise of coeducation is that all forms of discrimination in schools must be eliminated. It is based on the principle that the education schools provide should not have as its sole aim the attainment of objective knowledge, because this knowledge is imbued with the social values—including gender discrimination—that are generated through the hidden curriculum (Torres Santomé, 1991). Gender discrimination is one of the factors that most conditions individual lives, and it perpetuates stereotypes that discriminate against women (Arnot, 2002).

Data on the situation of women in our society indicates that the socialization process girls undergo in schools continues to be unequal and discriminatory due to the prevailing cultural habitus that determines the ideological patterns transmitted through educational practice. Data on sexualization in terms of the choice of optional subjects, postsecondary educational choices, and the sexual polarization of technical and occupational training programs indicates that despite the legislated changes, socialization continues to take place within a binary system based on the differentiation of sexual roles.

Schools have developed practical proposals designed to foster gender equity. The point of departure is a holistic perspective, because several interrelated factors are responsible for keeping women at a disadvantage. Various feminist theories have been taken into account in constructing experiences aimed at a single objective—to improve women's social position.

Dealing with Gender Violence in Schools

One of the issues progressive governments in Spain have prioritized is the eradication of gender-based violence. Interventions with women who have been mistreated or abused, mainly as a result of partner violence and sexual aggression, have been carried out in Spain for the past twenty years.

Pressure from women's movements has focused public attention on gender, making intervention a priority for public institutions; some private organizations also participate in this endeavor. In response, the Spanish government, presided over by the Socialist Party and its leader José L. Rodriguez Zapatero, approved new legislation against gender violence. The law of Integral Protection Measures Against Gender Violence, enacted on December 28, 2004, establishes sensitization, prevention, and detection measures, as well as sanctions against those who violate these measures. It maintains that violence against women is a cultural problem, and emphasizes the important role education plays in eradicating gender-based violence. Article 4 of the act, which addresses integrated protection measures against violence, establishes that "the Spanish education system shall include the teaching of respect for fundamental rights and liberties and the equality of men and women as part of its objectives, along with the exercise of tolerance and freedom within the democratic principles of peaceful coexistence."

Information provided by various organizations working within the schools reveals a situation that points to the need for primary and secondary school curricula that include actions to help young people re-examine concepts associated with gender violence, such as love, emotional relations, and affective and emotional bonds. The most relevant study in Spain reveals that 80% of young women and 75% of young men do not associate abuse with a lack of love; they believe it is possible to treat someone you love in a violent manner (Commission for the Research of Gender Violence, 2005). The same percentages of young people maintain that men who engage in this type of violence have serious difficulties controlling their aggression due to hormonal imbalances and thirty-two percent of boys and 14.4% of girls consider it normal for a boy to force a girl to have a sexual relationship (Commission for the Research of Gender Violence, 2005). Between 15% and 25% of the girls believe happiness, security, and protection can only be attained if they have a partner (Meras, 2003). Faced with these data, several organizations working to raise awareness and eliminate gender violence have become involved in schools by setting up workshops and theater groups and organizing talks on the subject. These activities aim to promote equal relationships between men and women and to foster a critical attitude toward the practice of differentiated socialization based on gender. The subjects addressed include:

- differentiated socialization
- social roles and gender stereotypes
- aspects of discrimination and sexism
- sexist language; male and female chauvinism
- feminism and coeducation

- equality in affective education
- prevention of gender violence
- myths about gender violence
- types of violence
- the stages in the cycle of violence
- conflict resolution through peaceful means

It is important to highlight the role these associations played in working with educators who voluntarily stay beyond class time to carry out activities in their schools. Unfortunately, educators have yet to develop a systematic approach to promoting gender equality that encompasses all aspects of the curriculum and puts a truly interdisciplinary perspective into practice.

Searching for a New Relational Model for the Classroom

The relationships that develop in educational environments are strongly influenced by gender. In other words, the interaction among the individuals involved in the teaching-learning process is always conditioned by the traditions and value judgments ascribed to what it means—or should mean—to belong to one sex or another. It is precisely through gestures, jokes, and comments (whether intentional or not), flyers on the bulletin board, and graffiti on desks and on blackboards throughout the school that we find different valuations of masculine and feminine culture (Jourdan, 1998). The dominant culture implicitly adopts a position in which patriarchal hegemony is the norm, and attitudes and behavior considered to be feminine are devalued. Educators can target the relationships students establish at school as a key part of an educational process that fosters the development of individuals who are autonomous and collaborative in both the public and private sphere.

Consequently, several proposals for research and educational policy designed to promote a model that values the contributions of girls have been put forward in the last ten years. They have highlighted the need for a critical review of the values and attitudes that we, as a society, want schools to teach, and that educators agree are a priority: reducing the level of violence in schools; offering boys and girls the same opportunities to express and develop their personal interests; fostering mutual respect and empathy; and promoting cooperative rather than competitive attitudes. However, neither educational practice nor the relationship dynamics established in schools reflect these ideals.

Evidence indicates that the fundamental construct on which today's society is based is masculine. This also applies in the classroom, and it is transmitted through behavior such as competing to see who is the strongest, fastest, or most intelligent. Therefore, from the point of view of education, the values cited above are considered essential to counteract the dominant values of a society whose axiology favors a patriarchal model.

Changing our model of education requires that both teachers and students eliminate certain sexist behaviors. One of the first steps taken in this direction was to extend the concept of violence to include what Dan Olweus (1998) refers to as "negative actions," which include threatening or mocking someone, hair pulling, and using insulting nicknames. Hitting, pushing, kicking, pinching, and physically blocking someone's way are other examples. Negative actions do not necessarily require the use of words or physical contact—they also include making faces, obscene gestures, or intentionally excluding someone from a group.

Violence in the classroom is taken seriously only when the level of aggression, whether between students or directed at teachers, becomes particularly alarming and merits news coverage. Both violent and nonviolent victimization can undermine an individual's self-esteem and make him/her particularly vulnerable, yet more subtle instances of violence are often overlooked and do not receive the attention they should. Movements that advocate for gender equality in the schools have attempted to draw attention to these situations, working on the premise that modifying violent attitudes involves prevention as well as penalties.

Implementing nondiscriminatory educational practices that promote gender equality requires questioning the implicit values of the dominant culture, which are developed and transmitted in the classroom through a process of visualization that leads to an awareness of what is accepted as "normal." Changing dominant attitudes involves reflecting on our own actions and those of others in order to clarify exactly what type of values, norms, and attitudes are being promoted in the classroom and which ones should be eliminated.

Androcentrism in Schools

Feminist movements have exposed the extent to which scientific constructs are conditioned by gender bias and therefore produce an androcentric perspective that involves the objectivization of the masculine point of view and a failure to consider the feminine (Fox Keller, 1985; Haraway, 1989; Harding, 1986).

This androcentric bias in the sciences has brought about the configuration of a male perspective that classifies scientific knowledge into categories based on dichotomies such as public and private, objectivity and subjectivity, reason and emotion. This compartmentalization of reality establishes a hierarchy of social values that prioritizes the values that historically have been constructed as masculine, while overlooking or undervaluing those considered feminine.

The massive increase of women in the scientific fields has brought about a revision of these scientific categories. A conceptual shift has taken place in the educational sciences not only in the predominant scientific epistemology, but also in terms of content and methodology, thereby presenting an alternative view of education. Consequently, different courses of action are now proposed. The influx of women scientists has given women a voice and paved the way for a plural perspective in terms of epistemological categories. However, it is not simply a question of adding a feminine perspective to this androcentric view of science: What is required is a general reconceptualization of science in a way that makes it more human and more comprehensive, because androcentrism results in a partial view of knowledge.

Pedagogy has been a harsh critic of androcentrism. It questioned the so-called neutrality of traditional knowledge and the idea that knowledge is theoretically value free, and it challenged the notion that educational science is not based on masculine values and interests and, ultimately, on the male perspective of the world.

Pedagogical action tends to put into practice the perceptions and convictions previously assigned to men and women, a practice that is also implemented in the area of science. Consequently, revising the scientific concepts that influence what is taught in schools is paramount.

The science that is studied in schools is, in fact, the sum of the various sciences, and therefore it has a direct impact on educational practice. An androcentric perspective biases students' interpretation of the world, which in turn conditions how gender roles are learned and internalized. This explains how students learn that sexual identity is assigned in accordance with two pre-established social models, the masculine and the feminine. The subjects taught in Spanish schools have a clear androcentric bias. History, art, literature, and mathematics, for example, provide ample evidence of the fact that such bias persists to this day.

The first steps toward making women more visible in curricular content have been taken, and women have begun to be treated as producers and actors in social events. However, their representation remains androcentric, since women often are relegated to the category of a minority group that is detached from the predominant social order of any given society. Thus women's role is presented as a subtopic in a specific section, but not as an integral part of the whole. For example, "human" history is presented as a whole, while a separate section deals specifically with the history of women. Moreover, women who have entered the public sphere often are considered an oddity.

Women's involvement in scientific fields has raised new questions. Consider, for example, the role women play in Rousseau's conception of citizenship. In what way are the gods of the Judeo-Christian religion relevant to women? What implications does the configuration of a specific spatial and temporal order have for women? How is social time defined? Is the private-domestic sphere included? Would the Marxist concept of the worker be redefined if this theory were to incorporate the notion of the female worker? Finding the answer to these and other questions related to teaching would require a reconceptualization of the science along non-androcentric terms.

Re-Examining Curriculum Materials

In our society, the first contact boys and girls have with the written language is usually an elementary school textbook. Students receive images of the world beyond their immediate experience through these books, whose images represent situations outside the family context that has defined their world up to the time they enter an educational institution. The textbook plays a fundamental role in the teaching and learning process in that it is the type of curriculum material used most frequently in the classroom at all levels and in every educational setting. Moreover, few schools use textbooks in conjunction with other curriculum materials and resources, making these texts one of the major means by which boys and girls acquire knowledge (Apple, 1986, 1991). Given the importance of textbooks in the educational realm, certain aspects of them must be re-examined if we are to establish criteria for evaluating quality. These aspects include the type of information offered, the worldview presented, the experiences proposed, and which models are legitimized and which are silenced. These are only a few of the questions tackled by research in this field over the last few decades.

The need to neutralize curriculum materials requires the teacher to play the role of an intellectual. For example, the educator must expose the patriarchal ideology represented in a textbook by analyzing how it constructs gender relations, the hidden and explicit discourse on sexual roles, and the stereotypes it portrays. Thus, the educator is empowered to participate actively in evaluating the education imparted to students. This notion of the teacher as researcher implies that he or she examines the sexist bias reproduced in textbooks and the various other resources students come into contact with.

Important work has been done to unmask the sexist stereotypes boys and girls learn through the models represented in school textbooks, and to analyze the process of "invisibilization" of girls' experience when they find they are not represented in the language and images of their textbooks (Subirats, 1993). Sexism in textbooks occurs when the references to men and women are unequal, and when the feminine symbolic order (women's lives, their feelings, dreams, social order, family-work organization, etc.) is devalued by the rarity of its representation in textbooks. This situation simply does not depict reality, as women in real life represent at least 50% of the population in any society or ethnic community.

Research such as that conducted by Nieves Blanco (2000) on a sampling of textbooks demonstrates that women continue to be underrepresented in these books, to the extent that only 10 out of 100 characters that appear are female. Moreover, only 255 women characters in the more than 5,000 textbook pages Blanco studied had individual identities, compared to the 2,468 male characters.

Analysis of the character traits depicted in textbooks allows us to determine the social models they currently portray. We have selected those we consider to be most relevant to the analysis of sexism: marital status, family status, occupation, and age.

We find numerous examples of gender bias in terms of marital status. Textbooks usually represent women as married, while the marital status of males is typically unknown. Closely linked to this is the identification of women as mothers and/or housewives. In contrast, there are few instances in which men are defined by their roles as fathers and/or husbands. This encourages the misleading notion that men and women have different interests and legitimizes the sociobiological differentiation of men and women to social roles upon which restrictive gender stereotypes are based.

Another trait that underscores gender inequality in textbooks is occupation. In practically every instance, males are defined in relation to paid work, which is not the case for women. In most cases, women are not represented within a professional framework at all, except in relation to domestic tasks, and symbolic equity does not extend to this area. Both quantitative and qualitative analyses of women's professional activities indicate that when women are represented within a professional framework, it is usually in so-called feminine roles such as nurses, hairdressers, or flight attendants. In contrast, males are represented within a much wider range of professional contexts, in roles that reinforce the masculine stereotype such as carpenter, executive, judge, lorry driver, or footballer. In the last few years, a greater number of images of men performing traditionally feminine roles, and vice versa, have found their way into textbooks, but when women are represented in jobs traditionally assigned to males, certain symbols usually are included to remind us of women's condition of mother-housewife-caretaker. For example, a woman doctor will appear surrounded by children in an affectionate stance, whereas a male doctor appears in more formal and professional situations. These images have a negative impact not only on the perception of women as a social group, but also on men. Failing to present men as having a range of emotions limits the opportunities boys have to explore the rich world of emotions and learn to express their feelings.

From a democratic standpoint, quality textbooks can be achieved only if they present more diverse social models. Representing female models more equitably would be an important step toward complying with democratic principles, without which boys and girls will lose a fundamental part of their development as individuals, as gender bias limits and diminishes their social roles.

Women Teachers in Positions of Authority in School Management

The traditional division of labor along gender lines is one major reason why women currently find themselves in a disadvantaged position. Not only is the feminization of work directly associated with the lowest paying jobs, but the unequal distribution of work actively reinforces the image of woman as subordinates within the social order. This is clearly evident in Spain's educational system, where there is a great disparity between the number of women teachers and the number of women in positions of authority.

Research on this subject in Spain (Caballero & Salvador, 2004; Carrasco, 2004; Gómez et al., 2004; Grañeras, 2003) reveals that there are more male principals than female principals. Research on gender and school management has focused on analyzing cultural factors that explain the low representation of women in school management positions, including difficulties reconciling work and family life; social or family pressure on women who attempt to take on professional positions of responsibility; confrontation with the masculine corporate culture, which clashes with women's management styles; and low expectations about women's management skills. Studies show that these are the main reasons for the low number of women in school management, but the research has not been able to confirm which reasons are most critical. Therefore, it appears that it is a combination of these factors inherited from the patriarchal past that is responsible for the fact that women are not promoted to positions of authority within the educational system.

Another line of research involves exploring whether there are any significant differences in management styles between men and women. School management does not follow a particular management model, but Sacristán (1995) discusses three types: strong management, in which the principal has significant power within the school; a type of collegial management; and management that is subject to external control such as school boards or, in the case of private schools, a board of trustees. Studies on women managers in the Spanish context reveal that women have developed a management style that favors participation, teamwork, consensus, and the sharing of power and information (Coronel, 1996; Díez et al., 2006; Guerra, 2000; Sarrió et al., 2004). This distinctive approach seems to be related to the socialization process women experience that teaches them that attending to others' needs and multitasking are important.

The relationship between a management model and patriarchal culture can also be observed in terms of legislation. The 1990 Law on Education introduced innovations regarding school management that called for a more open model based on participation and collaboration. After the law was enacted, the number of women principals increased (Al-Kalifa, 1989; Gómez et al., 2003). Yet, the 2002 Law on Quality in Education advocated a hierarchical structure based on strong individual leadership, and granted principals the autonomy required to stimulate and implement its Educational Quality Improvement Program (2002). The 2002 law, which was more conservative and authoritarian than its predecessors, does not mention a school board, only the principal. In order to strengthen the status of new principals within the educational community, the new law established that those who wish to take on the position of principal must receive specific training, and it also provides for salary increases. This salary differential is maintained as long as a principal remains in the teaching profession and receives positive evaluations by the educational administration. Principals are exempt from all or at least some teaching hours, and their new status also provides career recognition when they apply to other positions within the public school system or when they seek other professional opportunities.

If we take into account that, due to the socialization process they have experienced, women's management style emphasizes collaboration over control, the current educational legislation that opts for an individualistic approach to school management is, in fact, a step backwards in terms of the integration of women into management positions in public schools.

Notes

1. This paper was funded by Research and Development Project EDU2008–04858, corresponding to the Sixth National Plan for Scientific Research, Technological Development and Innovation 2008–2011, sponsored by the Ministry of Science and Innovation of Spain.
2. Pioneering Spanish feminists included Concepción Arenal (1820–1893); Emilia Pardo Bazán (1851–1921); Teresa Claramunt (1862–1931); Clara Campoamor (1888–1972); Victoria Kent (1897–1987); Margarita Nelken (1898–1986); Federica Montseny (1905–1994).

References

Acker, S. (1994). *Gendered education*. Buckingham, UK: Open University Press.

Al-Khalifa, E. (1989). Management by halves: Women teachers and school management. In H. Lyon & Y. F. Migniudo (Eds.), *Women teachers: Issues and experiences*. Milton Keynes, UK: Open University Press.

Apple, M. W. (1986). *Teachers and texts: A political economy of class and gender relations in education*. New York: Routledge.

Apple, M. W., & Christian-Smith, L. (1991). *The politics of the textbooks*. New York: Routledge.

Arnot, M. (2002). *Reproducing gender?: Critical essays on educational theory and feminist politics*. London: RoutledgeFalmer.

Blanco, N. (2000). *El sexismo en los materiales educativos de la E.S.O.* Seville, Spain: Instituto Andaluz de la Mujer.

Caballero, J., & Salvador, F. (2004). Satisfacción e insatisfacción de los directores escolares. *Revista de Educación, 333*, 363–384.

Carrasco, M. J. (2004). Análisis de los estilos directivos de las mujeres en centros educativos. *Revista Iberoamericana de Educación, 33*(3), 1–13.

Commission for the Research of Gender Violence, 2005. www.educarenigualdad.org/Upload/Mat_29_Informe%20menores.doc

Coronel, J. M. (1996). La investigacición sobre el liderazgo y procesos de cambio en los centros educativos. Huelva, Spain: Servicio de Publicaciones.

Díez, E., et al. (2006). *La cultura de género en las organizaciones escolares*. Barcelona: Octaedro.

Gimeno Sacristán, J. (1995). *La dirección de centros. Análisis de tareas*. Madrid: CIDE.

Gómez, C., et al. (2003). *Mujeres en cargos de representación del sistema educativo*. Madrid: Instituto de la Mujer.

Grañeras, M. (2003). Las mujeres en los equipos directivos de los centros escolares en España. *Organización y Gestión Educativa, 3*, 15–20.

Haraway, D. (1989). *Primate visions: Gender, race, and nature in the world of modern science*. New York: Routledge.

Harding, S. (1986). *The science question in feminism*. New York: Cornell University Press.

Jourdan, C. (1998). Las relaciones en la escuela. In Instituto de la Mujer (Ed,), *Educar en relación*. Madrid: Instituto de la Mujer.

Keller, E. F. (1985). *Reflections on gender and science*. New Haven, CT: Yale University Press.

Meras, A. (2003, September). Prevención de la violencia de género en adolescentes. *Revista de Estudios de Juventud, 62*, 143–150.

Olweus, D. (1993). *Bullying at school: What we know and what we can do*. Oxford, UK: Blackwell.

Santos Guerra, M. Á. (2000). Yo tengo que hacer la cena. La mujer y el gobierno de los centros escolares. In M. Á. Santos Guerra (Ed.), *El harén pedagógic. Perspectiva de género en la organización escolar* (pp. 53–69). Barcelona: Graó.

Sarrió, M., et al. (2004). Género, trabajo y poder. In E. Barerá & I. Martínez (Eds.), *Psicología y género* (pp. 193–216). Madrid: Pearson, Prentice Hall.

Subirats, M. (Ed.). (1993). *El sexismo en los libros de texto. Análisis y propuesta de un sistema de indicadores*. Madrid: Ministerio de Asuntos Sociales. Instituto de la Mujer.

Torres Santomé, J. (1991). *El curriculum oculto*. Madrid: Morata.

Name Index

Subject Index

GLOBAL STUDIES IN EDUCATION

A.C. (Tina) Besley, Michael A. Peters,
Cameron McCarthy, Fazal Rizvi
General Editors

Global Studies in Education is a book series that addresses the implications of the powerful dynamics associated with globalization for re-conceptualizing educational theory, policy and practice. The general orientation of the series is interdisciplinary. It welcomes conceptual, empirical and critical studies that explore the dynamics of the rapidly changing global processes, connectivities and imagination, and how these are reshaping issues of knowledge creation and management and economic and political institutions, leading to new social identities and cultural formations associated with education.

We are particularly interested in manuscripts that offer: a) new theoretical, and methodological, approaches to the study of globalization and its impact on education; b) ethnographic case studies or textual/discourse based analyses that examine the cultural identity experiences of youth and educators inside and outside of educational institutions; c) studies of education policy processes that address the impact and operation of global agencies and networks; d) analyses of the nature and scope of transnational flows of capital, people and ideas and how these are affecting educational processes; e) studies of shifts in knowledge and media formations, and how these point to new conceptions of educational processes; f) exploration of global economic, social and educational inequalities and social movements promoting ethical renewal.

For additional information about this series or for the submission of manuscripts, please contact one of the series editors:

A.C. (Tina) Besley: tbesley@illinois.edu
Cameron McCarthy: cmccart1@illinois.edu
Michael A. Peters: mpet001@illinois.edu
Fazal Rizvi: frizvi@unimelb.edu.au

Department of Educational Policy Studies
University of Illinois at Urbana-Champaign
1310 South Sixth Street
Champaign, IL 61820   USA

To order other books in this series, please contact our Customer Service Department:

(800) 770-LANG (within the U.S.)
(212) 647-7706 (outside the U.S.)
(212) 647-7707 FAX

Or browse online by series:
www.peterlang.com